First World War
and Army of Occupation
War Diary
France, Belgium and Germany

38 DIVISION
Divisional Troops
151 Field Company Royal Engineers
3 December 1915 - 31 December 1918

WO95/2547/3

The Naval & Military Press Ltd
www.nmarchive.com
Published in association with The National Archives

Published by

The Naval & Military Press Ltd

Unit 10 Ridgewood Industrial Park,

Uckfield, East Sussex,

TN22 5QE England

Tel: +44 (0) 1825 749494

www.naval-military-press.com

www.nmarchive.com

This diary has been reprinted in facsimile from the original. Any imperfections are inevitably reproduced and the quality may fall short of modern type and cartographic standards.

© **Crown Copyright**
Images reproduced by permission of The National Archives, London, England, 2015.

Contents

Document type	Place/Title	Date From	Date To
Heading	WO95/2547/2 124 Field Company Royal Engineers		
Heading	38th Division Divl Engineers 151st Field Coy R.E. Dec 1915-Jun 1919		
Heading	38th Div. 151th F.C.R.E. Vol I		
Heading	War Diary Of 151 Field Company Royal Engineers. for month of December 1915 Volume 1		
War Diary	Winchester	03/12/1915	03/12/1915
War Diary	Le Havre	03/12/1915	05/12/1915
War Diary	St Omer	06/12/1915	06/12/1915
War Diary	Mametz	07/12/1915	19/12/1915
War Diary	Robecq	20/12/1915	20/12/1915
War Diary	Les 8 Maisons	21/12/1915	31/12/1915
Heading	151st F.C.R.E. Vol. 2 Jan		
Heading	War Diary Of 151 Field Company R.E. for month of January 1916 Volume II		
War Diary	Les 8 Maisons	01/01/1916	05/01/1916
War Diary	Robecq	06/01/1916	15/01/1916
War Diary	Les 8 Maisons	16/01/1916	31/01/1916
War Diary	Guards Division	05/01/1916	16/01/1916
War Diary	Guards Div	17/01/1916	22/01/1916
Heading	War Diary Of 151 Field Company R.E. for month of February 1916 Volume III		
Heading	151st F.C.R.E. Vol 3		
War Diary	Les 8 Maisons	01/02/1916	16/02/1916
War Diary	Gorre	17/02/1916	29/02/1916
Miscellaneous	Appendix 2. Work In Progress Handed Over By 151st Field Coy, R.E. to 24th Field Coy, R.E.	15/02/1916	15/02/1916
Miscellaneous	Appendix 3. Work In Progress Taken Over From The 5th Field Coy, R.E. By The 151st Field Company, R.E.	16/02/1916	16/02/1916
Miscellaneous	Statement Referred To In Appendix 3 Para. 8		
Miscellaneous	Statement Referred To In Appendix 3. Para 9		
Heading	War Diary Of 151 Field Company R.E. for month of March 1916 volume iv		
Heading	151 F.C.R.E. Vol 4		
War Diary	Gorre	01/03/1916	31/03/1916
Miscellaneous	Routine Orders By Major General Ivor Phillipps, D.S.O., Commanding 38th (Welsh) Division. Appendix I	08/03/1916	08/03/1916
Miscellaneous	To The General Officer Commanding, 115th Infantry Brigade. Appendix II	17/02/1916	17/02/1916
Heading	War Diary Of 151 Field Company R.E. for month of April 1916 Volume V		
War Diary	Gorre	01/04/1916	14/04/1916
War Diary	Estaires	15/04/1916	15/04/1916
War Diary	Lavantie	16/04/1916	30/04/1916
Miscellaneous	Hd Qrs, 38th Welsh Division.	01/04/1916	01/04/1916
Miscellaneous	To Brigade Major, R.A. 38th Division.		
Miscellaneous	38th Division No. G. 73/ Appendix I	03/04/1916	03/04/1916

Miscellaneous	Reference Operation Order No. 98 by Lieut Colonel F.H. Gaskell, Comdg 16th Battn, Welsh Regt Appendix 2	09/04/1916	09/04/1916
Operation(al) Order(s)	Operation Orders No. 98 by Lieut Colonel F.H. Gaskell, Commanding 16th Battn, Welsh Regt, (Cardiff City).		
Miscellaneous	Work In Progress Handed Over To The 227th Field Coy, Royal Engineers, on relief, by 151st Field Coy, R.E. Appendix III	14/04/1916	14/04/1916
Miscellaneous	To Headquarters, 38th Division. Appendix IV	13/04/1916	13/04/1916
Miscellaneous	204th Field Company, Royal Engineers. Appendix V	13/04/1916	13/04/1916
Miscellaneous	204th Field Company, Royal Engineers.		
Miscellaneous	Appendix VI	25/04/1916	25/04/1916
Heading	War Diary Of 151st Field Company R.E. For Month Of May 1916 Volume 6		
War Diary	Laventie	01/05/1916	31/05/1916
Miscellaneous	O.C. 151st Field Coy, R.E.	18/05/1916	18/05/1916
Miscellaneous	Report On The Work In Connection With Sap Running Approximately From Point N.8.C. 1/2. 41/2 to point N.8.D.2.4 on The Night of The 27th-28th May, 1916. Appendix II.	27/05/1916	27/05/1916
Diagram etc			
Diagram etc	151 Fld Coy RE		
Miscellaneous	To The General Officer Commanding, 114th Infantry Brigade. Appendix III	28/05/1916	28/05/1916
Heading	War Diary Of 151 Field Company R.E. For Month Of June 1916 Volume VII		
War Diary	Lavantie	01/06/1916	11/06/1916
War Diary	Robecq	12/06/1916	14/06/1916
War Diary	La Clarence	15/06/1916	15/06/1916
War Diary	Guestreville	16/06/1916	26/06/1916
War Diary	Barry	27/06/1916	27/06/1916
War Diary	Bretel (Gezaincourt)	28/06/1916	30/06/1916
Miscellaneous	Handing Over Report of The 151st Field Company, Royal Engineers, on relief in the Fauquissart Section by 1/3 Field Company, South Midland Division. Appendix I	10/06/1916	10/06/1916
Miscellaneous	Special Order Of The Day By Major-General Ivor Philipps, D.S.O., Commanding 38th (Welsh) Division. Appendix II	14/06/1916	14/06/1916
Heading	War Diary Of 151st Field Company Royal Engineers For Month Of July 1916 Volume II		
War Diary	Toutencourt	01/07/1916	03/07/1916
War Diary	Mericourt-L'abbe	04/07/1916	05/07/1916
War Diary	Minden Post	06/07/1916	09/07/1916
War Diary	Mametz Wood	11/07/1916	11/07/1916
War Diary	Pommiers Redoubt	10/07/1916	10/07/1916
War Diary	Pommiers Redoubt to Mametz Wood	11/07/1916	13/07/1916
War Diary	Robempre	14/07/1916	14/07/1916
War Diary	Courcelles. Au-Bois	15/07/1916	29/07/1916
War Diary	Bus-Les-Artois	30/07/1916	30/07/1916
War Diary	Beauval	31/07/1916	31/07/1916
Map	War Diary July Appendix I		
Miscellaneous	Notes On Mametz Wood Obtained By Patrol, 2nd Battn, Royal Irish Regiment, On Night 3/4th. July.	03/07/1916	03/07/1916
Map	War Diary July Appendix II		

Miscellaneous	Handing Over Notes of Centre Section of the 38th Division front on relief by 20th Div. 151st (Field) Coy, R.E. to be relieved by 83rd (Field) Coy, Royal Engrs. Appendix III		
Miscellaneous	Machine Gun Emplacements		
Miscellaneous	Deep Dug-Outs.	28/07/1916	28/07/1916
Miscellaneous	Forward Water Supply.		
Heading	War Diary Of 151st Field Company Royal Engineers For Month Of August 1916 Vol 9		
War Diary	Millain	01/08/1916	03/08/1916
War Diary	Worm Houdt	04/08/1916	05/08/1916
War Diary	Ypres	06/08/1916	31/08/1916
Heading	War Diary 151st Field Coy RE September 1916 Vol 10		
War Diary	Ypres	01/09/1916	30/09/1916
Heading	War Diary-October-1916 151 Field Coy. R.E. 38th (Welsh) Divn		
War Diary	Ypres	01/10/1916	31/10/1916
Heading	War Diary-Novr 1916 151st (Field) Company, Royal Engineers. 38th (Welsh) Division. Vol 12		
War Diary	Ypres	01/11/1916	30/11/1916
Heading	War Diary December 1916 151st Field Company Royal Engineers 38th (Welsh) Division Vol 13		
War Diary	Poperinghe	10/12/1916	10/12/1916
War Diary	Houlle	02/12/1916	31/12/1916
Miscellaneous	151st Field Company, R.E. Appendix		
Miscellaneous	List of Articles Handed over by 151st Field Coy, R.E. to 225th Field Coy, R.E. on relief-1st Dec. 16	01/12/1916	01/12/1916
Miscellaneous	List of Plans and Drawings handed over by 151st Field Company, R.E. to the 225th Field Company, R.E. on relief 1/12/1916	01/12/1916	01/12/1916
Heading	War Diary January-1917 151st Field Company Royal Engineers 38th (Welsh) Division Vol 14		
War Diary	Houlle	01/01/1917	12/01/1917
War Diary	Elverdinghe	13/01/1917	17/01/1917
War Diary	B 18b 28	18/01/1917	31/01/1917
Heading	War Diary February 1917 151st Field Company Royal Engineers 38th (Welsh) Division Vol 15		
Heading	War Diary February 1917 151st Field Company Royal Engineers 38th (Welsh) Division		
War Diary	Cardoen Farm	01/02/1917	28/02/1917
Heading	War Diary For March 1917. 151st Field Coy, Royal Engineers		
War Diary	Cardoen Farm	01/03/1917	30/03/1917
Heading	War Diary-April 1917 151st Field Company, Royal Engineers 38th (Welsh) Division Vol 17		
War Diary	In The Field	02/04/1917	30/04/1917
Heading	War Diary-May, 1917 151st Field Coy, Royal Engineers 38th (Welsh) Division. Vol 18		
War Diary	In The Field	01/05/1917	29/05/1917
Heading	War Diary-June 1917 151st Field Coy, Royal Engineers 38th (Welsh) Division Vol 19		
War Diary	In The Field	03/06/1917	30/06/1917
Heading	War Diary-July, 1917. 151st Field Company, Royal Engineers 38th (Welsh) Division. Vol 20		
War Diary	In The Field	01/07/1917	31/07/1917

Heading	War Diary-August. 151st Field Company Royal Engineers 38th (Welsh) Division Vol 21		
War Diary	Canal Bank (Essex Farm)	01/08/1917	06/08/1917
War Diary	Proven F.10.b.5.2 Sheet 27 N.E.	07/08/1917	17/08/1917
War Diary	Canal Bank C 19. C. 2.b Sheet 28 N.W.	18/08/1917	18/08/1917
War Diary	Canal Bank	19/08/1917	23/08/1917
War Diary	Orderly Room C.19.a.0.7 Horse Lines B, 23, d, 3, 4	25/08/1917	25/08/1917
War Diary	Canal Bank	26/08/1917	31/08/1917
War Diary	Canal Bank	01/08/1917	31/08/1917
Heading	War Diary Unit: 151st Field Coy. RE (38) Welsh Division (September) Vol 22		
War Diary	Canal Bank C.19.a.0.7 Sheet 28 NW	01/09/1917	05/09/1917
War Diary	Canal Bank	05/09/1917	09/09/1917
War Diary	Proven	10/09/1917	15/09/1917
War Diary	Armentieres	16/09/1917	30/10/1917
Heading	War Diary Of 151st Field Co. R.E. From 1st Nov. 1917 To 30th Nov. 1917		
War Diary	Armentieres Sector	03/11/1917	17/11/1917
War Diary	Armentieres Sector	18/11/1917	30/11/1917
Heading	War Diary of 151st. Field Company R.E. From 1-12-17 To 31-12-17 Vol 25		
War Diary	Armentieres	01/12/1917	20/12/1917
War Diary	Nouveau Monde	21/12/1917	31/12/1917
Heading	War Diary. 151st Field Coy, R.E. From 1st January To 31st January 1918 Vol 26		
War Diary		01/01/1918	31/01/1918
War Diary		01/02/1918	12/02/1918
War Diary		13/02/1918	28/02/1918
War Diary		23/02/1918	23/02/1918
War Diary		01/02/1918	31/03/1918
War Diary		01/03/1918	31/03/1918
Heading	38th Div. V. Corps. 151st Field Company, R.E. April 1918		
War Diary	Boeseghem	01/04/1918	03/04/1918
War Diary	Varennes	04/04/1918	04/04/1918
War Diary	Warloy Baillon	05/04/1918	10/04/1918
War Diary	Senlis	11/04/1918	12/04/1918
War Diary	Henencourt	13/04/1918	13/04/1918
War Diary	Henencourt & Contay	15/04/1918	23/04/1918
War Diary	Toutencourt	24/04/1918	24/04/1918
War Diary	Henencourt & Contay	25/04/1918	26/04/1918
War Diary	Toutencourt	27/04/1918	30/04/1918
Heading	151st Field Coy R.E. War Diary For Month Of May Vol 30		
War Diary	V, 2, d And Harponville	01/05/1918	16/05/1918
War Diary	V, 5, a and Harponville	17/05/1918	19/05/1918
War Diary	Toutencourt	20/05/1918	31/05/1918
Heading	War Diary June 1917 151 Field Company R.E. 38 (Welsh) Division.		
War Diary	Toutencourt P. 30.d.9.3 & Clairfaye	05/06/1917	11/06/1917
War Diary	P.26.d.7.8 & Clairfaye	15/06/1917	22/06/1917
Heading	War Diary July 1918. 151 Field Coy RE Vol 32		
War Diary	Sheet 57 D Adv HQ & 4 Sections P 26d 78 Rear HQ-Horse Lines O30a 37 Clairfaye	01/07/1918	20/07/1918
War Diary	Sheet 57 D HQ P 26d 78 Detachment V 8.a.66 Horse Line O 30a.37	20/07/1918	31/07/1918

War Diary	Toutencourt	31/07/1918	31/07/1918
Heading	151st. Field Coy. R.E. War Diary. August 1st To 31st 1918 Vol 33		
War Diary	Sheet 57D U1	01/08/1918	05/08/1918
War Diary	Sheet 57 B V 17a 82	06/08/1918	25/08/1918
War Diary	Sheet 57 B W 10d 22	27/08/1918	31/08/1918
War Diary	Sheet 57D W 10d 22	01/09/1918	01/09/1918
War Diary	Sheet 57 C T 13C 18	02/09/1918	05/09/1918
War Diary	V 8 C 88	06/09/1918	06/09/1918
War Diary	S 10d. 55	06/09/1918	08/09/1918
War Diary	O 7C	09/09/1918	11/09/1918
War Diary	P. 32 C Rd.	11/09/1918	15/09/1918
War Diary	Sheet 57 C. P 32 D.C	16/09/1918	28/09/1918
War Diary	W. 20 C	29/09/1918	30/09/1918
War Diary	Sheet 57 C. W. 20.c	01/10/1918	03/10/1918
War Diary	F. 15.a.5.8	03/10/1918	03/10/1918
War Diary	F.17.d. F.21.b.9.5	04/10/1918	05/10/1918
War Diary	Sheet b. 24. N.W. A. 4.d.4.7	06/10/1918	07/10/1918
War Diary	Sheet 57.b. 6.24.a. T.16.b	08/10/1918	11/10/1918
War Diary	Sheet 57b P.4.b. 05.90	12/10/1918	21/10/1918
War Diary	K. 12.a.8.8	23/10/1918	25/10/1918
War Diary	F.4.a	26/10/1918	31/10/1918
War Diary	Sheet 57 B. F.4.a	01/11/1918	04/11/1918
War Diary	Sheet 57 A A.1.b.8.6	05/11/1918	06/11/1918
War Diary	C.2	07/11/1918	08/11/1918
War Diary	U.29	08/11/1918	09/11/1918
War Diary	Sheet 57 A. F.12. C.	10/11/1918	13/11/1918
War Diary	X.22. C. 0.7	14/11/1918	21/11/1918
War Diary	U. 21. C.	22/11/1918	24/11/1918
War Diary	Sheet 57 A	25/11/1918	02/12/1918
War Diary	Sheet 62. D N. 6. C. 9.3	05/12/1918	31/12/1918

WO95/2547/2
124 Field Company
Royal Engineers

38TH DIVISION
DIVL ENGINEERS

151ST FIELD COY R.E.
DEC 1915 - JUN 1919.

157th FCRE.
Vol: I

121/1928

38h/15w

Dec '15
June '19

Volume I.

WAR DIARY OF

151 FIELD COMPANY. ROYAL ENGINEERS.

for month of DECEMBER 1915

Page 1.
Army Form C. 2118.

WAR DIARY of 151 (Field) Company. R.E.

INTELLIGENCE SUMMARY.

(Erase heading not required.)

Instructions regarding War Diaries and Intelligence Summaries are contained in F. S. Regs., Part II. and the Staff Manual respectively. Title pages will be prepared in manuscript.

Place	Date	Hour	Summary of Events and Information	Remarks and references to Appendices
WINCHESTER	3/xii/15	6:30 a.m.	Marched to Southampton for embarkation. Weather heavy rain. Arrived SOUTHAMPTON DOCKS. 1.30 p.m.	
	3/xii/15	1.30 p.m. 4.30 p.m.	Embarked on S.S. ANGLO CANADIAN. Sailed at 6.15 p.m. Part of personnel crossed on S.S.C. 102	Sgnf.
LE HAVRE			S.S.C. 102 arrived LE HAVRE. 12 midnight 3rd - 4th/xii/1915. S.S. ANGLO CANADIAN arrived LE HAVRE 7.30 a.m.	
	4th/xii/15		Passage across the Channel fair.	
LE HAVRE	4/xii/15	8.0 a.m to 12 midday	Disembarking from S.S. ANGLO CANADIAN. Equipment drawn as far as possible from Ordnance but equipment far from complete.	Sgnf.
LE HAVRE	4/xii/15	1.0 p.m.	Arrived No 5 Rest Camp. Weather turned to heavy rain and wind.	
LE HAVRE	5/xii/15	6.30 a.m	Paraded and marched off for entrainment. Entrained at Point No 3. GARE DES MERCHANDISES. with 35th Divisional Cyclist Company. Train left 10.39 a.m. Weather fine.	Sgnf.
ST OMER	6/xii/15	8.10 a.m	Arrived ST OMER and detrained.	
	6/xii/15	11.60 a.m	Marched from ST OMER via BLENDECQUES. HEURINGHEM. (Long halt for dinner at 12.0 noon to 1.0 p.m.). ECQUES. CLARQUES to MAMETZ. Weather fine, turned to heavy rain after passing ECQUES. Arrived MAMETZ at 4.0 p.m. and billeted.	Sgnf.
MAMETZ	7/xii/15		Rested in billets. Distributed mobilization equipment obtained at LEHAVRE between sections. Weather fine in morning, but again turned to rain and wind.	Sgnf.
MAMETZ	8/xii/15		Rested in billets. Made arrangements with G.O.C. 115th Brigade for instruction of infantry in military engineering.	

T2134. Wt. W708—776. 500000. 4/15. Sir J. C. & S.

Army Form C. 2118.
Page 2.

WAR DIARY
of 151 (Field) Co. R.E.
INTELLIGENCE SUMMARY.
(Erase heading not required.)

Instructions regarding War Diaries and Intelligence Summaries are contained in F.S. Regs., Part II. and the Staff Manual respectively. Title pages will be prepared in manuscript.

Place	Date	Hour	Summary of Events and Information	Remarks and references to Appendices
MAMETZ	8/11/15 (cont.)		In afternoon route march under section officers. Weather fine.	GWF
MAMETZ	9/11/15		Company sent for route march by sections in the morning. N.C.O's made to guide their sections by map and find their way about. Programme prepared for training with 115th Infantry Brigade, and submitted to G.O.C. and approved. No 2 section in afternoon instructed in Grenades & Bombs throwing. Remainder of sections lectured by their Section Officers. Weather raining in morning. Turning to storm in afternoon & evening. Mens kits in trenches all cleaning and had to be changed. Horse picket lines had to be re-excavated at night and horses re-picketed owing to water.	GWF
MAMETZ	10/11/15	10.0 am	Instruction section in military engineering to officers 115th Infantry Brigade Company route march under Captain Cory R.E. No 3 Section took over instruction of 113th Infantry Brigade in military engineering under Lieut. J. Haviside R.E. No 4 section under Lieut Morgan took over from 126th Field Company instruction of 114th Infantry Brigade in military engineering. Officer Commanding & Lieut Morgan met G.O.C. 114th Infantry Brigade on the subject in afternoon. No 4 Section Section Officers Commanding Nos 1 & 2 Sections made arrangements with units in 115th Infantry Brigade for instruction to their battalions in military engineering. Nominal Roll of Officers etc of 151 (Field) Co. R.E. on embarking from England	

Officer Commanding :- Captain S.C.Y Fenton R.E. Captain :- Captain F.H. Cory. R.E. Captain :- Captain F.H. Cory. R.E.
No 907
H.Q. Sergeant :- No 67524 Sergeant S.W. Davis. C.S.M:- C.S.M. J. Paulman R.E.
C.Q.M.S :- No 99995 C.Q.M.S. W.D. — No 88531 Mounted Sergeant C. Harburg
Farrier Sergeant :- No 67524 Sergeant C.E. Morgan. No 67468 Sergeant S. Thomas
No 1 Section :- Officer Lieut. W.E. Willis. Sergeant No 62414 Sergeant J.S. Cook.

T2134. Wt. W708—776. 500000. 4/15. Sir J. C. & S.

Army Form C. 2118.

Page 3.

WAR DIARY
of 151 (Field) Co. R.E.
INTELLIGENCE SUMMARY

(Erase heading not required.)

Instructions regarding War Diaries and Intelligence Summaries are contained in F. S. Regs., Part II. and the Staff Manual respectively. Title pages will be prepared in manuscript.

Place	Date	Hour	Summary of Events and Information	Remarks and references to Appendices
MAMETZ	10/xii/15 (cont)		No 2 Section Officer :- 2 Lieut D.O. JONES. No 3 Section Officer :- No 67515 Sergeant I.M. Edwards. Lieut J. Howels. Sergeant No 62688 Sergeant J.S. Griffiths. No 4 Section Officer Lieut. G.V. Morgan. Sergeant No 62724 Sergeant F Owen.	GVF.
MAMETZ	11/xii/15		No 3 Section at work instructing 113th Infantry Brigade. No 4 Section instructing 114th Infantry Brigade. Nos 1 & 2 Sections employed making bombing range. Weather very heavy showers all day. Country flooded.	GVF.
MAMETZ	12/xii/15		No 3 Section employed instructional practice for 113th Infantry Brigade, without infantry. Remainder company employed in construction of a bombing range. 1000 bombs received for instructional purpose.	GVF.
MAMETZ	13/xii/15		Nos 1 & 2 sections employed under Section Officers giving instruction in military engineering to 115th Infantry Brigade. No 3 Section with 113th Infantry Brigade. No 4 Section with 114th Infantry Brigade. Work is being carried out with one or two exceptions in a satisfactory manner.	GVF.
MAMETZ	14/xii/15		In morning, sections employed under Section Officers as yesterday instructing infantry in military engineering. At 12.30 p.m. to 2.30 p.m were at FLECHINELLE (during talons, as many of all ranks as possible). Nos 1, 3, and 4 Sections employed giving night instruction.	GVF.
MAMETZ	15/xii/15		In morning, sections employed instructing infantry brigades in military engineering. At 12.30 p.m. to 4.0 a.m musketry practice at ranges between BLESSY and ESTRÉE BLANCHE. No 3 Section employed on night operations.	GVF.

T2134. Wt. W708—776. 500000. 4/15. Sir J. C. & S.

Army Form C. 2118.

Page 4.

WAR DIARY
of 151 (Field) Co. R.E.
INTELLIGENCE SUMMARY

(Erase heading not required.)

Instructions regarding War Diaries and Intelligence Summaries are contained in F. S. Regs., Part II. and the Staff Manual respectively. Title pages will be prepared in manuscript.

Place	Date	Hour	Summary of Events and Information	Remarks and references to Appendices
MAMETZ.	16/xii/15		Instruction continued in military Engineering to Infantry Brigade. Nos 1 and 3 Sections gave night instruction. Classes for bombing started under Captain CORY R.E.	Sgnf.
MAMETZ.	17/xii/15		Instruction continued in military Engineering to Infantry Brigade. No 4 Section gave night instruction. Bombing Classes were continued.	Sgnf.
MAMETZ.	18/xii/15		All work closed down and Stores collected at MAMETZ. 50 men sent to demonstration in use of gun cotton. Is given by an Infant.	Sgnf.
MAMETZ.	19/xii/15	7.30 a.m.	Paraded and marched via AIRE - ISBERGUES - SAINT VENANT to new billets at ROBECQ. Arrived at 2.0 p.m. Weather fine and clear. Transport and men heavily loaded owing to extra blankets, and fur coats.	Sgnf.
ROBECQ.	20/xii/15	8.0 a.m.	Paraded and marched to new billets at LES 8 MAISONS. East of VIEILLE CHAPELLE, arriving at 1.0 p.m. Detachment left at ROBECQ with horses and light spring cart. Weather cloudy but fine.	Sgnf.
LES 8 MAISONS.	21/xii/15	-	Company rested in billets, and generally cleaned up the Mess. Commanding Officer and Section Officers taken round trenches by officers of 81st (Field) Company, R.E. Section employed in:- Left Section of 19th Division in front of NEUVE CHAPELLE GUARDS DIVISION on left. No 1 Section employed carrying material for 81st (Field) Co R.E.	Sgnf.
LES 8 MAISONS.	22/xii/15		Carpenters and Blacksmiths employed in making Dug out frames. Parties employed in drawing timber from C.R.E.'s store at LA FOSSE. All work carried by night by order of O.C. 81st (Field) Co R.E. owing to probable delay visible to be caused by artillery fire. Very wet weather.	

T2134. Wt. W708-776. 500000. 4/16. Sir J. C. & S.

Army Form C. 2118.

Page 5.

WAR DIARY
of 151 (Field) Co. R.E.
INTELLIGENCE SUMMARY
(Erase heading not required.)

Instructions regarding War Diaries and Intelligence Summaries are contained in F. S. Regs., Part II. and the Staff Manual respectively. Title pages will be prepared in manuscript.

Place	Date	Hour	Summary of Events and Information	Remarks and references to Appendices
LES 8 MAISONS.	23/XII/15		Received orders as to change of programme of work for the Company. To be employed on improving communication trenches, HUN STREET and CHURCH ROAD. Reconnoitred HUN STREET with O.C. No 1 Section (LIEUT WILLIS). This trench can be drained considerably by churns out when blocked and improving cross drains. Will then require frames and trench boards. Reconnoitred CHURCH ROAD. This road is a more serious problem as it is deep and does not lend itself to drainage except near NEUVE CHAPELLE. Frames and Trench boards required. No 2 Section employed on RESERVE WORK South of BOUT DEVILLE at night. Heavy rain at night and early morning of 24/XII/15.	GUF.
LES 8 MAISONS.	24/XII/15		No 1 Section started work on HUN STREET. Nos 3 and 4 Sections on CHURCH ROAD. All carpenters and blacksmiths employed in billets making up frames. No 2 Section provided loading parties for material from R.E. Store at LA FOSSE. Considerable progress made in drainage of HUN STREET. Water also drained from CHURCH ROAD behind and in NEUVE CHAPELLE village. One man of No 4 Section wounded at this work. No 2 Section continued on Reserve Work at night. Nos 1, 3 and 4 Sections employed taking up material to work at night, by wagon to EUSTON POST and thence to CHURCH ROAD by trolley and HUN STREET by carrying parties. Weather showery. Water draining freely.	GUF
LES 8 MAISONS	25/XII/15		No 1 Section employed on draining HUN STREET and started fixing trench frames and trench boards. The majority of drainage of this trench completed. Carpenters and blacksmiths employed on trench frames and brickets in	

Army Form C. 2118.

Page 6

WAR DIARY
of 151 (Field) Company R.E.
INTELLIGENCE SUMMARY.
(Erase heading not required.)

Instructions regarding War Diaries and Intelligence Summaries are contained in F. S. Regs., Part II. and the Staff Manual respectively. Title pages will be prepared in manuscript.

Place	Date	Hour	Summary of Events and Information	Remarks and references to Appendices
			Company Workshops. Nos 3 and 4 Sections employed on CHURCH ROAD. Commenced trestling and frames behind NEUVE CHAPELLE. Drainage to within 60 yards of the firing line nearly completed. No 2 Section provided working parties during day, and conveyed material from EUSTON POST at night to site of work. Company workshops employed on preparing material for work.	Geot.
LES 8 MAISONS	26/11/15		No 1 Section continued work at HUN STREET. Drainage started in places to front steps. Walls were cleaned. Trestling, legs of floor boards, etc continued for 50 yards. No 3 Section employed on drainage of CHURCH ROAD between EDGEWARE ROAD and firing line. Proceeding satisfactorily, the trench being drained by a parallel drain and shoots to nearly dry. No 4 Section employed on cleaning steps and trestling from STREAM North of CHURCH REDOUBT to EDGEWARE ROAD. Said poorly waterlogged and steps continually wrecked. Work started by Said fire on the bottom at 3.0 p.m. Hours of work 8.30 a.m. to 5.0 p.m. Weather Rainy, rain at night, showery during day.	
LES 8 MAISONS	27/11/15		No 1 Section continued work at HUN STREET. Trestling and lifting old boards continued to second stream. Work started continually by enemy shell fire in afternoon. No 2 Section paraded at 8.0 a.m and marched to R A DIVISIONAL H.Q. GUARDS DIVISION for strengthening Artillery Observation Posts. No 3 Section paraded at 8.0 a.m and worked at CHURCH ROAD communication trench commencing at EDGEWARE ROAD and working towards firing line with trestling and trench boards. Shelled heavily in afternoon and	Geot.

Army Form C. 2118.

Page 7.

WAR DIARY
of 151 (FIELD) COMPANY R.E.
INTELLIGENCE / SUMMARY.
(Erase heading not required.)

Instructions regarding War Diaries and Intelligence Summaries are contained in F. S. Regs., Part II. and the Staff Manual respectively. Title pages will be prepared in manuscript.

Place	Date	Hour	Summary of Events and Information	Remarks and references to Appendices
			Work in consequence delayed. No 4 Section paraded at 3.0 a.m. and took up material to EUSTON POST (called from then through NEUVE CHAPELLE Valley to EDGEWARE ROAD) material for No 3 Section in CHURCH ROAD. Carpenters shop employed on making trench frames and preparing pickets. Wratten Party used with heavy rain in early morning and towards midday. Fine in afternoon.	9am GMF
LES 8 MAISONS	28/xi/15		Extra detachment of 12 N.C.O.'s and men sent off at 8.0 a.m. to join No 2 Section, for preparing alarmation posts. No 1 Section continued work at HUN STREET. Nos 3 and 4 Sections continued at the replacing portions of CHURCH ROAD. All work carried out by day. No 2 Section allotted to various groups of battalions preparing alarmation posts, on the line in front of LAVANTIE. Weather fair and clear all day. Heavy bombardment of NEUVE CHAPELLE about 3.15 p.m. Bombarded work on CHURCH ROAD near CHURCH REDOUBT. At 8.0 p.m. Head-Quarter Section and carpenters employed on carting material to CHURCH ROAD and HUN STREET.	GMF
LES 8 MAISONS	29/xi/15		Sections employed on HUN STREET and CHURCH ROAD as on previous day. HUN STREET heavily shelled between 10.30 AM and 11.0 AM and also between 2.0 p.m and 2.30 p.m. No casualties. No 2 Section employed on alarmation posts of GUARDS DIVISION. WORKSHOPS employed on preparation of material for work on HUN STREET and CHURCH ROAD.	
LES 8 MAISONS	30/xi/15		Sections employed on HUN STREET and CHURCH ROAD as on previous day. HUN STREET again shelled between 1.30 p.m and 2.45 p.m Considerably delaying work. Men prevented from carrying material.	

Army Form C. 2118.

Page 8.

WAR DIARY
of 151 FIELD COMPANY. R.E.
INTELLIGENCE SUMMARY.
(Erase heading not required.)

Instructions regarding War Diaries and Intelligence Summaries are contained in F. S. Regs., Part II. and the Staff Manual respectively. Title pages will be prepared in manuscript.

Place	Date	Hour	Summary of Events and Information	Remarks and references to Appendices
LES 8 MAISONS	31/12/15		Along the LA BASSÉE Road by day CHURCH ROAD in vicinity of NEUVE CHAPELLE was shelled between 12 noon and 1.30 p.m and also between 2.0 p.m and 3.0 p.m. No 2 Section continued work at Royal Artillery Observation Posts of the GUARDS DIVISION. Details similar from ROBECQ. Nos 1 and 4 Sections paraded at 3.0 a.m in order to carry down material before day break, starting work on completion of carrying. Sections continued on HUN STREET and CHURCH ROAD as yesterday, especially PONT LOGY DRAIN owing to finer weather for a couple of days, water level in streams has fallen considerably. No 2 Section employed as yesterday on Observation Posts. In turn came men war shelled out of their work	Sgt. G.C.V Fenton Captain R.E. O.C. 151 (FIELD) COMPANY. R.E.
	31-XII-15			

151st F.C. R.E.
Vol: 2

JAN.

Volume II

War Diary

OF 151 FIELD COMPANY. R.E.

for month of January 1916.

Army Form C. 2118.

WAR DIARY
of 151 FIELD COMPANY. R.E.
INTELLIGENCE SUMMARY.
(Erase heading not required.)

Volume II page 1.

Instructions regarding War Diaries and Intelligence Summaries are contained in F.S. Regs., Part II. and the Staff Manual respectively. Title pages will be prepared in manuscript.

Place	Date	Hour	Summary of Events and Information	Remarks and references to Appendices
LES B. MAISONS	1/1/16		Nos 1, 2 and 3 Sections continued work at HUN STREET and CHURCH ROAD. There is heavy earthwork to be carried out, but no infantry working parties to assist. Nos 1 & 4 Sections paraded at 8.0 a.m. No 3 Section at 8.0 a.m. Work practically uninterrupted, as no hostile artillery fire. No 2 Section employed on Observation Posts for GUARDS DIVISION, Royal Artillery. Posts in buildings along RUE TILLELOY at CHAPIGNY, FAUQUISSART, LE TILLELOY and PICANTIN. Insufficient working parties supplied by R.A. and complaint made to C.R.E. GUARDS DIVISION, who referred to G.O.C. R.A. Very heavy wind all day. Some rain.	GUNT.
LES B MAISONS	2/1/16		Work on HUN STREET and CHURCH ROAD continued as on previous day. No infantry working parties on being provided, although asked for, and certain wastage of skilled labour in employing sappers on earth work. Progress slow on this account. Day quiet from artillery interruption, there being only some High Explosive shells on head of CHURCH ROAD about 10 b.m. No 2 Section employed on Royal Artillery Observation Posts as yesterday. On no representation to the R.A.H.Q. of GUARDS DIVISION, larger working parties are being provided to assist. Weather fine in morning, but heavy rain in afternoon and night.	GUNT.
LES B MAISONS	3/1/16		Work on HUN STREET and CHURCH ROAD continued. Progress slow owing to heavy earthwork. Very little artillery fire to interrupt work. No 2 Section on artillery observation posts for GUARDS DIVISION. The Section officer complained that there was insufficient trench, brick hammers and saws for his work, and C.R.E. GUARDS DIVISION	

Army Form C. 2118.

WAR DIARY
of 151 Field Company R.E.
INTELLIGENCE/SUMMARY
(Erase heading not required.)

Volume II Page 2.

Instructions regarding War Diaries and Intelligence Summaries are contained in F.S. Regs., Part II. and the Staff Manual respectively. Title pages will be prepared in manuscript.

Place	Date	Hour	Summary of Events and Information	Remarks and references to Appendices
LES 8. MAISONS.	4/1/16		refund to issue any. This must be a misunderstanding. Weather fine all day and clear. Nos. 1.3 and 4 Sections continued work of already commenced on HUN STREET and CHURCH ROAD. No 1 Section also advanced 30 80 feet. The total work carried out by No 1 Section in HUN STREET since commencement was laying 158 new trench boards and frames 8'0" in length, and laying 67 old trench, in addition to improvements to drainage and putting the revetments in order. No 3 Section worked with No 4 Section at front. The whole drainage of CHURCH ROAD was taken by then sections and put in a satisfactory condition. The trench was nearly completely put in passable order up to 100 yards of the firing line, and the work still remaining to be done was laying of trench boards and clearing of falls. A sketch of the trench work referred to to date is attached to this volume. The weather was fine, and work was not interrupted by artillery fire. No 2 Section employed on installing observation Posts. Lieut. G.U. Morgan was sent to take charge.	
LES S. MAISONS	5/1/16	8.04am	Paraded for return to ROBECQ. Arrived at ROBECQ about 2.30 p.m. Good day for marching, but met 113th Infantry Brigade on road, which caused delay, and also caused the units wagon to go too near the ditch and got bogged by edge of road giving way. The need for extra transport is now evident. The loads given in the F.S. Manual are very complete, but with the addition of an extra blanket for men, which the men cannot be expected to carry in the march in the winter in addition	GUM

T2134. Wt. W708—776. 500000. 4/15. Sir J. C. & S.

Army Form C. 2118.

WAR DIARY
of 151 (FIELD) Company R.E.

INTELLIGENCE SUMMARY.
(Erase heading not required.)

Volume II page 3.

Instructions regarding War Diaries and Intelligence Summaries are contained in F.S. Regs., Part II. and the Staff Manual respectively. Title pages will be prepared in manuscript.

Place	Date	Hour	Summary of Events and Information	Remarks and references to Appendices
ROBECQ.	6/1/16		to enter charge, fire extinguishers, etc. The cleaning of all vehicles is greatly in arrear of that Calculated. No 2 Section continued with GUARDS DIVISION.	GNF
ROBECQ.	7/1/16		Sections employed in cleaning vehicles and equipment. Some N.C.O's instructed in use of instruments in the afternoon.	GNF
ROBECQ.	8/1/16		The cleaning of all vehicles, bicycles, and equipment continued. The cleaning and repairing of billets also continued. An order was sent to LIEUT MORGAN to commence a separate WAR DIARY from 5th January 1916 for the detachment in Observation Posts, and this will be attached as an Appendix.	GNF
ROBECQ.	9/1/16		The company was given a holiday in lieu of Christmas Day. Nothing of interest occurred during the day as far as the portion of the Company was concerned.	GNF
ROBECQ.	10/1/16		Company went to Church Parade in the morning. Holiday remainder of the day, nothing of interest.	GNF
ROBECQ.			Paraded at 8.0 a.m. No 1 Section did gas helmet drill in the morning. Nos 3 & 4 Sections were given instruction in Demolitions. Company trained in afternoon at the Brigade Battle Officers. Attended a conference with 115th Brigade Officers and was shown to by the Corps Commander. Nothing further of interest.	GNF
ROBECQ.	11/1/16		Paraded at 8.0 a.m. Lieut HOWELLS with N.C.O's of Nos 3 & 4 Sections carried out some demolition	GNF

Army Form C. 2118.

WAR DIARY
of 151 (FIELD) COMPANY. R.E
INTELLIGENCE SUMMARY
(Erase heading not required.)

Volume II Page 4

Instructions regarding War Diaries and Intelligence Summaries are contained in F. S. Regs., Part II. and the Staff Manual respectively. Title pages will be prepared in manuscript.

Place	Date	Hour	Summary of Events and Information	Remarks and references to Appendices
ROBECQ	11/1/16		Reconnaissance work to the North West of AIRE; LIEUT WILLIS similar work with No 1 Section N.C.O's in the village. The remainder of the men entrained on trestles with gas helmets and bombing, and unloading and	GMF
ROBECQ	12/1/16		improvements to equipment and vehicles. Also musketry and judging distance. Continued instruction as yesterday. Nothing of note during day.	GMF.
ROBECQ	13/1/16		Continued instruction as yesterday. Nothing of note.	
ROBECQ	14/1/16		Continued instruction in the morning. In afternoon received orders to move east to billet at LES 8 MAISONS to work under 19th DIVISION and to arrive by 10 h.m. Packed all stores and equipment before dark.	GMF
ROBECQ	15/1/16	6:30am	Completed attestations respecting to various recruits and repairs. Paraded and marched troops by the following route. DOUCE CRÈME FERME - South Bank of canal - RIEZ-DU-VINAGE - LE CORNET MALO - ZELOBES - VIEILLE CHAPELLE. Arrived 12:30 p.m. Dull day but fine	GMF
LES 8 MAISONS	16/1/16		men of sections employed on work repairing billets, building kitchens, incinerators, ablution rooms, making straw mats etc. Went round LORETTO road with O.C. 81st Field Company in the morning to see about the erection of steel arched corrugated shelters in various towns. In afternoon went round with O.C. 62nd FIELD Co about the erection of similar shelters at village south of RICHEBOURG-ST-VAST near RUE DES BERCEAUX. This latter work can commence to-morrow, but there is no material for LORETTO ROAD.	GMF.

T2134. Wt. W708-776. 500000. 4/15. Sir J.C. & S.

Army Form C. 2118.

WAR DIARY
of 151 FIELD COMPANY R.E.
INTELLIGENCE SUMMARY
(Erase heading not required.)

Volume II Aug 5

Place	Date	Hour	Summary of Events and Information	Remarks and references to Appendices
LES 8 MAISONS	17/1/16	—	No 1 Section employed on the preparation of sites for STEEL SHELTERS on the RUE DES BERCEAUX. The remainder of the company with Head Quarters employed on the improvement of billets.	GWF
LES 8 MAISONS	18/1/16		No 1 Section with 3 Steel Shelters continued. No 3 Section, and men furnished from howitzers will work trying to bank of material for the working of the same shelters on the LORETTO ROAD. No 3 Section continuing the work of the 81st FIELD COMPANY on the same shelters, and No 4 Section furnishing the unloading party. No 4 Section employed on work about billets. The RIGHT GROUP DIVISION R.A. GUARDS DIVISION Telegraphed to ask for more bricklayers for urgent work required on tactical grounds. Telegram sent to (R.E. 38th WELSH DIVISION) asking when O.P. entrenchment was to be relieved.	GWF
LES 8 MAISONS	19/1/16		No 1 Section continued at work on RUE DES BERCEAUX erecting Steel Shelters, completing the whole of the steel work for that section for 1 Company, (11 shelters). No 3 Section employed on similar work on the LORETTO ROAD, completing all they had material for. On LORETTO ROAD a large infantry working party had been provided, which carried on similar work. Some shelters of the ST YAST STN, when men were at work, but no remedies. Sent extra bricklayers to Artillery, GUARDS DIVISION, as C.R.E., 38th (WELSH) DIVISION notified that whips would not take place until 24th inst. Weather fine and bright all day.	GWF
LES 8 MAISONS	20/1/16		No 1 Section continued work on the RUE DES BERCEAUX, working at completion work on the steel shelters and	

T2134. Wt. W708—776. 500000. 4/15. Sir J. C. & S.

Army Form C. 2118.

WAR DIARY
of 151 FIELD COMPANY R.E.
INTELLIGENCE SUMMARY.
(Erase heading not required.)

Volume II page 6.

Instructions regarding War Diaries and Intelligence Summaries are contained in F. S. Regs., Part II. and the Staff Manual respectively. Title pages will be prepared in manuscript.

Place	Date	Hour	Summary of Events and Information	Remarks and references to Appendices
			also submarine during infantry on sand bagging. No 3 Section also worked on the RORETTE ROAD, with a large infantry working party. The erection of shelters was stopped owing to lack of small stores, which could not be obtained. C.R.E. held a conference as to carrying on of work on taking over and an extension of the line. Also the question of stores, etc. An appreciation of the work of the 38th DIVISION was read out on parade. Some stones at midday.	GWF.
LES 8 MAISONS	21/1/16		The details of the company were employed on improvements to billets. No 1 Section employed on steel shelters at RUE DES BERCEAUX. Remainder employed on improving billets. Presumably inhabited on new line with Captain Cory R.E.	SWF.
LES 8 MAISONS	22/1/16		No 1 Section sent up a small detachment to supervise the sandbagging of the Steel shelters on the RUE DES BERCEAUX. The remainder of the men employed on billets. No 2 Section and details under LIEUT MORGAN returned to H.Q. from the GUARDS DIVISIONAL ARTILLERY. Took over from the 81st FIELD COMPANY from the arrival of the 114th Infantry Brigade this night. Also received orders from C.R.E. 38th WELSH DIVISION to take over the erection of all steel shelters for the present.	GWF
LES 8 MAISONS	23/1/16		All officers of sections were sent with a few men to study 114th Infantry Brigade at work. No 1 Section was allotted to the right battalion of the Sub-Division. No 3 Section allotted to Left battalion. No 4 Section was given the communication Trenches. No 3 Section employed on Steel shelters for Cook area of 113th Brigade. O.C. made	

Army Form C. 2118.

WAR DIARY
of 151 FIELD COMPANY R.E
INTELLIGENCE SUMMARY
(Erase heading not required.)

Volume II Page 7

Instructions regarding War Diaries and Intelligence Summaries are contained in F.S. Regs., Part II. and the Staff Manual respectively. Title pages will be prepared in manuscript.

Place	Date	Hour	Summary of Events and Information	Remarks and references to Appendices
LES 8 MAISONS	24/1/16	—	A reconnaissance of work required with G.O.C 114th Brigade, and also the selection of strong posts. Colder, frosty weather in morning into fog. Clear bright day. Nothing of note. Men not taken in wires employed in the cellars.	GWF.
LES 8 MAISONS	25/1/16	—	Work continued on yesterday. Good progress of work by 15th Welsh, the Left Battalion. Work in HIGHLAND TRENCH commenced to connect with MOGG'S HOLE, then connecting up BALUCHI, and CHURCH with Left Battalion Head-Quarters. G.O.C 114th Brigade continued his reconnaissance. 4 Strong Posts decided on. Weather warmer again and clean. All spare men employed in cellars.	GWF.
			WORK was carried out as follows. No 1 and 2 sections were employed working with infantry in front trenches. The revetment of the front trenches was continued. The parapet is being broadened by throwing earth over. Some dug-outs have been commenced, but this work is not so urgent as the parapet work, and traverses. Considerable difficulty is being experienced in getting infantry to understand this. No 6 Section employed on trench communication trenches, was nothing's return to trench. Eighteen shorts at BALUCHI Trench heightened by night watering, firstly. Turfing and traversing of HIGHLAND and SANDBAG ALLEY continued. No 2 Section continued their work in the DIVISIONAL AREA at Steel Station and H.Q. for 2nd RIGHT BRIGADE. C.R.E 38th WELSH DIVISION watched work. Division on Steel Station in LORETTO ROAD	3.?
LES 8 MAISONS	26/1/16	—	Continued work as previous day. Working by night on BALUCHI TRENCH. C.R.E. inspected steel shelters	

Army Form C. 2118.

WAR DIARY
of 151 FIELD COMPANY R.E.
INTELLIGENCE SUMMARY.
(Erase heading not required.)

Volume II. Pay. 8.

Instructions regarding War Diaries and Intelligence Summaries are contained in F. S. Regs., Part II. and the Staff Manual respectively. Title pages will be prepared in manuscript.

Place	Date	Hour	Summary of Events and Information	Remarks and references to Appendices
LES 8 MAISONS	27/1/16	—	Being carried out by No 2 Section. Sections employed as before. No 4 Section will in twenty workmen firstly at night improved BALUCHI TRENCH. Officer the Working Party was wounded. No 1 Section put in a new machine gun emplacement and improved an existing one, moving it slightly and widening its arc of fire. Found that the type of machine gun teams are very fussy and cumbersome to carry.	GWF
LES 8 MAISONS	28/1/16		Sections still employed on the same work. No 1 Section put in two new machine gun emplacements, wiring 3 at night, and finishing at 5.0 a.m. Altogether many VERY lights and a stand light fired by Germans. Work not interfered with.	GWF
LES 8 MAISONS	29/1/16		Section continued at work as previous day. Cameron sources wished to shield EDGEWARE ROAD during hours killed. Staff sheltered carried up for right battalion H.Q. at the end of HUN STREET. Tried the company Patrick field standlights at night in front line, but not satisfactory. Beam is not strong enough and too concentrated.	GWF
LES 8 MAISONS	30/1/16		Sections continued at work on before. All the covering screens to protect EDGEWARE ROAD were completed. The work on the front line is progressing slowly, but it is a question of continual instruction on the part of the R.E. officers concerned to induce work to be carried out satisfactorily. The officers do not trouble to inspect and carry on work with their men, and thereby causes all the onus of work to fall on the R.E. An additional machine gun	GWF

T2134. Wt. W708—776. 500000. 4/15. Sir J. C. & S.

Army Form C. 2118.

WAR DIARY
or
INTELLIGENCE SUMMARY.
(Erase heading not required.)

Volume II. Aug 9

Place	Date	Hour	Summary of Events and Information	Remarks and references to Appendices
			Emplacement was finished with the exception of sandbag work. Work on communication trenches was also continued, men employed on BALUCHI Trench at night section 6 up. Work inspected by Chief Engineer, XI Corps.	Sect.
LES 8 MAISONS	3/1/16		All sections continued their work as previously. HIGHLAND Trench was linked up with BALUCHI Trench at one end and progress is being made to hook the work on to MOGGS HOLE. No 1 Section continued at night putting in two extra dugouts for machine gun emplacements in the front line. No 7 entanglement which is designed to flank the N.E.B. and also an all round field of fire. Very heavy British artillery fire on German front lines during day.	Sf.
			The Diary of the work carried out by the Brown Detachment attached to the GUARDS DIVISION on artillery Renovation Posts is attached to this report as Appendix I.	

G.V. Fenton
Captain R.E.
O.C. 151 (FIELD) Co. R.E.

Army Form C. 2118.

WAR DIARY
or
INTELLIGENCE SUMMARY.
(Erase heading not required.)

Appendix I page 1.

Place	Date	Hour	Summary of Events and Information	Remarks and references to Appendices
Guards Division	5/1/916		Working parties proceeded the work, building observation posts along the Rue Tilleloy. The chief work being ame.io, Timbers rooms with 12"×12" Timbers & 9"×8", and building up Sandbag revetments for F.O.Os dugout, and observation posts along. The R.E. party attached to the Guards Division for this work consists of 2 Officers 50 Sappers N.C.Os & men and 1 mounted section with R.E. Tool Cart and R.E. Limbered Wagon.	Detachment of 2 officers 50 Sappers & mounted section of the 151st Field Coy Royal Engineers
"	6/1/916		Working parties employed building O.P. and dugouts for 11 Batteries, along the Rue Tilleloy and on the right of the Division. Good progress was made generally. The C.R.A. personally inspected the work and complimented on the good work done by the R.E. The C.R.A. wishes to have a large number of built chimney observation posts, but difficulty is experienced in obtaining the necessary material. It is estimated that 30,000 Bricks will be required for each brick chimney O.P. The quantity of Cement and Sand required depends largely on the quality of Bricks used, if new bricks are used the quantity required will be less than if any and the work also pushes along much more rapidly.	

Army Form C. 2118.

WAR DIARY
or
INTELLIGENCE SUMMARY.
(Erase heading not required.)

Instructions regarding War Diaries and Intelligence Summaries are contained in F.S. Regs., Part II. and the Staff Manual respectively. Title pages will be prepared in manuscript.

Appendix I page 2.

Place	Date	Hour	Summary of Events and Information	Remarks and references to Appendices
Guards Division	7/1/1916		Working parties paraded at 8am for work on observation posts, with R.F.A. working parties assisting and filled sandbags Etc. Slow progress was made on Brickwork due to shortage of material and — only 3 Trowels to work with. Good progress was made with the heavy timbering and also sandbag laying. Night parties were employed getting material and fixing the roof slates where the O.P. or Sandbag work was observed by the enemy.	
"	8/1/1916		R.E. working parties from detachment, paraded at 8am and proceeded for work on artillery observation posts, with working parties of R.F.A. men. Good progress was made on Bristol, No.112 Slow O.P. and Stint Farm, and F.O.O.s dugout near Ebenza Farm. Night party was employed sandbag laying on Chatigny, and getting material to the other O.P.s.	

Army Form C. 2118.

Appendix I Aug 3

WAR DIARY
or
INTELLIGENCE/SUMMARY
(Erase heading not required.)

Instructions regarding War Diaries and Intelligence Summaries are contained in F. S. Regs., Part II. and the Staff Manual respectively. Title pages will be prepared in manuscript.

Place	Date	Hour	Summary of Events and Information	Remarks and references to Appendices
Guards Div.	9/5/96		Working parties of the Detachment paraded at 8 am to proceed to work on Observation posts. A supply of Timber was received from the O.C. to put on the work on Brickwork. The Enemy shelled The C.R.A.'s zone and got a direct hit on the Sandbags & Bricks protecting the front of the O.P. but caused no damage. This place was well packed with bricks & sandbags from floor to floor and is a cube of about 8ft, The shell was apparently a 4.15" H.E.	
Guards Div.	10/5/96		Working parties of the Detachment paraded at 8 am to proceed on Observation posts and F.O.O's Dug outs. The Farm O.P. was shelled during the previous night and damaged. Bristol, Barclay, Christ Farm & Chevigny were shelled during the day, but no damage was done. Night parties were employed on The Lounge, & Bristol O.P's fixing Roof Tiles to cover up new work Etc, a party was also employed on Chevigny O.P. Sandbag laying in front of the Christ Chimney. Good progress was made generally except for lack of material for the Double Brick Chimney O.P's	

T2134. Wt. W708—776. 500000. 4/15. Sir J. C. & S.

Army Form C. 2118.

Appendix I page 4

WAR DIARY
or
INTELLIGENCE SUMMARY

(Erase heading not required.)

Instructions regarding War Diaries and Intelligence Summaries are contained in F. S. Regs., Part II. and the Staff Manual respectively. Title pages will be prepared in manuscript.

Place	Date	Hour	Summary of Events and Information	Remarks and references to Appendices
Guards Division	11/1/16		Working parties proceeded at 8am to carry out work on new Observation Posts on the Rue Tilleloy. Satisfactory progress was made with the work generally, except on the new design Back Chimney O.P's which we could not procure with though lack of material. Small parties were employed last night with fatigue parties of R.F.A. men carrying material to O.P.s and one working party was employed laying sandbags at Chupigny O.P.	
"	12/1/16		Working parties proceeded at 8am to carry on work on new Observation Posts along the Rue Tilleloy and on the right of the Division. The Lounge & The Farm O.P's were damaged by the Enemy Guns 5·9 shells, but no casualties.	
"	13/1/16		Working parties proceeded at 8am to work on O.P's. Five N.C.O's and men reported sick and was attended by the R.F.A. medical officer. Good progress was made generally. R.E. Limbered Wagon was sent to Robecq for new construction for Store etc.	

Army Form C. 2118.

WAR DIARY
or
INTELLIGENCE SUMMARY.
(Erase heading not required.)

Instructions regarding War Diaries and Intelligence Summaries are contained in F. S. Regs., Part II. and the Staff Manual respectively. Title pages will be prepared in manuscript.

Appendix I pp 5.

Place	Date	Hour	Summary of Events and Information	Remarks and references to Appendices
Guards Division	14/1/96		Working parties employed building observation posts. No1. HQ staff O.P. finished. Two N.C.Os and men reported sick and were treated by the R.F.A. M.O. All Gas Helmets were examined and Gas Helmet Drill carried out, and the whole detachment were lectured on the use & care of Helmets.	
"	15/1/96		Working parties employed building O.Ps. Two N.C.Os & men again reported sick. Three O.Ps were shelled heavily during the morning but slight damage done. Three rifle parties were employed sandbag laying, timbering, etc., work that was not possible in day light. Good progress was made generally.	
"	16/1/96		Working parties employed building O.Ps. Two N.C.Os & 2 men reported sick. Concrete foundation laid for Chapigny O.P. Good progress was made generally.	

Army Form C. 2118.

Appendix I Aug 6

WAR DIARY
or
INTELLIGENCE SUMMARY

(Erase heading not required.)

Place	Date	Hour	Summary of Events and Information	Remarks and references to Appendices
Guards Div	17/1/16		Working parties from sedentary battalions were employed with R.F.A. working parties building observation posts and F.O.O. dugouts. The "Daan" observation could not before sufficient timbering could be erected, last night. Good progress was made generally.	
"	18/1/16		Working parties were employed with R.F.A. working parties building observation posts and "Dug outs" for forward observation officers.	
"	19/1/16		R.E. working parties employed with R.F.A. working parties building observation posts for Right and Left Groups R.F.A. Guards Division. Good progress was made on the Brick Chimney type. The material required for these is supplied much better than formerly.	

WAR DIARY
or
INTELLIGENCE SUMMARY

(Erase heading not required.)

Army Form C. 2118.

Appendix I Part 7

Place	Date	Hour	Summary of Events and Information	Remarks and references to Appendices
Guards Div.	28/1/16		Detachment employed building observation posts with R.E.A. working parties. One R.E.A. man assisting the party building "The Barclay" Observation Post was killed by enemy shell. Work on changing O.P. was resumed though shortage of materials. Otherwise good progress was made generally. The F.O.O.'s "Dug out" at Glen's Farm was finished.	
	29/1/16		Detachment employed building observation posts with R.E.O. working parties. O.C. Detachment 19th Div. R.E.O. reported at 12 oclock noon. He arrived motor store taking over. Received telegraphic news from O.C. to return to the Company at 10 a.m. tomorrow. Pieries further news at 8.30 P.M. from left Group. C.O. that relief would take place at 5 P.M. Bridge O.P. and Sagar's framework finished except for brickwork. 1st Barn O.P. complete half framework for new O.P. Barclay complete O.P. except for signal Room which required temporary sandbagging. Lourge O.P. all timber work finished except for two days work on sandbagging and covering passage. No 1 star O.P. Brick (single) chimney completed at temporary observation stage.	

Army Form C. 2118.

Appendix I Page 8.

WAR DIARY
or
INTELLIGENCE SUMMARY.
(Erase heading not required.)

Instructions regarding War Diaries and Intelligence Summaries are contained in F.S. Regs., Part II. and the Staff Manual respectively. Title pages will be prepared in manuscript.

Place	Date	Hour	Summary of Events and Information	Remarks and references to Appendices
Guards Div	31/1/1916		No 2 Spare O.P. completed, except for proposed brick buttress.	
			The Farm O.P. Practically completed, except for little timbering in O.P. and "Dugout".	
			6. R.A. Horse O.P. completed except for sandbags on top floor.	
			6. Rohigny O.P. Double brick chimney in course of erection.	
			Stork Farm O.P completed.	
			D 75 Battery dugout. completed.	
			George Liaison officers Dugout in course of erection.	
			B.75 Battery dugout at O.P. completed.	
Guards Div.	23/1/16		The Detachment paraded 8am and proceeded to pack up and clean billet. The O.C. Battery gave orders not to march the Detachment from the Battery until 4 pm. Two officers and 4 n.c.o's from the 81st field Coy R.E. reported at 10 am and were shown over the O.P.'s under construction. The Detachment returned to Les 8 Maisons billets at 9 pm.	

Geo. Morgan
Lt. R.E.

G.C.V Fenton
Captain R.E.
³¹/₁/16.
O.C. 151 (F.D) Co R.E.

Volume III.

WAR DIARY

OF 151 FIELD COMPANY. R.E.

for month of February 1916.

157th F.C.R.E.

Vol: 3

Army Form C. 2118.

WAR DIARY
of 151 FIELD COMPANY. R.E.
INTELLIGENCE SUMMARY
(Erase heading not required.)

Volume III page 1.

Instructions regarding War Diaries and Intelligence Summaries are contained in F.S. Regs., Part II and the Staff Manual respectively. Title pages will be prepared in manuscript.

Place	Date	Hour	Summary of Events and Information	Remarks and references to Appendices
LES 8 MAISONS	1/2/16	—	No 2 Section took over the left battalion of the front line. No 3 section took over steel stations in the RICHEBOURG ST VAAST. RUE DES TIERCEAUX area. Work proceeding in a satisfactory manner generally, but the drainage of the front line is not making much progress. A permanent party for drainage is necessary, so it is not found to change the whole of the drainage parties every 3 days or so on relief.	GUFF.
LES 8 MAISONS	2/2/16	—	Work continued as yesterday. No Reserve Brigade Working parties, so work at LORETTO ROAD and night work on BALUCHI trench not carried out. Same alignment and No 2 Section commenced putting in a new machine gun emplacement to cover the DUKE'S BILL. Heavy shelling near CHATEAU ROAD in the morning. 4 casualties among infantry owing to back blast of a H.E. Shell blowing into a dug-out open at the back. Entrance to dug-outs should be well screened or curved.	GUFF
LES 8 MAISONS	3/2/16.	—	Work continued as previous day. CHURCH ROAD completed through to King's Lane. Machine Gun emplacement completed by No 2 Section on far as to truth the box covered. Night party in HUN STREET, improving parapets. Sandbag work continued on all steel shelters. This work is delayed owing to shortage of stores. Commenced work on lifting and putting NORTH WESTERN Trolley track and laying trench branch.	GUFF.
LES 8 MAISONS	4/2/16	—	Work carried on as previous days, except that owing to inter battalion relief in the Brigade, there were no working parties. Agreement to the permanent drainage parties given by the Division and 40 men under an N.C.O. to be detailed by 115th Brigade for this work. This will be most satisfactory.	ans.

Army Form C. 2118.

WAR DIARY
of 151 FIELD CO. R.E.
INTELLIGENCE SUMMARY.
(Erase heading not required.)

Volume III. Page 2.

Instructions regarding War Diaries and Intelligence Summaries are contained in F. S. Regs., Part II. and the Staff Manual respectively. Title pages will be prepared in manuscript.

Place	Date	Hour	Summary of Events and Information	Remarks and references to Appendices
LES 8 MAISONS	5/2/16	—	Work carried on by all sections as on previous day. Working parties provided. Progress of work satisfactory. One Bomb hit by a bullet at EUSTON POST. Some shells fired by Germans fell in vicinity of trenches, but no damage done.	G.W.F.
LES 8 MAISONS	6/2/16	—	Work carried on by all sections as before. Sort the men a half holiday. HIGHLAND Trench completed as far as MOGGS HOLE, thus making complete communication from Left Battalion H.Q. to firing line via CHURCH ROAD. Artillery actions on each side.	G.W.F.
LES 8 MAISONS	7/2/16	—	Continued work as day before. All work progressing satisfactorily. The erection of dug-outs in reserve army in frames being available. The extraction of HUM STREET is proceeding, revetments being carried up by day and carried up by night. Clear day with a few shower of rain. Little artillery action.	G.W.F.
LES 8 MAISONS	8/2/16	—	Work continued as previous day. Nothing of note, and very little progress as there was no infantry parties at all, as Brigade relief was taking place with the Right Brigade and Battalion relief with the Left Brigade. Command trench tramway from RUE TILLELOY to SANDBAG ALLEY, Cuyere's ride. Weather showery. Fairly quiet as far as artillery is concerned.	G.W.F.
LES 8 MAISONS	9/2/16	—	Carried on the work on the trenches and communication trenches. New permanent drainage parties started work and made good progress for first day's work. Artillery firing active on both sides. Weather fine and clear.	G.W.F.

Army Form C. 2118.

WAR DIARY
of 151 (FLD) COMPANY. R.E.
INTELLIGENCE SUMMARY.
(Erase heading not required.)

Volume III   Aug. 3

Instructions regarding War Diaries and Intelligence Summaries are contained in F.S. Regs., Part II. and the Staff Manual respectively. Title pages will be prepared in manuscript.

Place	Date	Hour	Summary of Events and Information	Remarks and references to Appendices
LES B. MAISONS.	10/2/16		Work continued on all trenches and still shelters as on previous dates. Infantry drainage party attended also carrying on with work. Nothing of note during day. Weather fine, clear, mild and sunny.	Sgnd.
LES B. MAISONS.	11/2/16		Carried on work on the front line and communication trenches as usual. No progress on still shelters as no further stores received. Rained heavily all day and dull and wet. Nothing of note.	Sgnd.
LES B. MAISONS	12/2/16		Work on front line and communication trenches continued. The General Staff put up a scheme for improvement of the line, of which we had information was much. Arrangements made to commence work on the trenches of DUG-OUTS for MOGGS HOLE and HUN STREET, the latter on or near EDGEWARE ROAD. The majority of the work is known quite beyond the time that the DIVISION will remain in this part of the line. Cold, rainy weather. Dull and not good for observation.	Sgnd.
LES B. MAISONS	13/2/16		Work on front line and communication trenches continued. Nos 1 and 4 Sections commenced the erection of extra dug-outs at HUN STREET, right battalion H.Q. and MOGGS HOLE respectively. LIEUT WILLIS with a detachment of No1 Section and a carrying party of infantry proceeded at night to tramway at POPES NOSE. They remained out until 6.0 a.m of 14-2-16, but in spite of extensive digging in the bank of the work, they were unable to find any trace of them. O.C. company proceeded to GORRE to go round the new Brigade Section allotted us. GIVENCHY-LEZ-BASSÉE.	Sgnd.
LES B MAISONS	14/2/16		Work continued on previous days. Near SIGN POST LANE, improvements to the foundation of the tramway put in hand. O.C. examined new Brigade Trenches with C.R.E. and also drainage.	Sgnd.

Army Form C. 2118.

WAR DIARY
of 151 FIELD Co. R.E.
INTELLIGENCE SUMMARY
(Erase heading not required.)

Volume VIII pages 4.

Instructions regarding War Diaries and Intelligence Summaries are contained in F.S. Regs., Part II. and the Staff Manual respectively. Title pages will be prepared in manuscript.

Place	Date	Hour	Summary of Events and Information	Remarks and references to Appendices
LES 8 MAISONS	15/2/16	—	Work carried on as usual until midday. No infantry parties owing to relief taking place. In afternoon paraded equipment ready for moving tomorrow. Handed over front line to O.C. 94th FIELD COMPANY, preparatory to move tomorrow morning. Windy, rainy day.	gust
LES 8 MAISONS	16/2/16	—	Marched at 8.0 a.m. by sections in departments to GORRE. Bad day for marching, very high wind and heavy rain. Arrived at GORRE by midday and billetted in the BREWERY. In afternoon officers went out to see the work and line. At night party employed on COVENTRY STREET improvement to parapet and also a sapping party on relief.	
GORRE	17/2/16	—	The company took on and continued the work of the 5th Field Company R.E. until definite arrangement could be made for work. No 1 Section employed on machine gun Emplacement at LE PLANTIN in the village line of defence. No 2 Section employed on the production of the roof of the First Aid Post at LONE FARM. No 3 Section employed on COVENTRY STREET. No 4 Section employed on machine gun emplacements at SIDBURY Defences. The G.O.C. 113th Brigade went round the work with the Officer Commanding and pointed out work to visual exploitation and the order. Consequently the work is subdivided among the sections as follows:— No 1 Section Machine Gun Emplacements. No 2 Section. Reserve line work. No 3 Section Right Battalion work in front line and communication trenches. No 4 Section Left Battalion work in front line and communication trenches. Appendices to this diary. I. map of NEUVE CHAPELLE and surrounding trenches to illustrate previous diaries to date.	gust P. Mi...y

Army Form C. 2118.

WAR DIARY
of 151 Field Company R.E.
INTELLIGENCE/SUMMARY.
(Erase heading not required.)

Volume III Part 5.

Place	Date	Hour	Summary of Events and Information	Remarks and references to Appendices
GORRE	18/2/16	—	Attention II. Work in progress handed over to 94th Field Company R.E. on 15/2/16. Attention III. Work in progress taken over from 5th Field Company R.E.	
			Sections commenced work as detailed on previous day. Owing to the Brigade relief, there was no working parties to be attached and all work had to be carried out by R.E. The chief work carried out by No.1 Section was on machine gun emplacements of work and repairs on SIDBURY Redoubt, WINDY CORNER. No.2 Section employed on the continued defence of SIDBURY and the construction work on the shutters of DEVILS CASTLE. Worked over No.3 Section concentrated on COVENTRY STREET (night work), QUEEN'S ROAD, HATFIELD ROAD and WOLFE ROAD communication trenches. No.4 Section worked at the front and support line on GIVENCHY HILL. Also NEW ROSE STREET.	Genl.
GORRE	19/2/16	—	Work continued as on previous day. No.1 Section also commenced repairs to WINDY CORNER HOUSE. WINDY CORNER barricade intended by No.1 Section to shield the corner from machine gun fire. O C visited Artillery observation Posts with Artillery officer to examine them as to importance and work required on each.	Genl.
GORRE	20/2/16	—	All work carried on as on previous day. BELLE VUE O.P. damaged by shell fire and repaired at night. Also examined with a view of taking over work on them from the mining company, commencing in the night groups of section.	Genl.
GORRE	21/2/16	—	All work carried on as on previous day. No.1 Section commenced additional work at SAPPERS HOUSE in GIVENCHY, clearing. Two sections of 203rd Field Company R.E. arrived for instructional work.	Genl.

Army Form C. 2118.

WAR DIARY
of 151 FIELD COMPANY. R.E
INTELLIGENCE SUMMARY.
(Erase heading not required.)

Volume III pages 6.

Instructions regarding War Diaries and Intelligence Summaries are contained in F. S. Regs., Part II. and the Staff Manual respectively. Title pages will be prepared in manuscript.

Place	Date	Hour	Summary of Events and Information	Remarks and references to Appendices
GORRE	22/2/16	—	All work continued except that 1 section of 203rd Field Company took over the continuation of the NEW ROSE TRENCH, while the other commenced on WOLFE ROAD. No 1 Section erected steel ladder up the back of GIVENCHY CHURCH TOWER at night and made observation hole for O.P. No 2 Section commenced work shuttering up curbing of the SOUP KITCHEN near WINDY CORNER to make shelter proof and also the erection of a bunker well inside. No 4 Section took over work on the left group of sapes to craters, in charge of infantry working at night. C.R.E. visited the lines, going along railway line.	GWF
GORRE.	23/2/16		All work continued so an hurried day, bright brickwork and concrete stopped owing to frost and snow. LE PLANTIN W Observation Post and WINDY HOUSE Observation Post commenced, the shuttering up of the former and the clearing for a brick tower at the latter by No 1 Section. No 2 Section took in hand the WINDY CORNER SOUP KITCHEN and the protection of the Advanced Brigade office. Weather snow during day, cold and frosty. Continued in section by C.R.E. 38th DIVISION, G.S.O 2 and G.O.C. of 113th Brigade.	GWF
GORRE.	24/2/16	—	Owing to frost all brickwork and concrete making gun emplacements and observation posts stopped. No 1 Section carried on with ironwork and timbering at Artillery Observation Posts. No 2 Section completed R.E. work at Windy Corner Soup Kitchen. Also carried on at Windy Corner and the Advanced Brigade office. No Bomb 4 Sections employed with the front line Battalions improving trenches. Also No 4 Section employed sapping; all work was delayed owing to trenches and sapes being cleared of deposits. 203rd Field Company attached, carried	

T2134. Wt. W708—776. 500000. 4/15. Sir J. C. & S.

Army Form C. 2118.

WAR DIARY
of 151 FIELD COMPANY R.E.
INTELLIGENCE SUMMARY
(Erase heading not required.)

Volume III Aug 7

Instructions regarding War Diaries and Intelligence Summaries are contained in F. S. Regs., Part II. and the Staff Manual respectively. Title pages will be prepared in manuscript.

Place	Date	Hour	Summary of Events and Information	Remarks and references to Appendices
GORRE.	25/2/16	-	on work at WOLFE ROAD and NEW ROSE TRENCH. Continued work as on previous day with all sections, and with section of 203rd Field Company R.E. Commenced work on No. 1, 2 and 3 First Aid Posts in WINDY CORNER ROAD. No 2 Section shuttering and covering cellars. The weather still frosty and snow. Site for machine gun emplacement at PRINCES ISLAND cleared at night.	GWF.
GORRE.	26/2/16	-	Work carried on as on previous days, but all work delayed by efforts to prevent injury to personnel by German artillery. The closing of all the front area to prevent injury to personnel by German artillery. The weather started to get milder and thaw started. No 2 Section started the erection of steel shelters.	GWF.
GORRE	27/2/16	-	Work continued. Thaw having set in masonry work and cement was recommenced on Artillery Observation Posts and Machine Gun emplacements by No 1 Section. No 2 Section continued their work in the Village area, erecting steel shelters. Covering cellars for front aid posts, &c. No 3 Section employed on night section front line. Special work transferred covered station in Ac. Sapa for observation for trench mortar fire. No 4 Section continued saps with left Battalion and dug-outs for trench mortar battery, in addition to other work. All unwanted trenches falling in on sides owing to thaw. 2 extra sections of 203rd Field Company arrived, two sections details.	GWF.
GORRE	28/2/16	-	Started a redistribution of work. Nos 1 & 2 Sections employed on O.P.'s machine gun emplacements and defence scheme of GIVENCHY village. Nos 3 & 4 Sections continued then employed on front line defence and communication Trenches. 1 Section of 203rd Field Company employed on WOLFE ROAD; 1 section employed on COVENTRY STREET. 1 section on the Sapa	GWF.

Army Form C. 2118.

WAR DIARY
of 151 FIELD COMPANY R.E.

~~INTELLIGENCE SUMMARY.~~

Volume III Page 8

(Erase heading not required.)

Instructions regarding War Diaries and Intelligence Summaries are contained in F. S. Regs., Part II. and the Staff Manual respectively. Title pages will be prepared in manuscript.

Place	Date	Hour	Summary of Events and Information	Remarks and references to Appendices
			of the Right Group of trenches and 1 section on the Reserve line. Chief work of interest during day was the construction of a trench bridge observation post in AC Sap for trench mortar battery. Frame thoroughly set in and weather mild with rain at intervals.	GVF.
GORRE	29/2/16		No 1 Section continued work, on making gun emplacements and communication trenches No 1 SIDBURY DEFENCES and LE PLANTIN No 6. No 2 Section employed in clearing cellars for GIVENCHY dugout Scheme, and machine gun emplacements. No 3 Section continued with right battalion, on communication trenches front line, etc. No 4 Section continued with left battalion and also pushing forward F.H.J. & K. Saps. 203rd Field Company working up on Saps to Right Group of trenches. WOLFE ROAD, COVENTRY STREET and Village Line. Fine clear day, quite mild.	GVF.

G.V. Fenton
Captain R.E.
O C 151 FLD Co RE.

APPENDIX 2.

WORK IN PROGRESS HANDED OVER BY 151st
FIELD COY, R.E. to 24th FIELD COY, R.E.
15th Feby 1916.

1. TRAMWAY.— Trench boarding and raising and packing. New Branch Line to SANDBAG ALLEY in abeyance.

2. CHURCH ROAD.— Improvement and heightening of parapets.

3. KINGSWAY.— Clearing and floorboarding.

4. HUN STREET.— Improvement and heightening of parapets.

5. CRESCENT COMMUNICATION TRENCH WITH BRANCHES ALONG ROOME TRENCH.— Clearing and floorboarding.

6. MOGGS HOLE,-AND HUN STREET.— Erection of extra dugouts.

7. B. LINE.— Clearing and revetting from MOGGS HOLE to BALUCHI TRENCH.

8. LORETTO ROAD.— Erection of steel shelters.

9. BOMB ROW.— Clearing and floorboarding (just commenced).

10. HIGHLAND TRENCH.— Improvement to parapet.

11. NEUVE CHAPELLE CHATEAU
    and
    PORT ARTHUR KEEP.— Strong points near NEUVE CHAPELLE CHATEAU, and the preparation of scheme for strengthening PORT ARTHUR KEEP handed over.

G.V. Fenton
Captain, R.E.,
O.C. 151st Field Coy, R.E.

APPENDIX 3.

WORK IN PROGRESS TAKEN OVER FROM THE
5th FIELD COY, R.E. BY THE 151st FIELD
COMPANY, R.E., 16th February 1916.

1. Machine Gun Emplacements (a) W.C. No.3 at WINDY CORNER, inner nearly up to loophole height, outer walls complete. A large number of the rails for the roof are at site. Wall in front of loophole will require clearing when M.G. is complete. Its arc is intended to fire just in front of the wire of village line, and 150° about to E. of wire only.

2. SIDBURY. Two steel and concrete M.Gs. are proposed here, as per plate A. Of these, one has been commenced, and has made good progress. A tramway had to be constructed to bring up materials. The other M.G.E. should be started as soon as possible, so as to free the tramway for work at other M.G. Arcs of fire are wide, and are shewn on the plate.

3. Other M.G.Es Ordered.
    (a) One in house near GUNNER SIDING and WOLFE ROAD.
    (b) Two in MARIE REDOUBT.
    Arcs of fire of these are shewn in plate B. When building these redoubt should be carefully considered, and renovated with dog-legging entrance.

4. OBSERVATION STATIONS. Please see separate list attached.

5. R.A.GUN POSITIONS. We have been giving advice, materials, and a skilled assistance in the construction of bomb proof shelter for guns and telephone operators. These were under construction in four places. Route B X 24a., F.11.d., F.10.d., F.4.d.

6. DEVILS CASTLE (LONE FARM) FIELD AMBULANCE DRESSING STATION. Repairs of walls completed. Provision of bursting roof over cellars (in progress).

7. NEW ROSE STREET. Sapping platoons have been worken on sandbag revetment in the southern portion. The remainder has been revetted, with wire frames up to the Brigade Boundary. This needs repairs and parapet thickening almost throughout. Tools and Baskets are dumped at site of work.

8. SAPS D.G.H.J.K. Please see separate statement attached.

9. COVENTRY STREET, HOPE STREET, CAMBRIDGE TERRACE, HATFIELD. Please see separate statements attached.
    COVENTRY STREET is passable from SHAFTESBURY AVENUE to HATFIELD ROAD. It must be reclaimed up to front line, and HOPE STREET must be made passable by floor boarding, and parapet raised to give protection. The eastern end is to be firestepped to fire N.

10. WOLFE ROAD. This is passable throughout, but will require

Appendix 3 (continued).

revetting, and a little more floor boarding to make a permanent job.

11. DRAINAGE.   I have handed to O.C. 151st Field Coy, R.E. a copy of Drainage map, and have taken O.C. C. Coy, 19th Welsh round drains in our area. He also went with O.C. 226th Fd Coy, R.E. round drains in C (Left   area, and he has been given a copy of drainage map.   Drains that require especial watching:-
    (1) SUEZ CANAL and its tributaries.
    (2) SUNKEN ROAD DRAIN. The drains running from DUCKS BILL to the Canal vitally affects this area, but lies almost entirely outside it. When I last saw C.R.E. 33rd Divn he told me that a considerable amount of work was being done on it.

There is only one R.E. Stores, viz. GORRE BREWERY. List of contents herewith. There is a dump at WINDY CORNER only for immediate use.

STATEMENT REFERRED TO IN APPENDIX 3,
PARA. 8.

Sap F.   Reference map handed over. The main gallery
         should go along the crest between the two
         craters with a gallery and loophole to each.

Sap G.   This is abondoned, and is of no importance from
         the point of view of the miners.

Sap H.   O.C. 180th Co. wishes same work done as at Sap
         F. He wishes the sap to be pushed on as an open
         Sap first up to the old sap head commanding the
         crater.

Sap J.   Site of new sap was shewn on the ground, but no
         work has been started. It was considered advisable
         to clear the connection J-K first. This is in
         progress.

Sap K.   This has two heads, one filled in, the other partially
         cleared out. O.C. 180th Coy wants to get the Southern
         Sap cleared out first so as to command one crater.
         He also wants a gallery run from the Northern Sap with
         a loophole into each crater. All work on this sap
         must be very silent, as the enemy bombs the sap head
         at any sign of work.

STATEMENT REFERRED TO IN APPENDIX 3, PARA 9.

COVENTRY STREET.   Has been floorboarded throughout.
Present floorboards are at level of old
firing step. Work has been commenced on
building up parapet.
Parados needs revetting.
The continuation past HATFIELD ROAD keeping
E. of WILLOW ROAD has not been worked on.

HOPE STREET.   This has not been worked on, but should
be reclaimed. At present it is very narrow,
and wet, with one big shell hole in the
middle.

HATFIELD ROAD.   Floorboarded throughout. It has not been
graded properly, so gets very wet. Old
floorboards will probably have to come up
and be raised on transoms, the parapet being
raised also. The parapet is already very
low indeed near WOLFE ROAD.

CAMBRIDGE TERRACE.   An old lateral communication with four T
heads for firing purposes. This has been
allowed to lapse badly at present. A fair
amount to the mud has been cleared out, but
there is still a good deal to get out.
The question of revetment has not been
settled.

Water level in this area fluctuates, rising rapidly
if the drain to the canal gets blocked.   The drain
is in the next Division's hands.

Volume IV.

War Diary of

151 FIELD COMPANY. R.E.

for month of March 1916

38

151 FCRE

Vol 4

Army Form C. 2118.

WAR DIARY
of 151 FIELD COMPANY. R.E.
INTELLIGENCE SUMMARY.
(Erase heading not required.)

Volume IV page 1.

Place	Date	Hour	Summary of Events and Information	Remarks and references to Appendices
GORRE.	1/3/16	—	Sections continued at work as usual. No 1 Section completed LE PLANTIN'S No 6 Machine Gun emplacement and made considerable progress with the LE PLANTIN and WINDY CORNER Observation Posts. Also the provision and strengthening of Dugouts in ARTILLERY HOUSE and BELLE VUE Observation Posts. No 2 Section employed on the GIVENCHY Village Defences, chiefly on cellars in the various keeps. No 3 Section continued work on the right battalion area, cleaning communication trenches. Also continued at work at some minor alterations in GIVENCHY KEEP. No 4 Section employed on work with the left Battalion Defences, supervising working in front line work and communication trenches. Also continued with F, H, J, & K Saps. All ready for tunnelling for look-out places. 1 known boring driven through by vibration of steel pin and being driven by Ramming. 203rd Field Company attacked for instruction carried on with work on night groups of saps, COVENTRY STREET, WOLFE ROAD and the works in the Rumor line.	
GORRE	2/3/16	—	Continued work on as previous day by all sections. Nothing of interest or note.	
GORRE.	3/3/16	—	Sections continued work as previously. No 1 Section is so far as possible completing Machine Gun emplacements and Observation Posts in the village lines before working in cement on the GIVENCHY defences. No 2 Section employed on the cleaning and clearing of cellars in the village of GIVENCHY for defence purposes. No 3 Section employed on right battalion defences and communication trenches. No 4 Section on left centre saps and left battalion front line and	

Army Form C. 2118.

Volume IV. Page 2.

WAR DIARY
of 151 F.D. Co. R.E
INTELLIGENCE SUMMARY.
(Erase heading not required.)

Place	Date	Hour	Summary of Events and Information	Remarks and references to Appendices
GORRE.	4/3/16	—	Communication trenches. 203rd Field Company attended workings on village tram, COVENTRY STREET, Right Centre Sap, and WOLFE ROAD communication trenches. Weather dull and some rain. Continued work as on previous days, but owing to heavy snow and not many of the unrevetted communication trenches, and most of the bad revetment in the front line and supports collapsed, causing the trenches to become flooded, drainage blocked and generally in a very bad state. No 4 Section working on revett. sups in the left extension arm. Tunnelling under the lips of the craters, changing direction to broken craters at angle. Heavy snow and sleet all forenoon, night and day. A very nasty day from all points of view.	Supt
GORRE.	5/3/16		Sections continued at work as usual. The falls on all trenches still continued, and although the weather was better, the state of the trenches was bad. O.C. went round the trenches to be taken over as far as the canal with the O.C. 11th Field Company. They are in a bad state and in places impassable. The work also fell heavily on the company taking over. 124th Field Company arrived taking over the billets from 203rd Field Company, which left in the morning.	Supt
GORRE.	6/3/16		Continued work by all sections as on previous days. Communication trenches and other trenches very bad condition. Men were extended about midnight 6" - 7" snow 1916, showing its arm in a satisfactory manner. Very little drainage done to sups or trenches from the extension. Suffering faulties of No 3 Section were forward to carry out when work necessary. All jobs delayed by difficulties of transport in the slush and snow. 1 N.C.O. wounded	Supt

Army Form C. 2118.

WAR DIARY
of 151. F.D. Co. R.E.
INTELLIGENCE SUMMARY.
(Erase heading not required.)

Volume IV Page 3.

Place	Date	Hour	Summary of Events and Information	Remarks and references to Appendices
GORRE.	7/3/16	—	At work on LE PLANTIN W. O.P. by Sapper.	GWE
GORRE.	8/3/16	—	All sections carried on with work as on previous day. There was a continuation of snow and sleet that made the trenches very bad and all work considerably delayed. W39/P/5/G41 P05 Despatched by WAR Bagan 124 Field Company prepared to commence work on part of 7th line from midnight 7th-8th March 1915. Continued with work, No 4 Section Knocking our work on the left of the line to 124 FIELD COMPANY R.E. Took over new trenches as far as the LA BASSÉE Canal on the South. 113th Infantry Brigade relieved by 114th Infantry Brigade in the front line, the former going into rest billets. A battalion of the 33rd DIVISION was also relieved on the night of our line by the 114th Brigade. An improvement in the weather, the snow stopping, but a sharp frost at night. Received orders at night from C.R.E. that new entanglements in the LE TOURET and TUNING FORK lines would be strengthened and constructed under the supervision of the 151 FLD Co, the former by the RESERVE Brigade and the latter by the 19th Battalion (PIONEERS) WELSH REGIMENT.	GWE
GORRE.	9/3/16	—	Work continued as usual on Communication Posts and GIVENCHY Defences. Sappers sparing men on both groups of section, but no damage of any consequence to the trenches, sides or parapets. Reconnaissance carried out of lining required for TUNING FORK and LE TOURET LINES, with a view to putting the work in hand tomorrow. Better weather during day, but going very heavy owing to snow and thaw. Order of the day issued as an Appreciation of the work done by 38th DIVISION during the time they have been in the Trenches. No 4 Section at rest.	GWE Appendix I

Army Form C. 2118.

WAR DIARY
of 151 FIELD COMPANY. R.E.
INTELLIGENCE SUMMARY.
(Erase heading not required.)

Volume IV page 4

Place	Date	Hour	Summary of Events and Information	Remarks and references to Appendices
GORRE	10/3/16		Continued work as in previous days. Work on entailing observation commenced at first wall in Keans and a new trench will be commenced on completion. (No.1 Section) (No.2 Section) New trenches on GIVENCHY Defences owing to very considerable difficulty in disposing of floating earth, etc. Many allies being situated and strengthened. Steps to right grants of culvert still in Keans by No.3 Section. No.4 Section in rest, employed on strengthening wire to the Reserve line of defence. Water still came of trenches, weather being warm, snow melting etc.	Genl
GORRE	11/3/16		Work continued as usual. No.1 Section commenced two new observation posts in GIVENCHY village. Remainder of work as on previous day. DIVISIONAL CAVALRY employed under R.E. supervision on ORCHARD STREET, while the Brigade draining party employed on front end of WOLFE ROAD. Weather milder and finer, but very bad going under foot. Nothing occurred of much interest. West strength infantry employed on Reserve lines.	
GORRE	12/3/16		Work continued as usual. Owing to dryer weather, with pumping and draining of drains, the water level in ORCHARD ROAD STREET and front end of WOLFE ROAD considerably lowered. Owing to non-arrival of sufficient material, working parties on the Reserve lines delayed in strengthening work. No.4 Section in rest employed on cleaning rifles, in addition to usual wire work.	Genl
GORRE	13/3/16		All sections continued at work as on previous day. No.1 Section completing observation posts at village farm, and expect to finish them during the week. No.2 Section reaching trenches with allies in GIVENCHY village and machine gun emplacements. Ought to commence brickwork for latter in couple of days.	

T2134. Wt. W708—776. 500000. 4/15. Sir J. C. & S.

Army Form C. 2118.

WAR DIARY
of 151 FIELD COMPANY R.E.
INTELLIGENCE SUMMARY.
(Erase heading not required.)

Volume IV page 5

Place	Date	Hour	Summary of Events and Information	Remarks and references to Appendices
GORRE.	14/3/16		No 3 Section on Safs and COVENTRY STREET. Progress slow and not much to show for work done. No 4 Section still in rest. Work on LE TOURET and TURNING FORK LINES. 19th Platoon continued work, but no infantry parties on insufficient material available. Weather much warmer and dry. Will improve country and work generally.	Snf.
GORRE.	15/3/16		All sections continued work as on previous day. No infantry or equist working parties except for COVENTRY STREET either by day or night. Open from days much warmer. Work on TURNING FORK LINE continued, but owing to lack of stores no work in LE TOURET line.	Snf.
GORRE.	16/3/16		Work continued as on previous day by all sections. LIEUT A.L. CARROLL arrived and took over command of No 3 Section from LIEUT J. HOWELLS, who is transferred to 123rd FIELD COMPANY R.E. to date from 14/3/16. All work considerably improved owing to weather improvement. Trenches drying rapidly.	Snf.
GORRE.	17/3/16		Work continued on as previous day, except that owing to Brigade relief, there were no working parties on the TURNER lines from the Brigade in TRENCHES, owing to relief. Water in trenches and communication trenches considerably less owing to drier weather. Fine bright sunny day. Very little artillery action known.	Snf.
GORRE	17/3/16		Sections continued at work as usual. No 1 Section continued on Observation Posts. No 2 Section employed on the GIVENCHY Defences. No 3 Section on Safs and Coventry Street and No 4 Section in rest on forming Reserve lines, surrounding infantry at work. Nothing of interest during day. Weather fine warm and dry.	Cnf.

Army Form C. 2118.

WAR DIARY
of 151 FIELD COMPANY R.E.
INTELLIGENCE SUMMARY
(Erase heading not required.)

Volume IV page 6.

Instructions regarding War Diaries and Intelligence Summaries are contained in F.S. Regs., Part II. and the Staff Manual respectively. Title pages will be prepared in manuscript.

Place	Date	Hour	Summary of Events and Information	Remarks and references to Appendices
GORRE	18/3/16	—	No 1 Section went into rest. Held No 4 Section unusual work. The bricklayers, masons and plasterers of No 4 Section reported for work on Observation Posts, while remainder of section put on WOLFE ROAD and ORCHARD ROAD, drainage and general putting them in order. No 3 Section on COVENTRY STREET and Saps. Weather continued fine and warm, and dry. Recon. lines continued.	SWF
GORRE.	19/3/16	—	Sections continued work as on previous day. Sunday the men a half holiday for Sunday. No cyclists available. The drainage of the communication trenches is being continued by No 4 Section. Considerable difficulty is being caused by the infantry putting down the floor boards again and thus blocking the drains. Very small infantry working parties provided. Weather fine and warm, and counting day ing well.	SWF
GORRE	20/3/16	—	All sections carried on work as on previous day. No 3 Section was delayed on the site owing to "Stokes" mortar battery bombardment of turn opposite the Sonet section and the GERMAN retaliation. Working party on the LE TOURET RESERVE LINE near SOUTH TUNING FORK was shelled by H.E. and Shrapnel. Weather fine clear day, warm and sunny.	SWF
GORRE.	21/3/16	—	All the work was carried on as on previous days. Progress was made by bricklayers from various sections working on the Observation Posts, brick towers, in GIVENCHY village. No 2 Section continued work on the machine gun emplacements and cellars in the village. No 3 Section employed on the Saps and COVENTRY STREET and No 4 Section on WOLFE ROAD and ORCHARD STREET. drainage and floor boarding. Progress	SWF

T2134. Wt. W708—776. 500000. 4/15. Sir J. C. & S.

Army Form C. 2118.

WAR DIARY
of 151 FIELD COMPANY R.E.
INTELLIGENCE SUMMARY
(Erase heading not required.)

Volume IV page 7.

Instructions regarding War Diaries and Intelligence Summaries are contained in F.S. Regs., Part II. and the Staff Manual respectively. Title pages will be prepared in manuscript.

Place	Date	Hour	Summary of Events and Information	Remarks and references to Appendices
GORRE	22/3/16		slow, but satisfactory, water levels being very considerably lowered and water made to flow along trenches. No 1 Section in charge of wiring LE TOURET Reserve Line, with Reserve Brigade, with Captain Cory and LIEUT WILLIS.	G.M.F.
GORRE	23/3/16		All work continued on as in previous days. The work on ORCHARD road to be handed over the 19th (Infantry) Batt'n West Regiment, the Officer Commanding being warned. Weather was a cold and raining, and generally unpleasant. Very quiet on the front, owing to little or no artillery fire.	G.M.F.
GORRE	24/3/16		All sections carried on work as in previous days. Little of note during the day. The work on the Reserve Line South of ROUTE A. practically completed as far as wire entanglements are concerned. Weather fine but cold.	G.M.F.
GORRE	25/3/16		All sections continued working as in previous day. No infantry working parties on any work except the DIVISIONAL cyclists owing to with Brigade reliefs. Weather started to snow again and continued most of the day. CAPTAIN CORY went down on 10 days special leave at night.	G.M.F.
GORRE	25/3/16		Continued work with all sections as in previous days. Weather cold for good progress of work, being rainy and cold. No 4 Section took on the repair of Two maxim gun emplacements in PONT FIXE NORTH. No 2 Section went into rest instead of No 4 Section and took on the wiring of the RESERVE LINE at LE TOURET. Summers showing a man in the morning near D 3 Sap, until cannot very little damage. No attempt to occupy it. and it is full of water.	G.M.F.

T2134. Wt. W708—776. 500000. 4/15. Sir J. C. & S.

Army Form C. 2118.

WAR DIARY
of 151 FIELD COMPANY R.E.
INTELLIGENCE SUMMARY.
(Erase heading not required.)

Volume IV page 9.

Instructions regarding War Diaries and Intelligence Summaries are contained in F.S. Regs., Part II. and the Staff Manual respectively. Title pages will be prepared in manuscript.

Place	Date	Hour	Summary of Events and Information	Remarks and references to Appendices
GORRÉ	26/3/16		All sections continued work as on previous day. WINDY CORNER HOUSE O.P. completed by No 1 Section. Weather was raining and stormy with fairs intervals. No 4 Section completed tunnel branching off WOLFE ROAD and HATFIELD ROAD from their junction as far as COVENTRY STREET.	Sgnt
GORRÉ.	27/3/16		Work continued by sections as on previous day. The 19th Pioneers were heavily shelled in ORCHARD ROAD at work and had several casualties. The work in FINCHLEY ROAD has not been continued by them, and falls now to be undertaken. Orders given for No 4 Section to assist work on this branch. The work on mining the Russian Saps continued, but the progress delayed owing to lack of tools. Progress in COVENTRY STREET good by No 3 Section, but the work in the Sap is very bad, the work having to be re-done several times. Weather fine and bright in the morning, but rained and nasty in evening and night. 1 Section of the 234th Field Company R.E. attached for instruction, arriving the day.	Sgnt
GORRÉ	28/3/16		All work continued by sections as on previous day with the exception that No 4 Section detached a party for continuation of work on FINCHLEY ROAD and also started to open out and drain HOPE STREET. Work on the safe hut under LIEUT MORGAN, summary Sany. Continuation of the wiring of the LE TOURET system. Weather fine and dry.	Capt
GORRÉ	29/3/16		Sections carried out work as on previous days. 1 Section of 234th Field Company R.E. working with No 4 Section on communication in Trenches. No work carried on at the Minchew Saw Enfilement at the MAIRIE.	

Army Form C. 2118.

WAR DIARY
of 151 FLD Co R.E.
INTELLIGENCE SUMMARY.
(Erase heading not required.)

Volume IV page 4.

Instructions regarding War Diaries and Intelligence Summaries are contained in F. S. Regs., Part II. and the Staff Manual respectively. Title pages will be prepared in manuscript.

Place	Date	Hour	Summary of Events and Information	Remarks and references to Appendices
GORRE	30/1/16		Owing to No 2 Section being unable to supply sufficient sapper labour. No other incidents of note during day. Weather frost, bright and clear, and all conditions good for Engineer work.	GVF
GORRE	31/1/16		All work continued as on previous day, except that the section of the 234th Field Company was not available for work owing to trench baths. No work in wiring of the LE TOURET Line on this was no infantry working parties, due to an inspection of 114th Brigade by 1st Army Commander. Weather fine & warm, and quite dry.	GVF
			All work continued by sections as on previous days. Reduced infantry parties on wiring the Rouen Lines owing to intra Brigade reliefs. Weather fine and clear.	
			NB. Appendix II attached to War Diary is an appreciation of work carried out during January and February 1916 at NEUVE CHAPELLE.	

G.V. Fenton
Captain R.E.
O.C. 151 FLD Co R.E.

1/15/4

War Diary Volume IV.
Appendix I

Extract from

ROUTINE ORDERS.

BY

MAJOR GENERAL IVOR PHILLIPPS, D.S.O.,

Commanding 38th (Welsh) Division.

Wednesday, 8th March 1916.

ORDER OF THE DAY.

The Major-General Commanding has much pleasure in publishing the following Order. All ranks will, he feels sure receive this high testimony to the good work they have already done with feelings of pride and satisfaction, and will at the same time join with him in the determination to justify by continued good work the high opinion which the Corps Commander has already formed of the Division:-

"G.O.C., 38th Division.

I am anxious to express to all ranks in the Division under your Command my satisfaction at the progress they have made in fighting efficiency since the Division arrived in this country.

Part of the line taken over by the Division was in the most boggy part of Flanders, and another part has been subject to intense and active hostility from the enemy.

Both in working and fighting the Infantry, Artillery, and Engineers have distinguished themselves during the few weeks they have been in the line. They have overcome to a marked extent the great difficulties in the improvement and drainage of the wet part of the line, and by their highly commendable aggressive attitude in the other part they have succeeded in dominating the enemy in front of them.

I am sure that all ranks now appreciate the great value of offensive action, and I shall hope soon to be able to congratulate them on more successful raids in the enemy's trenches.

(Signed) R.HAKING, Lieutenant-General,
Commanding XIth Corps."

7-3-16.

Copy.

War Diary Volume IV
Appendix II

General Staff.
No. G. 467
38th Welsh Division.

To
The General Officer Commanding,
115th Infantry Brigade.

It is with much pleasure that I place on record my appreciation of the good work that has been put in by your Brigade in the improvement of the front line trenches and in the opening up of communication trenches during the time it has held the Left Section of the line occupied by the Division. Will you please convey to the Officers, N.C.Os and men of the Units under your command, including the 151st Field Company, R.E. attached to your Brigade, my thanks for the zeal, energy and soldierlike spirit shown by all ranks. The exigencies of the service prevent my giving your men the period of rest to which they would ordinarily have been entitled, but I feel sure that in calling again upon them to take over at short notice a new line of trenches I can look forward with confidence to their continuing to do their utmost to carry out efficiently the task allotted to them.

(Sd) Ivor Phillipps,
Major General.
Commanding 38th (Welsh) Division.

17/2/16.

(2)

O.C. 151st Fd Coy, R.E.

Forwarded for your information. The G.O.C., 115th Brigade desires to express his thanks to you for the assistance given by the 151st Field Company, R.E.

(Sd) C.L.Veal.
Captain,
Bgde. Major, 115th Brigade.

19/2/16.

1st FCR
Vol 3

XXXVIII

Volume V.

War Diary of

151 FIELD COMPANY R.E.

for month of April 1916.

Army Form C. 2118.

WAR DIARY
of 151 FIELD COMPANY, R.E.
INTELLIGENCE SUMMARY.
(Erase heading not required.)

Volume V page 1.

Instructions regarding War Diaries and Intelligence Summaries are contained in F.S. Regs., Part II. and the Staff Manual respectively. Title pages will be prepared in manuscript.

Place	Date	Hour	Summary of Events and Information	Remarks and references to Appendices
GORRE	1/4/16		No 1 Section continued its work on the Royal building Observation Posts in GIVENCHY Village. Two brick towers in hand. The erection of a painted screen in one house to shield the work does not appear to have been noticed by the enemy as they have taken no action. No 2 Section completed their arrival of not, and will continue to work at the GIVENCHY Village Defences. There was no wiring on the LE TOURET Reserve line as there was an inter Brigade relief. Disturbed portion of 2 NCO's and 3 Sections from Nos 1 & 2 Sections detailed to work in the morning, with LIEUT WILLIS and LIEUT JONES supervising in alternate days. No 3 Section continued work in the night group of craters, opening and clearing the sapes. Also the putting in order of COVENTRY STREET. No 4 Section employed on the communication trenches WOLFE ROAD and HATFIELD ROAD, and also FINCHLEY ROAD, at the continuation of which via ORCHARD ROAD. The 19th (PIONEER) WELSH REGIMENT are working. Weather fine, warm days, very calm.	Sapp F.
GORRE	2/4/16		All sections given a rest during the day, except those supervising working parties. Section of 234th Field Company R.E. employed on HOPE STREET and HATFIELD ROAD. Night work on COVENTRY STREET continued. Weather fine, day and sunny. Very hot for work. No wiring on LETOURET RESERVE line.	Capt.
GORRE	3/4/16		All section continued at work on Front and Reserve lines. No 1 Section on Observation Posts, No 2 Section on GIVENCHY Defences. No 3 Section in the Sapes and COVENTRY STREET and No 4 Section on COMMUNICATION TRENCHES and Machine Gun emplacements at POINT FIVE. Section of 234th Field Company employed on communication	

Army Form C. 2118.

WAR DIARY
of 151 Field Company R.E.
INTELLIGENCE SUMMARY.
(Erase heading not required.)

Volume V page 2

Instructions regarding War Diaries and Intelligence Summaries are contained in F. S. Regs., Part II. and the Staff Manual respectively. Title pages will be prepared in manuscript.

Place	Date	Hour	Summary of Events and Information	Remarks and references to Appendices
GORRE	4/4/16		trenches. The Germans sprang a mine under the left group of SAPS but did not affect our new section. Weather mostly in the morning, but clear, warm, fine and summery later.	GMT.
			All sections continued at work as during previous day. No 2 Section completed the trench boundaries of WOLFE ROAD between GUNNER SIDING and COVENTRY STREET. Great difficulties in obtaining working parties and in being delayed thereby. Weather fine and warm. Good progress being made on new entanglements on the Reserve line.	GMT.
GORRE	5/4/16		All sections continued at work as on previous day. Infantry working parties reduced on the wiring of the LETOURET Reserve line to 300 per day. No 4 Section completed the clearing and trench boarders of FINCHLEY ROAD. Complimentary letter received regarding the work of No 1 Section on Observation Posts, detail is attached. Weather fine all day, but rather breezy. Experiments carried out with a Bangalore Torpedo of Stout Tin, which was entirely satisfactory and very tight.	Appendix I GMT.
GORRE	6/4/16		Work continued as on previous day. Work on machine gun emplacements at PONT FIXE Nos 4 and 16 completed. Wiring continued in the Reserve line. Work at night very considerably delayed at times by very heavy rain storm. Weather during day quite fine, at times breezy. Further experiments of practice carried out with Bangalore Torpedoes, to demonstrate to infantry why last had a failure on previous night.	GMT.

T2134. Wt. W708—776. 500000. 4/15. Sir J. C. & S.

Army Form C. 2118.

WAR DIARY
of 151 FIELD COMPANY. R.E.
INTELLIGENCE SUMMARY

(Erase heading not required.)

Volume V page 3.

Instructions regarding War Diaries and Intelligence Summaries are contained in F. S. Regs., Part II. and the Staff Manual respectively. Title pages will be prepared in manuscript.

Place	Date	Hour	Summary of Events and Information	Remarks and references to Appendices
GORRE.	7/4/16	—	The work on the Sap was transferred to the Section of the 226th Field Company under instruction. Also the construction of a machine gun emplacement at PONT FIXE NORTH. The remainder of the work carried on as on previous days under HATFIELD ROAD was carried on by No 2 Section, and the Section men of No 3 Section employed on KINGS ROAD to get that trench in order. Weather fine and clear.	Gun
GORRE	8/4/16	—	All work continued on as on previous day by the Sections. No wiring parties for the LE TOURET Redoubt done. No 4 Section committed to by trench trunks between junction of ORCHARD ROAD and OXFORD TERRACE to front line. Carried out operations at night to place a Bangalore Torpedo under the German wire to cut to be a working party. Operation arduous and officers combt report to 115th Brigade and attached. Weather fine but cold. Clear front & night, but cold & misty in early morning. Conditions ideal.	Appendices II Gun
GORRE	9/4/16	—	Work continued on as on previous day, except that No 4 Section commenced work on front line to clear up returns centre and right entrance of right salient. This necessitates the clearing of ORCHARD ROAD return WILLOW drain and front line, which is in hand. Artillery were endeavouring to explode Bangalore Torpedo in the enemy's wire without success. Owing to this. H.Q 38th Division decided it was not advisable to try and explode it by night. Fine Clear day and no interruptions to work	Gun
GORRE.	10/4/16		Section continued work on their usual programme. No 1 Section started trench work on the shaft of the	

Army Form C. 2118.

Volume V page 4

WAR DIARY
of 151 FIELD COMPANY. R.E.
INTELLIGENCE SUMMARY
(Erase heading not required.)

Instructions regarding War Diaries and Intelligence Summaries are contained in F.S. Regs., Part II. and the Staff Manual respectively. Title pages will be prepared in manuscript.

Place	Date	Hour	Summary of Events and Information	Remarks and references to Appendices
GORRE.	11/4/16	—	Observation Post at LE PLANTIN 2. A new surface template was completed by the section of the 234th Field Company attached in the church yards at C and CA Sopa. Weather fine, bright and sunny morning, afternoon rainy and idle for work.	GWF
GORRE.	12/4/16	—	All sections continued work as in previous days. Nothing much of note during day, which was dull and raining the majority of the time. The intolerant will work.	GWF.
GORRE.	13/4/16	—	All sections remained in their work as in previous days. Orders received that the company were to leave the front area in a few days and go north near LAVANTIE. Special efforts made to finish as much as possible, especially on Observation Posts and strong machine gun emplacements. Weather much colder with rain and wind.	GWF.
			No 1 Section and No 2 Section employed on clearing as much as they can to finish up Observation Posts and Machine Gun emplacements. The team in GIVENCHY village and SAPPERS HOUSE were practically completed. No 3 and 4 sections employed on loading up pontoon and trestle wagons. On pontoon wagon sent on to LAVANTIE. All arrangements made to hand over to 227th Field Company R.E. Weather dull and cold, but fine.	GWF.
GORRE.	14/4/16	7.0 a.m	Company paraded and marched via LOCON and LA GORGUE to ESTAIRES. Handed over all work to 227th Field Company R.E., notes of the work in progress attached. Captain Long in command on the line of march. Officer	Appendix III

Army Form C. 2118.

Volume V Aug 5.

WAR DIARY
of 151 FIELD COMPANY. R.E.
INTELLIGENCE SUMMARY.
(Erase heading not required.)

Instructions regarding War Diaries and Intelligence Summaries are contained in F. S. Regs., Part II. and the Staff Manual respectively. Title pages will be prepared in manuscript.

Place	Date	Hour	Summary of Events and Information	Remarks and references to Appendices
ESTAIRES	15/4/16	12 Noon	Commanding went round trenches with Adjutant, Divisional Royal Engineers, 39th DIVISION. Weather wet and showing all day. Heavy rain at night. Company billetted at ESTAIRES during night with 115th Brigade. Received report of the instruction of the D.D.V.S. of 1st Army. Copy of extracts from the report attached in which the company was specially mentioned as proven in particularly good condition.	Appendix IV GWF
			Company paraded and marched to LAVANTIE to take over part of the line from 201st Field Company R.E. Handing over notes of that company attached. In afternoon men employed on cleaning billets etc. The section officers and Officer Commanding going round the trenches in the evening. Bright sunny day, but breeze by a few rain and wind showers in morning.	Appendix V
LAVANTIE	16/4/16		Company employed in cleaning billets and making new and further scanty arrangements also the disposal of the accumulation of stable manure of many weeks. Weather fine and warm all day, at start to rain at night.	GWF
LAVANTIE	17/4/16		Company continued work on cleaning billets, and improvements generally. N.C.O's went round the trenches allotted most of work proposed and agreed where is as follows. No 1 Section Left Battalion. No 2 Section Right Battalion, in the front line to be employed in erection of dug outs, machine gun emplacements, and front communication trenches. No 3 Section to be employed on the 300x Reserve line and Third across the Rue Delvas Saliat. No 4 Section in posts and Keeps. Weather dropping rain last 4/th day, clearing up about midday and	Appendix VI GWF

Army Form C. 2118.

Volume I Part 6.

WAR DIARY
of 151 F.L.D Co R.E.
INTELLIGENCE SUMMARY.
(Erase heading not required.)

Instructions regarding War Diaries and Intelligence Summaries are contained in F.S. Regs., Part II and the Staff Manual respectively. Title pages will be prepared in manuscript.

Place	Date	Hour	Summary of Events and Information	Remarks and references to Appendices
LAVANTIE	18/4/16		Again thawing the snow at night. Officer Commanding went round with 2nd G.O.C. 115th Brigade the right posts and front line. East Section continued on work as detailed & work is quite satisfactory and the chief annoyance is not quite satisfactory and the exact position was inspected to the General Staff. The position of the chief annoyance is nothing of mud without the report during the day, as it is the company's first day in the new line. Very heavy showers of rain made going and work very heavy. The Germans did not seem to be very wide awake in the front and little in no sniping or action.	Sgnt.
LAVANTIE	19/4/16		Sections continued at work as on previous days will general reference to breastworks and parados. No 1 Section included in its work the reconstruction of the line near the RED LAMP Salient and the approach to No 9 Medium Gun Emplacement. Work also carried on in communication trenches on both right and left sub-divisions. No 3 Section continued work in the 300 Yard Reserve line. No 4 Section scattered throughout the front. Weather fine and sunny most of the day, but heavy showers rather cold. Many scattered clothing throughout the day, and one coffin slightly wounded by shrapnel in the leg.	Sgnt.
LAVANTIE	20/4/16		Sections continued at work as on previous day. A survey was made of all the observation Posts in the left sector in conjunction with the Artillery to ascertain what work was required. All work of return nature at present, as no firing can yet be observed. Weather dull and showery at first, but cleared later in day.	Sgnt.

T2134. Wt. W708—776. 500000. 4/15. Sir J. C. & S.

Army Form C. 2118.

WAR DIARY
or
INTELLIGENCE SUMMARY.
(Erase heading not required.)

Volume V Page 7

Instructions regarding War Diaries and Intelligence Summaries are contained in F. S. Regs., Part II. and the Staff Manual respectively. Title pages will be prepared in manuscript.

Place	Date	Hour	Summary of Events and Information	Remarks and references to Appendices
LAVANTIE.	21/4/16	—	Sections continued work on the line, but the detail was redistributed owing to 174 Field Company R.E. taking over the right sub-division. No 1 Section continued on the left front line and fixed communication trenches completing 5 No 9 machine gun emplacement. No 2 Section took over the inspection and return of the tents from No 4 Section in the left sub-division. No 3 Section continued work at the Reserve Line. No 4 Section took over the construction and repair of Observation Posts for the artillery. Weather being warm and work all day.	Sgt.
LAVANTIE.	22/4/16	—	Work continued and the sections settling down to the new distribution of work. CRA's Harem O.P. was destroyed by shell fire, and steps were taken to repair it. Nothing of note in the other work going on. Weather dull and showery all day. Very heavy at times. Officer Commanding on duty to LOCON to advise the 39th Division about Observation Posts in the GIVENCHY area.	Sgt.
LAVANTIE.	23/4/16	—	Sections continued at work, as on previous days. Little of interest during day, and work carried on. Weather fine clear day and sunny. At night had out the start to the salient across the RED LAMP for communication on following Moon night.	Sgt.
LAVANTIE.	24/4/16	—	All work carried on as on previous days. No 3 Section working in the Reserve line were shelled in the afternoon but no casualties. No 4 Section making good progress on Observation Posts. No 1 Section commenced with infantry workers party on the start from FIREWORKS POST to support line across the RED LAMP Salient. Weather fine and warm and very clear most of the day. With exception of slow artillery very quiet. The arrival of	

Army Form C. 2118.

WAR DIARY
of 151 FIELD COMPANY. R.E.
INTELLIGENCE SUMMARY.
(Erase heading not required.)

Volume V Aug 8

Place	Date	Hour	Summary of Events and Information	Remarks and references to Appendices
LAVANTIE	25/4/16	—	of a Dam to No 62724 Serjeant F. OWEN and particulars of same are attached. CAPTAIN GREY R.E. left unit on a previous day. Good progress was made on all work. Some of the concertinas posts on the RUE TILLELOY were filled, but very little dummy so far as could be constructed. Weather firm and warm all day and very cold. Some trouble in the provision of infantry working parties. Much rifle and machine gun fire at night, but it did not delay work.	* Appendix N. ✓
SWF.
LAVANTIE	26/4/15	—	All sections were employed as on previous days. Infantry working parties were turning up to work in little numbers. Little of infantry took place during day, but few frozen. Weather fine warm and sunny, and very clear, but not much artillery activity.	SWF.
LAVANTIE	27/4/16	—	Sections continued at work as on previous days. Owing to weather, the weather's parties by night were constantly interfered with. A new scheme for the mounting gun emplacements on the RUE TROUVEROT POSTS line was prepared for approval for the left sub-division, slightly amending the ground scheme by the Divisional General Staff. HOUGOUMONT POST was twenty filled dummy morning, but little dummy. At 10.30 p.m. an alarm was raised of a GAS attack. No further developments so the company was dismissed at 11.30 p.m.	SWF.
LAVANTIE	28/4/16	3.00 am	Heavy shelling of the front positions of the line. Weather fine, clear and warm all day. A bright clear night, and quite warm.	
LAVANTIE	29/4/16		Damage caused by above shelling not very important. No 3 Section was employed in repairing damage caused to	

Army Form C. 2118.

WAR DIARY
of 151 FIELD COMPANY R.E.
INTELLIGENCE SUMMARY.
(Erase heading not required.)

Volume V page 9.

Instructions regarding War Diaries and Intelligence Summaries are contained in F. S. Regs., Part II. and the Staff Manual respectively. Title pages will be prepared in manuscript.

Place	Date	Hour	Summary of Events and Information	Remarks and references to Appendices
			ROTTEN ROW. The remainder of the sections continued at their work. The Observation Post in LE TILLELOY, next to one under course of construction by No 4 Section was set on fire. The gutted main building, but left two standing. Fire started to spread to next Observation Post, but was got in hand and put out. Chief Engineer XI Corps ordered the company to carry out work on the town to endeavor to conceal it. This was done during night, as well as refinishing the clearings caused to an Observation Post. Rollers & tins of interest. Weather fine warm and sunny. Very clear.	
LAVANTIE	29/4/16		Sections continued at work as usual. No 1 Section completed new emplacement for No 8 Machine Gun, and commenced dug-out for No 6 Emplacement. Regarding Observation Post, having shelled the CONVENT, but did not do much damage. Some of the workmen faintly wounded. The C.R.E. inspected the positions of the machine gun emplacements for the RUE DE BACQUEROT, for the left sub-division. Weather fine sunny and warm. Rather hazy for observation. Watching quiet most of the day.	G.W.F.
LAVANTIE	30/4/16		Sections continued at the work as usual. No 4 Section completed the work required for the Observation Post of the Topographical Section R.E. at LAVANTIE. Remainder of work on Observation Posts progressing well. The work on the front line continued. Stormy day. cut nearly completed for No 6 Machine Gun emplacement attachment. This work carried out by No 1 Section. Cleared axon track of the RED LAMP SALIENT cut right through ready for revetment. No 2 Section completed the trench boarding right through the GREAT NORTH ROAD. No 3 Section carried on with the 300'	G.W.F.

Army Form C. 2118.

WAR DIARY
of 151 FIELD COMPANY R.E.

INTELLIGENCE SUMMARY
(Erase heading not required.)

Volume V page 10.

Place	Date	Hour	Summary of Events and Information	Remarks and references to Appendices
RESERVE LINE			and Communication Trenches. C.R.E. gave out a new scheme for the provision of extra Stokes mortar gun emplacements and sentry posts in the front line. Weather fair and warm, but rather scorp. Beyond the burn at PHANTOM POST being set on fire by artillery, the day was quiet. G C V Fenton Captain R.E. O 151 FLD C.o R.E.	GVF

Copy.

Hd Qrs, 38th Welsh Division.

In forwarding the attached letter from Lieut Colonel Pringle, Commanding "B" Group, R.A., I would like to add that I have also been much impressed by the excellent work of Captain Fenton, Lieutenant Willis, and the 151st Field Company, R.E. in connection with "B" Group, R.A., and also with that of Lieut McLean and the 123rd Coy, R.E. in connection with "C" Group.

The keenness and energy of these officers and men has been of the greatest assistance to the Artillery, and is much appreciated by them.

      (Sgd) W.A.M.Thompson,
        Brig. Genl, R.A.
April 1st 1916.
       C.R.A., 38th Division.

Copy.

To Brigade Major, R.A.
    38th Division.

I should very much like the G.O.C., R.A. to bring to the notice of the Major General Commanding, the very able assistance that has been given to me by the Officers and men of the 151st Field Coy, R.E. in this sector. They have always been most willing and keen in carrying out any work I have asked them to do.

Construction of O.Ps has been carried out very rapidly, and with great skill.

I would specially bring forward the names of Captain Fenton, R.E. and Lieut Willis, R.E. The latter has been in charge of the construction work, and I cannot speak too highly of the energy and skill he has displayed. Since arriving here on 16th February he has completed two new O.Ps, practically rebuilt two more, and another two will be finished in the course of the next fortnight, the result being that instead of being very badly off for O.Ps, this group will have several in reserve in a few days time.

(Sgd)   H.E.PRINGLE,
                Lieut.Col.
            Comdg "B" Group.

Appendix I

Copy.

38th Division No. G. & 73/

C.R.E.

Forwarded.

The Brigadier General Commanding is pleased to receive this good report regarding the Officers concerned, and desires that they be informed of the same.

(Sgd) H.E.Pryce,

Lieut. Colonel,

3-4-1916.   General Staff, 38th (Welsh) Division.

APPENDIX (2).

Copy.

SECRET.

115 Brigade.

Reference operation order No. 98 by Lieut Colonel
F.H.Gaskell, Comdg 16th Battn, Welsh Regt
(Cardiff City).

In accordance with instructions issued 1 N.C.O. and 1 Sapper accompanied the wire cutting party under Lieut BUIST.

They report the Bangalore torpedo fixed in position, detonator placed, and leads taken back to the exploder.

The N.C.O. asked permission to connect up the wires, but was ordered not to by LIEUT BUIST. This, I consider a mistake, as if the exploder had been connected the torpedo could have been fired at once.

The R.E. party remained in the SUMP, until ordered to retire by the Officer I/c, which they did, taking the exploder with them.

LIEUT WILLIS, who was in charge of R.E.arrangements, reports (1) That the electric current was tested before taking out with a Battery and Galvonometer, and found correct, and pointed this out to the Sapper who had to fire.

(2) That he asked permission to go out with the R.E. party to fire the torpedo after the retirement, but this was refused by O.C. 16th Battn, Welsh Regt.

(3) I have also to bring to your notice that Lieut Willis went out alone after the failure to search for 2nd Lt O.Williams, who was missing ; as he did not know the ground, and I understand went up to the German wire, and stayed out until nearly daybreak, and could stop no longer. I consider this is a matter worthy of consideration.

(4) In future operations, may I make the following suggestions.

(a) That the exploder should be connected ready for firing at once, so that in case of alarm or difficulty, the charge can be fired at once.

(b) That orders should be issued in future that in event of retirement, the torpedo should, if possible, be fired to create a diversion, and the enemy's wire could be cut, at any events and the torpedo not fall into the enemy's hands.

(Sgd) G.C.V.FENTON,
Capt,R.E.,
O.C. 151st Fd Coy, R.E.

9/4/16.

COPY.

Copy No. 7.

OPERATION ORDERS No. 98.

BY

Lieut-Colonel F. H. Gaskell,
Commanding 16th Battn Welsh Regt, (Cardiff City).

Reference B.T.Map Area E. Portion of Sheet 36.c.N.W. 1.

INFORMATION.

    (1) The enemy has a Machine Gun in an emplacement at A.16.c.55.64.

INTENTION.

    (2) To attack and capture this gun and to inflict the maximum of damage upon the enemy.

WIRE CUTTING
OPERATIONS.

    (3) At 11.0.p.m. on the 8th April, party as detailed in margin (less one Signaller who will remain with O.C. 16th Welsh at A.16.c.05.65.) will leave point A.16.c.05.65. in our trenches and proceed through our Sap.

2nd Lieut.Buist.
6 men to cut wire.
as covering party.
2 Signallers.
One R.E. N.C.O.

2nd Lieut Buist and wire cutting party, one signaller and one R.E. N.C.O. will go to SUMP at A.16.c.40.70.
The covering party will go to shelter of CANAL BANK about 15 yards from enemy wire.
The signaller with his instrument will stay in the SUMP.
He will lay his wire as he comes out.
He and the signaller who remains at A.16.c.05.65 will carefully test their instruments immediately before the start, and will from time to time ascertain wires are intact by sending through the "R.U."
The men to cut wire will be armed with a revolver each and will carry two bombs apiece.
They will also carry R.E. shears and hedging gloves.
One of these men will carry two blankets.
The other two men will take out a Bangalore torpedo 16 feet long, and the R.E.N.C.O. will carry a line detonator and exploder.
Signaller will have a revolver and two bombs.
R.E. N.C.O. will carry a revolver.
All the party will have blackened faces and hands and will be without headgear.
The N.C.O. and men of covering party will be armed with revolvers and 12 bombs per man carried in bombing waistcoats.
2nd Lieut Buist and his cutters with R.E.N.C.O. will proceed to enemy's wire crawling forward with the torpedo line and detonator.
They will proceed to cut the wire.
Signaller will signal "C.C." answered by "R.D." When this task is done the cutting party will place the torpedo in position, the R.E.N.C.O. will adjust the detonator and all will retire to the sump.
The signaller in SUMP will send "S.R.P." answered by "R.D." whereupon raiding parties under 2nd Lt O.Williams, detail as shewn in margin, will move.

ASSAULT.

RIGHT PARTY.
2nd Lt. L. Tregaskis.
No. 1 Bomber.
" 2 Carrier.
" 3 Bomber.
" 4 Carrier.
" 5 Bomber.
" 6 Carrier.
" 7 Searcher.
" 8 Searcher.
" 9 Guard.

LEFT PARTY.
2nd Lt O. Williams.
No. 1 Bomber.
" 2 Carrier.
" 3 Bomber.
" 4 Carrier.
" 5 Bomber.
" 6 Carrier.
" 7 Searcher.
" 8 Searcher.
" 9 Guard.

Parties will move out of Sap and proceed to SUMP advancing in two parallel lines in single file. All will have darkened faces and hands, and will be without headgear.
Each man will have a revolver.
Each bomber two bombs in pockets.
Nos 2,4,6,7,8 and 9 will have waistcoats with 12 bombs each.
Nos 5 and 6 will have 2 screwdrivers, hammer and chisel.
The R.E.N.C.O. on the command of 2nd Lt.O. Williams will explode the torpedo.
Immediately after explosion the two parties will rush the gap and pass over the enemy's parapet side by side in order shewn in margin.
The signaller will send "P.O.P" answered by "R.D." At the same time the covering party will throw one bomb each into trench at M.G. Emplacement and will retire to our Sap.
2nd Lt Buist and his wire cutters and the R.E. N.C.O. will also retire at once to Sap.
The signallers remain in SUMP.
On entering trench at A.16.c.55.65. the Right Party will drop No. 9 who will remain and guard point of entry, the remainder will rush down to their right to secure M.G. bombing any dugouts etc on their way.
On reaching A.16.c.53.63. Nos 1 and 2 will continue up TORTOISE TRENCH and proceed 20 yards to block approach from that/direction.
Nos 3 and 4 will stand by to guard the party at M.G. emplacement while Nos 5 and 6 will dismantle or destroy the gun.
Nos 7 and 8 will search Germans, removing all articles of value, badges, etc.
The gun having been dealt with, 2nd Lt Tregaskis or Senior effective will give a series of short whistle blasts.
These will be taken up at once by No.9 at point of entry.
On this signal all will retire to point of entry turn left and proceed 50 yards up trench bombing dugouts etc and doing all possible execution. Nos 7 and 8 acting as searchers.
The party will not in any event proceed beyond A.16.c.63.73.
On whistle sounding as stated, or, if not sounded or not heard at the end of 8 minutes from time of entry, 2nd Lt Williams or Senior effective will blow sharp blast on whistle, it will be taken up by No. 9 at point of entry and party will fall back to point of entry. If an unexpected communication trench is found to join main trench a guard (i.e., last bomber and carriers) will be dropped to block it.
Both parties having effected a junction at this point of entry will recross parapet retiring together.
Both parties must be out of front trench in 10 minutes from time of entry.
They will make for our Sap, using cover of BANK.
The Signaller, the moment raiding parties are clear of wire will give "G.I." answered by "R.D." and immediately he receives his answer he will make for Sap with his instrument.
All badges, distinguishing marks, papers and identification discs will be discarded.

The password will be "CARDIFF"

REPORTS.   The O.C. 16th Battn, Welsh Regt. (Cardiff City) will be at A.16.c.05.65.

Copies to:-
No. 1 War Diary.
 " 2 115th Brigade.
    3 O.C. B.Group R.A. 31th Division.
    4 O.C. No.5 M.M.G.Battery.
    5 O.C. Y/38 T.M.Battery.
    6 A/115 T.M.Battery.
    7 O.C 151st Field Coy,R.E.
    8 O.C: Raiding Party.

Appendix III

14th April 1916.

WORK IN PROGRESS HANDED OVER TO THE 227th FIELD COY,
ROYAL ENGINEERS, on relief, by 151st FIELD COY, R.E.
----

1. OBSERVATION POSTS.

   (a) HOUSE IN GIVENCHY VILLAGE. Repair roof of cellar, and erect burster roof.
   (b) SAPPERS HOUSE. Erect burster roof over cellar.
   (c) PONT FIXE DISTILLERY. Erection of O.P. Plan handed over.
   (d) SPOIL BANK. Erection of O.P., as per plan approved by R.A. Wood frame-work for same, and periscopes commenced and in yard at Company Workshops.

2. GIVENCHY VILLAGE.

   (a) HOUSE AT A.15.a.4.9. Completion of roofs to Machine Gun Emplacements; cellars to be cleaned, and made water tight, and entrance to be made.
   (b) MAIRIE. Completion of Machine Gun Emplacement, and connecting up cellars to this.
   (c) Completion of repairs to cellars. List of cellars and condition were submitted to C.R.E., 38th Division, and will be handed over to C.R.E., 39th Division on relief.
   (d) Placing the front edge of GIVENCHY VILLAGE in a state of defence. Scheme for this work is not yet made out, nor has the work been commenced, but will require careful consideration.

3. FRONT LINE DEFENCES - RIGHT SUB-SECTION.

   (a) SAPS. The chord between D Sap and C Sap through Ac Sap has been carried out, but a large amount of extra work is required to make this really satisfactory. It is suggested that on the north these three saps should be connected to the front line, while on the South C.1 sap should be joined by a chord to the existing front line, thus transferring the front line from the existing position to the edge of the craters.
   (b) COVENTRY STREET. This communication trench should be completed from PICADILLY to the front line as far as the existing alignment.
   (c) FRONT LINE. This should be connected up between Centre and Right Companies of this sub-section.
   (d) COMMUNICATION TRENCHES:-
      1. WOLFE ROAD. Trench boarding completed throughout. Much revetment requires doing, and care should be taken to prevent falls occurring, thus blocking front line.
      2. ORCHARD ROAD. Work on this trench between the WILLOW DRAIN and the Junction with OXFORD TERRACE has been carried out by the Pioneers. This work needs careful consideration, as it is doubtful whether the existing work will be satisfactory. Between the WILLOW DRAIN and front line this trench should be cleared and floor boarded thus enabling a large amount of the water to the front line to be drained off into the WILLOW DRAIN.
      3. OXFORD TERRACE and FINCHLEY ROAD. These trenches have been floor-boarded throughout, but requires revetment in many places. Drainage requires careful watching in these trenches.
      4. HATFIELD ROAD. Floor boarding completed between KING'S ROAD and COVENTRY STREET. Much revetment

required. Trench requires watching.

6. <u>HOPE STREET</u>. A large amount of the floor boarding and clearing has been carried out. This requires completion to the front line.

7. <u>KING'S ROAD</u>. Repairs to trench boarding on this road has been commenced, but requires completion.

(e) <u>GUNNER SIDING.</u> Considerable amount of repairs required to this trench, which at present contains a large amount of water, in which the floor boards are floating.

(f) <u>MACHINE GUN EMPLACEMENTS.</u> Many of the Machine Gun Emplacements in the front line are in a very poor design and condition, and require repairs.

(g) <u>WIRING.</u> The wiring of PICADILLY and COVENTRY STREET in accordance with the plan handed over has been pegged out, but very little progress has been made. This should be done by the Garrison, under the supervision of the R.E. to see that the wire is placed in the position as laid down in the drawing handed over.

(4). <u>LE TOURET RESERVE LINE.</u>

The wiring of this reserve line has been completed with the exception of festooning. This work will probably have to be undertaken by the Reserve Brigade of the 39th Division under R.E. supervision. It should only take a very short time.

(5). <u>DRAINAGE.</u>

The C.R.E., 39th Division desired that the drainage system of the area should be explained on paper to you for his information:-

The general water courses of the area are of three separate sub-divisions, namely:-

(a) The LE BASSE--BETHUNE CANAL.
(b) The DESECHEMENT, or main drain from the mines in BEUVRY.
(c) The RIVER LOISNE.

Consider first the canal. There is a dam at the point F.19.d.6.9½., also the locks at A.15.c.4.8. In normal times the canal between the dam and the locks is above the level of the LE PLANTIN Marsh and the country to the West of GUINCHY. By the instalment of powerful pumps on barges belonging to the Inland Water Transport near the dam this level in the canal has been reduced below the level of the surrounding country, and act as a drain to the marshes. The water through GIVENCHY HILL and the southern portion of LE PLANTIN Marsh by means of an artificial cut known as the SUEZ Canal has been diverted to flow into the Canal. The flow of the water through the lock is at present controlled by a Field Company of the 33rd Division. This is apparently done without consultation with the Inland Water Transport, and the latter is liably to be overpowered by a flow of water let through the lock when the pumps are not prepared for it. The level of the water East of the lock is governed by the Tunnelling Companies requirements but what mines are affected by this water is not known by me.

With regard to DESECHEMENT. In the winter months this water syphons under the canal near the dam, but before the instalment of the pumps by the Drainage Coy the outfall was not sufficient to deal with the volume of the water coming in from the syphon, and the excess overflowed into the LE PLANTIN Marshes. By the instalment of the Pumping machinery this excess water is pumped from the DESECHEMENT into the LE BASSE CANAL, and the flow of water has been reversed from the marsh into the outfall, and thence finds its way into the canal DE LAWAE.

The river LOISNE syphons on to the canal, and finds its way into the canal DE LAWAE, and it does not affect the front area.

Capt, R.E.,

O.C. 151st Fd Coy, R.E.

Appendix IV

COPY.

To Headquarters,
         38th Division.

         The following are some notes made at an inspection of the horses of the Division on the 6th, 7th and 8th inst.

         The health and condition of the horses was on the whole exceptionally good.

                xx   xx   xx   xx

         The other units of the Division were quite satisfactory, the following being particularly good:-

                151st Field Coy., R.E.

                xx   xx   xx   xx

                         (Signed) T.E.MARTIN,
                                  Lt Col., A.V.C.
Hd.Qrs.First Army,   D.D.V.S. First Army.
April 19th 1916.

To C.R.E.
    38th (Welsh) Division.

                    For your information.

                              Lieut.Colonel.
13-4-16.   A.A. & Q.M.G., 38th (Welsh) Division.

Appendix V.V

Copy.

204th FIELD COMPANY, ROYAL ENGINEERS.

HANDING OVER REPORT.

FAUQUISSART SECTION.

13th April 1916.

----------------------oOo--------------------

204th Field Company, Royal Engineers.

HANDING OVER REPORT.

FAUQUISSANT SECTION. (ROTTEN ROW to ELGIN STREET inclusive).

The Company has been engaged upon six principal works, which, in the opinion of 35th Division are of the following order of urgency.

(1). Reclamation and completion of 300 yards line and RESERVE TRENCH from A.1 Post to ELGIN POST.

(2). Repair and reclamation of communication trenches between this line and the Support Line, (i.e., that just behind the front line), and especially BONDSTREET, RIFLEMEN, FLEET STREET, PICANTIN, ROTTEN ROW, MASSELOT, and ELGIN.

(3). Construction of bomb-proof M.G. Emplacements and dugouts in the Front Line.

(4). The construction of a Cut off across the RED LAMP SALIENT.

(5). Extension of the Great Central Railway to MINEHEAD at RED LAMP.

(6). Completion of C.R.A's HOUSE and MASSELOT HOUSE.

In addition to constructing these new works, the Field Company in this section is responsible for supervising the maintenance by the Garrison of the Front Line and the following strongpoints:-

A.1, FLANK, FELON, FIREWORKS, FAUQUISSART, and, when handed over, C.R.A.s HOUSE and MASSELOT HOUSE.

FRONT LINE.

Dugouts.

The principal work in the front line consists in strengthening the existing dugouts in order to make them bomb-proof. At the present time most of the dugouts are not even splinter proof, having roofs consisting of one sheet of corrugated iron and a layer of sandbags. The Garrisons should be instructed to make the roof of every dugout bomb-proof. As there are probably not enough steel rails for doing them all, they should have a strong roof made of sleepers or thick timber, a row of sandbags, a sheet of corrugated iron, a layer of sandbags filled with broken bricks, and then two layers of sandbags or earth. In many cases, in order to prevent this thickness of roof rising above the height of the parapet it will be necessary to lower the roof of the dugout. 3 feet is the usual height of a dugout for an ordinary one, and 3ft 6ins for an Officers' dugout, but the drainage now will permit of the floors being lowered 6" in most cases should this prove necessary.

Firesteps.

These have been raised for the use of the 35th Division, but will need to be lowered about 5" by the incoming Division.

Parapet.

In some cases a single row of sandbags have been laid along the top of the parapet. This dangerous practice should be checked, and the parapet at the top should be at least 50" thick.

(2).

M.G. Emplacements.

A number of M.G. Emplacements are being reconstructed and a special report on this is attached.

Trenchboards and Drains.

The Infantry Garrisons are responsible for seeing that the existing trenchboards are in order, and for seeing that the drains from the front line back to the Support trench are clean and flowing freely.

Parados.

In several cases there are an unnecessary number of parados, and in other cases, especially at MINEHEAD near RED LAMP SALIENT, the number of sandbags used is excessive, with the result that the parapet has sunk down and closed in the bays. Two bays here are at present unoccupied for this reason, and should be reclaimed, and have firesteps put in them. At RED LAMP itself several casualties have occurred through shots from our own line coming in behind the parapet. A small wall has already been constructed to protect the garrison, within a few feet of the RED LAMP SALIENT. Further steps should be taken by building a parados for this purpose.
In the portion of the trench between RED LAMP and ROTTEN ROW it has been proposed to put small firesteps on each side to give enfilade fire, along the front of our parapet on the southern section, and along the rear of our parapet on the northern section.

RED LAMP CUT OFF.

The RED LAMP Cut Off consists of the reclamation of the Support trench for about 100 yards in a N.W. direction, and then a right angle bend into the front line near the Junction of N.13.7 and N.14.1. When this is completed, or contemporaneously if possible a line of trenches is to be cut from FIREWORKS POST to RIFLEMAN'S AVENUE. The wiring along the S.side of the trench from ROTTEN ROW to RED LAMP is to be doubled.

STRONGPOINTS.

These Posts have all been visited, and instructions given to the garrison with regard to the carrying out of certain small works by them, consisting chiefly of strengthening dugout roofs, thickening and raising of parapet where necessary, etc., etc. Particulars of these will be found in the Post Log Books, and should be continued by garrisons. Various other small works such as reconstruction of Bomb Stores, stronger roofs, etc., should be carried out in these Posts.

COMMUNICATION TRENCHES.

While in time the whole of the communication trenches from the RUE TILLELOY to the Front Line should be reclaimed, work is only being done at present on those mentioned in paragraph 2 page 1. Of these BOND STREET, PICANTIN, ROTTEN ROW, FLEET STREET, MASSELOT STREET, and ELGIN are fairly complete, although still needing some revetment in places. MASSELOT STREET needs a little draining. A separate report on these is attached.

RESERVE TRENCH.

The 300 Yard Line Reserve Trench runs from A.1 POST

to ROTTEN ROW on the S.E. side of RUE TILLELOY, and is known here as the '300 yard Line'. After its junction with ROTTEN ROW it follows that line in a right angle bend across the RUE TILLELOY, and then turns to the left in a S.W. direction parallel to TILLELOY, until it reaches ELGIN STREET. It is trenchboarded for nearly the whole distance now, excepting a small portion N.E. of the RUE TILLELOY crossing, which is now being drained. The arrangement proposed by this Division for the trench is attached, but in many cases the dugouts had been previously constructed, and this portion of the trench is being adapted as far as feasible to make up the proposed arrangements. On the greater part of this line work can be done by day, but near SUTHERLAND AVENUE unless some more screening is put up it will only be possible to work by night, as there have been casualties to working parties at this point by day.

The policy of the 35th Division Staff has been to press forward with a small section of the line between ELGIN and MASSELOT HOUSE, and to finish this off completely with dugouts, so that it may be habitable and occupied by the garrison before completing the trench right through. The garrison will then be able to finish off some of the dugout work, etc.

Special drains have been dug near RIFLEMAN TRENCH, ROTTEN ROW, both sides of TILLELOY, MASSELOT HOUSE, and C.E.A.s HOUSE, and should be maintained.

TRAMWAY.

The Great Central Railway is being continued along RUE TILLELOY under the hedge, through the house at ROTTEN ROW corner, on through or by FIREWORKS POST, along the western edge of the Salient and then cutting across behind the Cut Off to the front line. One of the principal objects of the tramway is to deal with the 1000 to 1500 sandbags per day which the mine at RED LAMP is producing, these being taken and used in the RESERVE TRENCH. A short line from MINEHEAD to RIFLEMAN has also been proposed.

DEFENDED HOUSES.

C.R.A.s House and MASSELOT HOUSE are being put in a state of defence, in accordance with attached plans. MASSELOT HOUSE is fairly well advanced, but C.R.A.s HOUSE still needs a good deal doing to it.

It has been proposed to make a defended house in RUE TILLELOY near ROTTEN ROW corner, report and plans of which are in the possession of the C.R.E.

BOMB STORES.

Bomb Stores are being constructed at various corners along the RUE TILLELOY, see separate report.

SCREENING.

A good deal of screening has been done, but more is required in the RUE TILLELOY, especially near the head of the Great Central Railway.

SOUP KITCHEN.

Soup Kitchen has been constructed near Great Central Rail Head, and is now used by the troops.

PONTOON BRIDGE.

A Pontoon Bridge at NOUVEAU MONDE has been moved some 300

(4).

yards, and a new wharf constructed. The maintenance of this bridge comes under the Field Company.

WATER SUPPLY.

A ~~Penkman×Bridge×al~~ system of water supply has been arranged for the watercarts of the troops in LAVENTIE. The source of supply is the well in the BREWERY which has been certified by the M.O. to be pure and the best in the district. From a small pump at the head of the well the water is pumped through 2" piping to a flexible delivery pipe outside the ablution house door, where the watercarts draw up and fill.

BATHS.

Arrangements have been made in the Brewery for bathing of troops billeted there, and a separate pump is used for this purpose. Most of the bathing hitherto has been done at the White Chateau (Transport H.Q.). A bath house is also ~~completed~~ being completed at the stables near LAVENTIE station, map ref. G.24.d.3.7. There is a portable boiler and an overhead tank already arranged.

WIRING.

The whole of the RESERVE TRENCH wire wants strengthening and notice boards are in hand indicating the way to the gaps. The wire round a number of the Posts and by the side of the communication trenches also needs strengthening.

OBSERVATION POSTS.

An O.P. for Infantry has been constructed in FLEET STREET.

PLANS.

Attached will be found plans of the Section, and Handing Over notes of previous Field Companies.

(Signed)   T.H.Marshall

Major, R.E.,

O.C. 204th Field Coy, R.E.

Appendix VI.

  62724 Sergeant F. Owen, 151st Field
Company, Royal Engineers.
   For conspicuous gallantry and initiative.
When acting as guide, Sergeant Owen observed a bomb
fall near a trench full of men. He instantly ran
forward and threw the bomb over the parapet.
In all probability he saved many lives.

151 FCRE
Vol. 6

XXXVIII

VOLUME 6

WAR DIARY

OF 151ˢᵗ FIELD COMPANY R.E.

FOR MONTH OF MAY 1916

Army Form C. 2118.

WAR DIARY
of 151 Field Company R.E.
INTELLIGENCE SUMMARY.
(Erase heading not required.)

Volume VI page 1.

Instructions regarding War Diaries and Intelligence Summaries are contained in F. S. Regs., Part II. and the Staff Manual respectively. Title pages will be prepared in manuscript.

Place	Date	Hour	Summary of Events and Information	Remarks and references to Appendices
LAVENTIE.	1.5.16.		CAPTAIN G.C.V. FENTON R.E. proceeded to England on leave. Lieut. W.E. WILLIS R.E. took over command of the Unit during the absence of the Officer Commanding. No 1 SECTION continued work on FRONT LINE and CORD at back of SALIENT. SECTION 2 continued work on COMMUNICATION TRENCHES + POSTS. No 3 SECTION on 300× TRENCH + RIFLEMANS AVENUE COMMUNICATION TRENCH. + No 4 SECTION on OBSERVATION POSTS. WORK on O.P. for TOPOGRAPHICAL SECTION completed. CAPTAIN OWEN 15th R.W.F. called at OFFICE ran 9.30 to ran two sappers for patrolling ground for 'RAID'. NOTHING of interest occurred. Weather FINE, WARM, SUNNY + very CLEAR.	SWF
"	2.5.16.	3 A.M.	Heavy shelling of the front portion of the Line. A bright clear night. Sections continued on work in hand. Progress slow owing to inter-Brigade reliefs & consequently few Infantry working parties being available for work. No 1 SECTION Commenced excavating for new M.G. dugout No 7. No 2 SECTION started making new dugout & preparing for construction of M.G. Emplacement at DEAD END POST FARM. O.P. No 4 SECTION commenced work preparing for erection of new double track chimney O.P. Weather fine, warm, but rather cloudy.	GWF

Army Form C. 2118.

WAR DIARY
of 151 FIELD COMPANY R.E.
INTELLIGENCE SUMMARY.
(Erase heading not required.)

Volume VI Page 2

Instructions regarding War Diaries and Intelligence Summaries are contained in F.S. Regs., Part II. and the Staff Manual respectively. Title pages will be prepared in manuscript.

Place	Date	Hour	Summary of Events and Information	Remarks and references to Appendices
LAVANTIE	3-5-16	—	1 Sapper killed on night of 2nd to 3rd May. Telegraphy station on GREAT NORTHERN RAILWAY. No 1 Section completed No 6 Machine Gun emplacement dug out. Strengthening of wiring on the RUE BACQUEROT Reserve Line commenced. Weather fine and warm and clear	gmf
LAVANTIE	4-5-16	—	Sections continued at work as on previous day. No 1 Section still continued concentrating work on the front and back of the RED LAMP Salient. Also work at No 7 Machine Gun dug-out. LIEUT WILLIS and 11 LIEUT JONES both wounded while inspecting wiring between JOCK'S LODGE and COPSE POST. LIEUT G.W MORGAN assumed command of the company. No 2 Section carrying on with the strengthening of the machine gun emplacements in the RUE BACQUEROT RESERVE LINE. Weather fine and warm but dull.	gmst.
LAVANTIE	5-5-16	—	Sections were employed as previously. Work on trench and concrete machine gun emplacements and wirework in connection with communication trench by Nos 2 and 4 Sections very considerably delayed by lack of cement. TEA HOUSE OBSERVATION POST completed. Considerable progress by attached men of drainage party on the swampy of the RUE TILLELOY. Weather fine and warm but cloudy at intervals.	gmst.
LAVANTIE	6-5-16	—	All work carried on by sections as on previous days. New registering platform for OP at the BERKELEY completed. Cement still not available for brickwork. LIEUT T.C FREETH R.E transferred from 123rd FIELD COMPANY and took over command of the company.	ssit.
LAVANTIE	7-5-16	—	CAPTAIN LLOYD·GORING G.W.W WILLIS PATON arrived from the line and took over the command of the company.	sst.

T.J.134. Wt. W708—776. 500000. 4/15. Sir J. C. & S.

Army Form C. 2118.

WAR DIARY
or
INTELLIGENCE SUMMARY.
(Erase heading not required.)

Volume VI page 3

Instructions regarding War Diaries and Intelligence Summaries are contained in F. S. Regs., Part II. and the Staff Manual respectively. Title pages will be prepared in manuscript.

Place	Date	Hour	Summary of Events and Information	Remarks and references to Appendices
LAVANTIE	8.5.16		Work by Nos 1, 2 and 3 Sections all considerably delayed by the num amount of infantry working parties. No 4 Section was delayed on Observation Posts by the lack of cement for trestlework and concrete. Weather showery and dull.	
			All work carried on as on previous days. No 2 Section continued wiring between MASSELOT POST and HOUDOUMONT. LIEUT PATON wounded from the town on patrons to the company. During the night of the 7th-8th a raid on the German trenches was successfully carried out owing to a gap in the wire being formed in R.E. party was detailed for demolition by Bangalore Torpedoes, or other destruction of the line. Weather mild colder, with rain and dull.	G.W.E.
LAVANTIE	9.5.16		All work continued by sections as on previous days. No 1 Section was prevented from working on the CHORD behind the RED LAMP SALIENT as no infantry parties were available. No 2 Section continued the wiring between HOUDOUMONT and MASSELOT POSTS. Conference at CRE's office attended by CAPTAIN LLOYD GORING and LIEUT FREETH regarding BANGALORE Torpedoes and Modern Sun emplacements. Weather showery and dull.	G.W.E.
LAVANTIE	10.5.16		All work continued at work as on previous days. Germans shelled RED LAMP Salient considerably delaying work of No 1 Section. Also work on CHORD behind delayed owing to infantry working parties not turning up. No cement so work by No 4 Section on Observation Posts was considerably delayed being at a stand still as	G.W.E.

T.134. Wt. W708—776. 500000. 4/15. Sir J. C. & S.

Army Form C. 2118.

WAR DIARY
of 151 FIELD COMPANY R.E.
INTELLIGENCE SUMMARY.
(Erase heading not required.)

Volume VI pages 4

Instructions regarding War Diaries and Intelligence Summaries are contained in F.S. Regs., Part II. and the Staff Manual respectively. Title pages will be prepared in manuscript.

Place	Date	Hour	Summary of Events and Information	Remarks and references to Appendices
LAVANTIE	11/5/16	—	For as all masonry work was concerned. Owing to heavy German shelling special parties had to be detailed on ROTTEN ROW and RED LAMP Salient to repair damage. No 1 Section concentrated on the work on the RED LAMP Salient cloud. Other section continued to carry on work as in previous days. No 3 Section continued repairing damage due to German shelling on ROTTEN ROW in addition to other communication trenches and Reserve line. Chief Engineer of XI Corps inspected the drainage of the company and found everything to two satisfactorie. Weather fine.	SWT.
LAVANTIE	12/5/16		All sections continued at their work as on previous day. A limited supply of cement enabled No 4 Section to continue wall masonry work, but not fully. At PICANTIN POST, an ammunition dug out was completed by No 2 Section. CRE inspected front line and other positions for Depots for ammunition and bombs, and Various other steps. Captain Foster returned from leave and took over command of the company. A fine day but dull.	SWT.
LAVANTIE	13/5/16		Sections were employed on work as on previous day. Allotment of officers to sections was made as follows:— No 1 Section Lieut FREETH, No 2 Section Lieut PATON No 3 and 4 Section continued under Lieut CARROLL and Lieut MORGAN respectively. Weather heavy rain in early morning and not throughout the day off and on. Not much work of interest carried out during day, as there were no infantry working parties, being day of relief, and the GOC of the Brigade did not wish the men to go out in the rain later relief.	SWT.

Army Form C. 2118.

WAR DIARY
of 151 FIELD COMPANY R.E.
INTELLIGENCE SUMMARY.
(Erase heading not required.)

Volume VI Appx 4

Instructions regarding War Diaries and Intelligence Summaries are contained in F. S. Regs., Part II. and the Staff Manual respectively. Title pages will be prepared in manuscript.

Place	Date	Hour	Summary of Events and Information	Remarks and references to Appendices
LAVANTIE	14/5/16	—	Sections continued at work as on previous days. Alterations made in the wire of No 2 Section with regard to the machine gun emplacements in the RUE BACQUEROT trench and also the wiring. No 3 Section carrying on with the RONNET shed and communication trenches. No 1 Section employed on the RED LAMP Salient. No 4 Section work was delayed on the demolition task owing to insufficient cement. Weather heavy snow in the morning, but cleared later in the day, and remained fine.	SEE
LAVANTIE	15/5/16		All work continued by sections as on previous days. Work on front of the line was stopped owing an operation for destroying front of the WICK SALIENT in U. GERMAN Line. Attended by the O.C. and several officers of the Company. A demonstration of a bonus apparatus by hydraulic power for driving forward tasks and fitting small explosive and making a continuous tunnel to demolition of front of the line. No 4 Section were delayed owing to shortage of cement. Weather warm in early morning, but cleared later. Dull and cloudy all day.	SEE
LAVANTIE	16/5/16		Sections continued at work as on previous day. No 1 Section used at posts in for new tunnel mortar platform, but the trench mortar battery was unable to furnish working parties to commence work. Heavy artilling fire all day on the right sub division and very intense about 4.30 p.m. FARM observation Post severely damaged in evening but during day. Weather fine clear and warm. No structure of much importance on left sub division ......missing in Comp. LIEUT MORGAN Escorted our Co work to CAPTAIN LLOYD GORING proceeding to join 5 in Comp.	SEE

Army Form C. 2118.

WAR DIARY
of 151 FIELD COMPANY R.E.
INTELLIGENCE SUMMARY.
(Erase heading not required.)

Volume VI. May 6.

Instructions regarding War Diaries and Intelligence Summaries are contained in F. S. Regs., Part II. and the Staff Manual respectively. Title pages will be prepared in manuscript.

Place	Date	Hour	Summary of Events and Information	Remarks and references to Appendices
LAVANTIE	17/5/16	—	Sections continued at work as on previous days. Owing to interi. brigade reliefs, the working parties were very considerably reduced, all infantry being cancelled except on front line. No 1 Section started work on the preparation of RENNER STN DUGOUTS in the front line. No 2 Section completed the widening of tunnels in PICCADILLY Communication Trench, and was relieved by tunnels that have floated away about midnight action. Some clearing was to being reformed by No 4 Section who carried on previous evening to CRA's HOUSE CONCENTRATION POST. LIEUT. COLONEL KNOX R.E. commenced to take over the duties of C.R.E. from COLONEL ATKINSON. Weather fine, warm and very clear. Not much shelling action, but aeroplanes active.	S.W.F.
LAVANTIE	18/5/16		Sections continued at work as on previous days. Owing to the large amount of other work in the front line, No 1 Section was unable to provide men for the examination of the front line tunnels. No 2 Section making good progress on the machine gun entrenchments on the RUE BACQUEROT alnd. The work on the RENNER 300" line is progressing slowly. No 4 Section concentrating their efforts on the CONVENT and SNOWDON CONCENTRATION POSTS, while preparing the limits for work, collecting material, etc. The new and old C.R.E's inspected the portion of the line to see the work in hand and for the former to see the lie of the land. No 2 Section started work on the Water Sidings on the GREAT NORTHERN and GREAT CENTRAL RAILWAYS. Weather fine warm, sunny and clear. Not much artillery activity, but aeroplanes busy. Much machine gun fire at night.	S.W.F.
LAVANTIE	19/5/16		Sections continued at work as on previous day. No 1 Section commenced in addition a new tunnel another	

T.2134. Wt. W.708—776. 500000. 4/15. Sir J.C. & S.

Army Form C. 2118.

WAR DIARY
of 151 Field Company R.E.
INTELLIGENCE SUMMARY.
(Erase heading not required.)

Volume VI Page 7.

Place	Date	Hour	Summary of Events and Information	Remarks and references to Appendices
LAVANTIE			emplacement to the right of ROTTEN ROW. No 2 Section completed the strengthening of No B.14 Machine Gun emplacement near PICANTIN POST in PICCADILLY Trench. No 4 Section started work on framework for new observation Post at th. FARM. A detachment under Lieut CARROLL was sent to the 255th Tunnelling company, to learn how to use the new tube driving hydraulic and mechanical apparatus. The SENTINEL and BARRETT Wheeler fans were tried and clean. Considerable aeroplane activity, but patrolling quiet. Much machine gun and a certain amount of artillery fire at nights on both sides.	
	20/5/16		Sections continued at work as on previous day. No 1 Section had to divert considerable number of men to repair damages to ROTTEN ROW, and some men and working parties of No 3 Section were detailed for the same work. No 2 Section completed the tunnel trenches of PICCADILLY communication Trench, and also commenced work on Nos B.11 and B.13 Machine Gun emplacement and dug out for former. No 4 Section employed on observation Post, progress is rather slow owing to organization not being as good as it might be. The disturbed party under LIEUT CARROLL continued work at boring with 255th Tunnelling Company. Weather fine, warm and sunny and clear, but inclined to be laggy for aeroplane reconnaissance. Artillery fired briskly against ROTTEN ROW in morning during considerable dummy to communication trench. C.R.E. inspecting defensive vicinity at junction of ROTTEN ROW and RUE TILLELOY, with 114th Brigade staff and G.S.O. 2 of the 36th DIVISION. C.R.E.'s farewell letter is attached as an Appendix.	Appendix I.

Army Form C. 2118.

WAR DIARY
of 151 FIELD COMPANY. R.E.
INTELLIGENCE SUMMARY.
(Erase heading not required.)

Volume VI page 8.

Instructions regarding War Diaries and Intelligence Summaries are contained in F. S. Regs., Part II. and the Staff Manual respectively. Title pages will be prepared in manuscript.

Place	Date	Hour	Summary of Events and Information	Remarks and references to Appendices
LAVANTIE.	21/5/16.		All work continued as on previous days. By sections. Owing to the battalion keep working parties constantly curtailed and work delayed. Nothing much of note during day. Weather warm and sunny. A little heavy owing to the heat. A little artillery action but not important.	Cont.
LAVANTIE	22/5/16		Sections continued as on previous day. Considerable amount of work on O.P's in hand. By no 2 section. Billets at LAVANTIE were shelled in the evening but no damage or casualties. Weather fine, warm and sunny with some rain in the afternoon and evening but not heavy.	Cont.
LAVANTIE	23/5/16.		All sections continued at work as on previous days. Comparatively quiet to day. Weather cooler and rather cloudy during day, but cleared towards evening. Heavy shelling during night, which damaged the lines in several of the farms we are visiting and new O.P. under construction on BLINAYM. A scheme was prepared for running out a sub from the end of BURLINGTON ARCADE, but owing to being Australian trenches being out, it was unfeasible to make reconnaissance. Nothing else of note was during day.	GMF.
LAVANTIE.	24/5/16		Sections continued at work as in previous days. Lieut CARROLL and a detachment from No 3 Section are employed daily on the construction of headquarters trench at MERILLON on the ESTAIRES - MERVILLE ROAD. A reconnaissance of a new safe was made and the work pegged out during night. Nothing event of interest during day. Weather cooler and some rain in the afternoon.	GMF

Army Form C. 2118.

WAR DIARY
of 151 FIELD COMPANY R.E.
INTELLIGENCE SUMMARY.
(Erase heading not required.)

Instructions regarding War Diaries and Intelligence Summaries are contained in F. S. Regs., Part II. and the Staff Manual respectively. Title pages will be prepared in manuscript.

Volume VI page 9.

Place	Date	Hour	Summary of Events and Information	Remarks and references to Appendices
LAVANTIE	25/5/16		Sections continued at work as on previous dates. Came to relief wagt, no infantry working parties often 12 Onoon. Nothing much of interest during day, and until the eruption of some trench mortar activity on the left by the AUSTRALIANS and retaliation by the artillery of the enemy all was fairly quiet. Officer Commanding and Lieut FREETH with LIEUT GREEN of 10th West Regiment went out on patrol to reconnoitre position of new sap. Position marked at with show yarn. Weather dull all day and evening. Heavy showers at night. Clear for aeroplane observation.	Quiet.
LAVANTIE	26/5/16		Sections continued work as usual. No 1 Section had a good proportion of men employed on practice for new sap to the new front Attractively fronts N 9 c 7.5 to N 8 d 24. No 2 Section continued work on the posts and new machine gun emplacements. No section on Communication Trenches and Reserve lines in front of RUE TILLELOY and No 4 Section on Convention Post. At night the work in front of the front line and bridges across the ditches were placed in position. Weather fine, but dull and cool. Comparatively quiet.	Quiet.
LAVANTIE	27/5/16		All sections continued at work as on previous dates. Supply of sand sheet so delay caused to masonry work on machine gun emplacements and observation posts. Other sections were also delayed owing to shortage in working parties. At night, men cut sods from front line, 250 yards long towards SUGAR LOAF. Work carried out in quite a satisfactory manner. Report on the operations attached as appendix.	Appendix II

T.J.134. Wt. W708-776. 500000. 4/15. Sir J. C. & S.

Army Form C. 2118.

WAR DIARY
of 151 FIELD COMPANY. R.E.
INTELLIGENCE SUMMARY.
(Erase heading not required.)

Volume VI Page 10.

Place	Date	Hour	Summary of Events and Information	Remarks and references to Appendices
LAVANTIE	28/5/16	-	Weather fine, but cool and clear all day. Aeroplanes active, but not much artillery. Clear, but dark at night. Ideal conditions for night work. Sections continued at work on their normal duties. Nothing of interest during day. Company received congratulations from many sources on the successful manner in which the work of the sap during the previous night was carried out. No 1 Section informed the histories to the sap during the night. Weather fine and clear, but cool. LIEUT MORGAN returned from leave in the evening and assumed command of No 4 Section 6 p.m.	GHF
LAVANTIE	29/5/16	-	Sections continued at work in their usual areas. No 1 Section were put on a new Trench mortar emplacement. A new signalling dug-out and the machine gun emplacements in the front line. Then are considered very urgent. Nothing of note so far as No 2 and 3 Sections are concerned. No 4 Section were suited out of work at the FARM observation Post, but without any casualties. Weather fine, but rather heavy rain of the day, and cloudy at other times. Artillery rather active between 1.0 p.m. and 2.30 p.m. shelling observation Posts in RUE TILLELOY without however any serious damage being done. Continuous active and observation balloons up. An attempt in	GHF
LAVANTIE	30/5/16	-	of work carried out by the G.O.C. 38th DIVISION on the new sap is attached as an appendix. All sections continued at work as usual. No 1 Section made great progress on Trench mortar emplacement and signallers dug-out. Nothing much of note during the day. At night very considerable hostile activity on right and left and a small amount shrapnel against our own line and communications. The carrying of was	Appendix III GHF

Army Form C. 2118.

WAR DIARY
of 151 FIELD COMPANY R.E.
INTELLIGENCE SUMMARY.
(Erase heading not required.)

Volume II page 11.

Instructions regarding War Diaries and Intelligence Summaries are contained in F. S. Regs., Part II. and the Staff Manual respectively. Title pages will be prepared in manuscript.

Place	Date	Hour	Summary of Events and Information	Remarks and references to Appendices
			to the front line was destroyed by the hostile artillery action. Weather being warm in the morning, but then to fine and warm in the afternoon & evening.	SMT
LAVENTIE	31/5/16		All sections continued at work as on previous days. Sections during morning were all detailed owing to their being insufficient sand to empty all sacks. Nothing much of note during day. The Tank Mortars and artillery carried out a scheme in the German trenches in the evening, which created considerable retaliation. Weather fine and sunny and clear.	SMT

G.C.V.Foster
Captain R.E.
O.C. 151 FLD Co R.E.

151 Fd Co R.E. War Diary

May 1916. Appendix I.

Copy.

O.C. 151st Field Coy, R.E.

Will you convey to the Officers, N.C.Os and men of the Company under your command my regret that owing to their duties in the field I am unable to say good-bye to them as a body.

My sorrow at leaving the Division is enhanced by the fact that I am handing over command of as reliable and zealous a body as could be wished for. The splendid way they have worked, their ability, cheerfulness and good discipline have gained for them a high place in the opinion of the rest of the Division.

I am sure when the Division comes to sterner work they will continue to keep up the glorious record of the Corps of ROYAL ENGINEERS.

I wish them Good Luck, and Good-Bye.

(Signed) E. Atkinson,
Brig. Genl.

18/5/1916.

151 FIELD COMPANY. R.E WAR DIARY.
May 1916. Appendix II.

Copy No 3

REPORT ON THE WORK IN CONNECTION WITH SAP RUNNING APPROXIMATELY FROM POINT N.8.C.7½.4½ to POINT N.8.D.2.4 ON THE NIGHT OF THE 27th-28th MAY, 1916.

The Alinement of the sap was laid out on the night of the 25th-26th May, 1916 by spunyarn pinned at intervals with French wire staples.

On 27th-28th inst.

Immediately after dark the Covering Party of the 13th Welsh Regiment was sent out along the line and dropped Covering Groups, in accordance with orders issued by the Officer Commanding the 13th Welsh Regiment.

Immediately following the Covering Party a Tracing Party, consisting of two N.C.Os and three men of the 151st Field Company, R.E., laid out the cutting line of the trench with tracing tapes. This party had the whole of the trench traced out by 9.30.p.m.

The Working Party of the 10th Welsh Regiment, consisting of 200 men, with a complement of N.C.Os and Officers, was sub-divided into eight parties, consisting of 25 men with a pick and shovel each under the command of an Officer, who was assisted by a sapper of the 151st Field Company, R.E.

At 9.30.p.m. these parties, under the command of Major M.A.NAPIER of the 10th Welsh Regiment, filed out from the parapet, and extended along the tracing tape. Every man on reaching his task immediately dug himself in as rapidly as possible, and by 10.15.p.m. every man was under cover along the whole length of the trench.

On arrival at the end of the trace it was found that No. 8 party and half of No. 7 party were not required at the extreme end, and they were immediately sent back to the front line to await orders.

At 11.15.p.m. rifle fire from our own front line was falling among the working party. I immediately consulted with Major Napier, and went back to the front line along the ditch joining the front line at point N.8.C.9½.6½. The Platoon Sergeant of that portion of the front line was warned that this was happening, and I at once went to the Officer Commanding the Left Company holding the front line, and warned him of the fact. On my return to the new trench I found that Major Napier and one man had been hit, and I assumed command of the working parties.

As bullets were continuing to fall among the working party, and another man was hit near me, I sent Lieut. Braithwaite of the 13th Welsh Regiment, to warn the Headquarters of the Right Company of the Australians, as I considered that this rifle fire might be coming from them.

About 12.30.a.m. I met Lieut.Colonel Ricketts, 10th Welsh Regiment, who informed me that he had taken charge of the work.

After reporting at the Company Headquarters of the Left Company of the 13th Welsh Regiment, the remainder of No. 7 party and No. 8 party were ordered by me to improve the

(2).

exit from the breastwork of the front line, the R.E. Tracing Party being left there to assist in this under Lieut T.C.FREETH, R.E., 151st Field Company, R.E.

Water was struck in three places along the trench at a depth of approximately 2'6". Extra men were sent out from the remaining men in No. 7 and 8 parties to assist in raising the parapet at these points by obtaining earth from a borrowing pit in front.

At 1.20.a.m. an inspection was made of the whole of the work, and it was found that, with the exception of several places being a few inches too narrow, or not quite deep enough, the whole of the trench was excavated to the full dimensions.

At 2.a.m. the whole of the work was completed, and the parties were withdrawn by order of the Officer Commanding, and were followed into the trench by the Covering Party.

A section of the trench, as excavated, and a small scaled line drawing shewing the approximate position, is attached.

Before closing this report I wish to bring to notice the excellent way in which the Infantry Working Parties extended along the tracing tape, and carried out their work. The extension was carried out with practically no noise of any description, and, with only one mistake, and the men had within half an hour of the commencement of the work dug themselves under cover all along the line. Taking into consideration that this is, as far as I know, their first actual experience of night digging in my opinion the work could not have been better performed.

G.C.V. Fenton

Captain, R.E.,
O.C. 151st Field Coy, R.E.

28/5/16

Copy No. 1 to C.R.E.
Copy No. 2 to 114th Brigade.
Copy No. 3) War Diary.
Copy No. 4)

NOTE

The height of a pick helve is 3'-0"

Each man to extend, drive his pick in on left of his task as pointed out by R.E. Commence digging from left to right getting cover dug on left as soon as possible. Traverse men divide work behind traverses. Throwing earth on to traverse.

Section

Ground line
Traverse
Traverse trench dotted ?
3'-0
3'-0

Plan

Tracing tape
25'-0
5 men's task
8'-0
2'-6"
8'-0
2'-6"

Sketch View

5 men's task

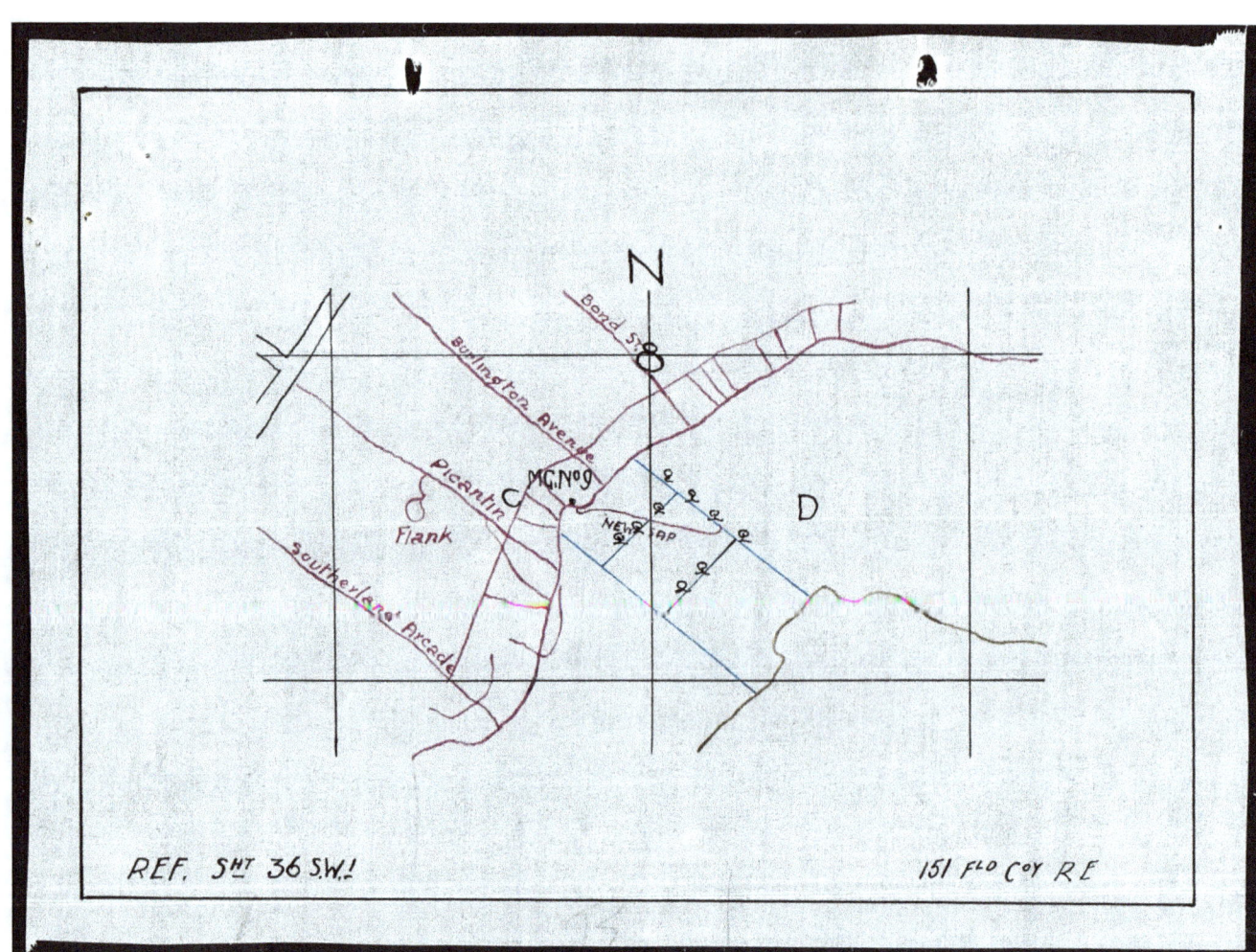

War Diary. 151 Field Company R.E.
May 1916. Appendix III.

Copy.

38th D/G/1013.
General Staff.

To
The General Officer Commanding,
114th Infantry Brigade.

I am directed by the Major General Commanding to acknowledge the receipt of Captain Fenton's report on digging the sap, and to say that he considers it a very fine piece of work, reflecting great credit on your Brigade and all concerned, especially on Captain Fenton, R.E. who reconnoitred the ground and superintended the work. The work done by the 10th Welsh Regiment was a fine piece of organisation and industry. Credit is also due to Major Edwardes and the 13th Welsh Regiment, who provided the covering party. The Major General Commanding will be obliged if you will convey his congratulations to Colonel Ricketts and all the officers, N.C.O's and men of the 151st Field Company, R.E., 10th Welsh Regiment and 13th Welsh Regiment who took part in the operation.

The Major General Commanding deeply regrets the unfortunate death of Major Napier, by which we lose the services of a gallant soldier and an officer of much promise.

A copy of the report is being forwarded to the Corps Commander, who ordered the work to be carried out.

(Sd) H.C.REES, Major,
for Lieut: Colonel,
General Staff, 38th (Welsh) Division.

28/5/16.

To O.C. 151st Company, R.E.

The above is a copy of a letter received this morning from the 38th Division. Please make the contents known to all concerned.

(Sd) A.P.BOWEN, Captain,
A/Brigade Major, 114th Inf: Bde.

29/5/1916.

French
vol 7
151. F.C. R.E.

~~XXXVIII~~

Volume VII

WAR DIARY OF

151 FIELD COMPANY R.E.

FOR MONTH OF JUNE 1916.

Army Form C. 2118.

WAR DIARY
of 151 FIELD COMPANY. R.E
INTELLIGENCE SUMMARY.
(Erase heading not required.)

Volume VII page 1.

Instructions regarding War Diaries and Intelligence Summaries are contained in F. S. Regs., Part II. and the Staff Manual respectively. Title pages will be prepared in manuscript.

Place	Date	Hour	Summary of Events and Information	Remarks and references to Appendices
LAVANTIE	1/6/16		Two Sections of the 1/3 Field Company, SOUTH MIDLAND R.E. arrived in previous evening and started work. One half Coy Section attached to one section of the Company. No 1 Section continued work in the front line, working at Machine gun emplacements Nos 31 and 33, Stokes signaller dug-out and Trench mortar Emplacements. No 2 Section employed in the Posts on the RUE BACQUEROT from various at all machine gun emplacements Nos 13.10.11.12 and 13. Also at EDGEWARE ROAD and the Tramways. Also improvements to Posts. No 3 Section employed on 300 Yards Reserve Line and machine gun emplacements in the TILLELOY Line. Also RIFLEMANS AVENUE. No 4 Section employed on Observation Posts. Put three at SPANTON, THE FARM, CONVENT. THE COTTAGE. Starting 5 up of CRA'S Horn and BERKELEY, and also erection of barriers in the SIEGE HOUSE. Weather fine, warm and sunny all day. Clear and aeroplanes a/gun fairly quiet as far as artillery is concerned.	Spot.
LAVANTIE	2/6/16		All work carried on as on previous days. The continued No 1 Section work on the Strong Dug-outs in the front line, and the cutting through of the sheet in addition to the other work. No 2 Section also commenced work on the extension of the Railway Line along the RUE TILLELOY for extension to the MINEHEAD. No 3 Section continued work at the Two new Machine gun emplacements in the 300 Yards Reserve Line, in addition to communication Trenches and Reserve Line. The CONVENT O.P. was spoilt, being damaged by shell fire, which was carried on during the day by 5.9" German Guns. The masonry work was generally altered, owing to insufficient sand being available to put all the sections emplaced Machine fire. Clear and Sunny all day. Aeroplanes not very active. Some shelling at times.	Spot.

T.134. Wt. W708—776. 500000. 4/15. Sir J. C. & S.

WAR DIARY
of 151 FIELD COMPANY. R.E.
INTELLIGENCE SUMMARY.
(Erase heading not required.)

Army Form C. 2118.

Volume VII page 2.

Instructions regarding War Diaries and Intelligence Summaries are contained in F.S. Regs., Part II. and the Staff Manual respectively. Title pages will be prepared in manuscript.

Place	Date	Hour	Summary of Events and Information	Remarks and references to Appendices
LAVANTIE	3/6/16	—	All sections continued as on previous days. No 1 Sections work delayed owing to no carrying parties for material during previous night. No watering parties this morning. No 3 Section finished on wall machine gun emplacements at avenue turn in ROTTEN ROW and also from near PICANTIN (communication Trench) No 4 Section managed to complete the drainage dam to CONVENT Cr. All mornings work delayed owing to supply of sand not being equal to the requirements of the bricklayer. Weather fine and bright and clear, but unruly. Heavy trench mortar activity during afternoon. Communication by our people and retaliation by the Germans.	SecF
LAVANTIE	4/6/16		All sections continued at work as on previous days. Owing to lack of carrying parties during previous night, and general report of work, all work was delayed. Fatting of road was during the day. CRE inspecting the work on our front in the afternoon. At night a bombing raid was carried out will heavy retalling fire on both sides. Weather, much rain will strong wind during day. Some rain. but not being.	5 WF.
LAVANTIE	5/6/16		All sections continued at work as on previous duties. No 1 Section commenced work on screening for a new Machine Gun emplacement to be erected No 33. Work was delayed owing to no workers parties due to the 116th Brigade being relieved in the FAUQUISSART section by the 115th Brigade. Also work on O.P.s by No 4 Section was delayed by no carrying parties on the previous night for material. Weather strong wind and cool will showers at intervals, little our wire-cutting or artilling either.	SecF
LAVENTIE	6/6/16		Work continued as on previous day. Hour of parade advanced two hours to obtain two interruption for the artilling	

T.1134. Wt. W.708—776. 500000. 4/15. Sir J. C. & S.

Army Form C. 2118.

WAR DIARY
of 151 FIELD COMPANY. R.E.
INTELLIGENCE SUMMARY.
(Erase heading not required.)

Volume VII Page 3

Instructions regarding War Diaries and Intelligence Summaries are contained in F.S. Regs., Part II. and the Staff Manual respectively. Title pages will be prepared in manuscript.

Place	Date	Hour	Summary of Events and Information	Remarks and references to Appendices
			activity, which generally occurs during afternoons. Most of the masonry work was hung up for want of sand, sufficient quantities of which is not yet obtainable. Heavy artillery shelling of RED LAMP SALIENT and ROTTEN ROW during the day. The wire front wire entanglement was damaged at expectation having knocked about by the shelling, but little material damage. Weather dull and cool all day with strong wind and heavy showers of rain.	
LAVENTIE	7/6/16		Sections were employed on the usual programme. No night parties were provided owing to large numbers of men being required for work with the 126 (Field) Company. Cutting off the corner on the right of the RED LAMP SALIENT. Sand was still not being in sufficient quantities to keep the masonry work going in all sections. Rolling mist are of rain during the day, which was very variable so far as weather is concerned, being sunny at times and at other times heavy rain showers. Generally mild, but strong wind not mire whirling or aeroplane activity.	GnF.
LAVENTIE	8/6/16		Sections continued at work as on previous day. Most of the work delayed owing to shortage of night parties and lack of material. No 4 Section got the roof completed of the CONVENT O.P. Masonry work unable to be carried out to full satisfactory owing to insufficient sand. A German aeroplane came over our line flying low, while none of our aeroplanes were about. Weather fine and sunny but rather cool, not much artillery activity.	GnF.
LAVENTIE	9/6/15		Sections continued at work as on previous days. No 2 Section with the end of the attached section commenced work on the Advanced Battalion Battle Head-Quarters. Owing to DIVISION shifts all working parties at night were	Cont.

T.2134. Wt. W708–776. 500000. 4/15. Sir J. C. & S.

Army Form C. 2118.

WAR DIARY
of 151 FIELD COMPANY R.E.

INTELLIGENCE SUMMARY.
(Erase heading not required.)

Volume VIII Page 4.

Instructions regarding War Diaries and Intelligence Summaries are contained in F.S. Regs., Part II. and the Staff Manual respectively. Title pages will be prepared in manuscript.

Place	Date	Hour	Summary of Events and Information	Remarks and references to Appendices
			Cancelled. Not much of interest occurred during the day. Weather fine, warm and bright and clear. Some rain in the very early morning. Aeroplanes active, and also some artillery action.	
LAVENTIE	10/6/16		Sections continued work as in previous days. No 1 Section completed No 31 machine gun emplacement on the front line. No 2 Section continued work on the posts, several jobs being practically completed. No 3 Section continued at 300ˣ Reserve line and Communication trenches. No 4 Section completed work as far as possible in Observation Posts. All bombing war shafts and distrib[ution?] guns to O C 1/3 Field Company. South Midland Division who have to take over the area from 11/6/16. Henceforth are not attached as an attachment. Weather some rain, but generally fine and warm.	Appendices I.
LAVENTIE	11/6/16		Snowshoe. The Company paraded at 8.00 a m with all transport cleaned its billets and paraded at 11.00 a m to LA GORGE. A halt was made at LA GORGE and at 12.30 pm moved off and marched via MERVILLE and (CALONNE-SUR-LA-LYS to ROBECQ, being billeted in an old billets. Weather good day for marching, but very heavy showers at intervals. And Some hail. Covered at billets at 4.0 pm, being attached to 115th Infantry Brigade.	
ROBECQ	12/6/15		Spent the morning cleaning rifles, and clothing tools and equipment. In afternoon gave the men a rest. Weather fine at intervals, but heavy showers. Nothing of interest occurred.	
ROBECQ	13/6/15		The morning was spent in clothing gas helmets and finishing the overhaul of equipment. Section officer also took their men for a short march. In afternoon rested. Weather heavy showers all day, and cool. At 7.0 pm attended	

Army Form C. 2118.

WAR DIARY
of 151 FLD Co. R.E.
INTELLIGENCE SUMMARY.
(Erase heading not required.)

Volume VII page 5.

Instructions regarding War Diaries and Intelligence Summaries are contained in F.S. Regs., Part II. and the Staff Manual respectively. Title pages will be prepared in manuscript.

Place	Date	Hour	Summary of Events and Information	Remarks and references to Appendices
ROBECQ	14/6/16		A conference at 115th Brigade H.Q to arrange details for march on following day. Nothing of interest.	GOC.
		7.0 a.m.	Paraded at 7.0 a.m. The whole company complete. Fell in with the 115th Brigade at the Starting Point at 9.0 a.m. following the Brigade Head Quarters and preceding the 16th (Cardiff City) Welsh Regiment. Marched via LILLERS, BERBURE, RAIMBERT, CAUCHY-A-LA-TOUR, CAMBLAIN-CHÂTELAIN, to FOSSE DE LA CLARENCE, where we billeted for the night. Arrived at 3.0 p.m. Weather slight showers, cold and windy. Good day for marching, except going rapid at first. Nothing of interest.	GOC
LA CLARENCE	15/6/16	6.30 a.m.	Paraded at 6.30 a.m. Clock advanced 1 hour at 11.0 p.m. previous night becoming midnight. 11th South Wales Borderers following 115th Brigade Head-Quarters and Aldengl column nearly 1 hour. Eventually got into our position in the column at 8.15 a.m. behind 115th Brigade Machine Gun Company. In DIVION. Bombed train on the line. The second R.E. Wagon of No.1 Section stuck in the hill out of DIVION. Column was halted by Royal Artillery at HOUDAIN. Thence via LA COMTE HOUVELIN, FRÉVILLERS to QUESTREVILLE, arriving at 1.30 p.m. Weather showery. Some sunshine. But good day for marching. Cool and windy, but roads a little greasy.	GOC
QUESTREVILLE	16/6/16		Started work on preparation of Gunners second line trenches, with 115th Infantry Brigade. Two visits, working in morning and afternoon. Weather fine and sunny. Prepared programme of training and instructions for the following day.	GOC
QUESTREVILLE	17/6/16		Commenced training. No.1 Section went for a route march with a view to instruction of N.C.O's and men in map reading, via VILLERS BRULIN, BETHES, PENIN, TINQUES, CHELERS and home. No 2 Section did a similar route.	GOC

Army Form C. 2118.

WAR DIARY
of 151 FIELD COMPANY, R.E.
INTELLIGENCE SUMMARY.
(Erase heading not required.)

Volume VII page 6.

Instructions regarding War Diaries and Intelligence Summaries are contained in F. S. Regs., Part II. and the Staff Manual respectively. Title pages will be prepared in manuscript.

Place	Date	Hour	Summary of Events and Information	Remarks and references to Appendices
GUESTREVILLE	18/6/16		March via CHELERS, TINQUES, AVERDOING, LA NEUVILLE PLANQUETTE, BAILLEUL-AUX-CORNAILLES, and home via CHELERS. Nos 3 and 4 Sections on the training ground making rouson fortification relics. The whole company had drill in the morning before breakfast. Kit inspection after dinner. A copy of a Special Order of the Day is attached as an appendix unit	Appendix D
GUESTREVILLE	19/6/16		An approximation of the work of the 38th Division on the XIth Corps. Weather fine warm and sunny all day. Sun, the whole company a complete rest and Sunday. Continued training on the programme. Nos 1 and 2 Sections were employed on ferry work and other fortification work on the training ground. No 3 section carried on as training routh month of the following routh, on the Same instruction as the previous day. CHELERS, MONCHY-BRETON, ROCOURT, HOUVELIN, FREVILLERS, and Zone. No 4 Section carried out a similar march on route FREVILLERS, HERMIN, CAUCOURT, BETHONSART, VILLERS BRULIN. In the morning before breakfast the company did squad and section drill and in afternoon numbering order and kit inspection.	SWF
GUESTREVILLE	20/6/16		In the morning, before breakfast, company drill as a complete unit. In the morning Nos 1 and 2 Sections went for a route march in marching order, with instruction as in previous days. No 1 Section via CHELERS, MAGNICOURT, FREVILLERS, and LE TIBLET. No 2 Section VILLERS BRULIN, MINGOVAL, VILLERS CHATEL, CAUCOURT, BETHONSART. No 3 and 4 Sections carried on ferry work at the training ground. Officer Commanding reconnoitred the route to march to PETIT HOUVIN, via TINQUES, PENIN and BUREVILLE for entrainment. The whole of the section were continued on their vehicles in the afternoon. Weather was warm and sunny. Making of note.	SWF
GUESTREVILLE	21/6/16		In the morning, before breakfast, company drill as a complete unit. In the morning, Nos 3 and 4 Sections carried	

Army Form C. 2118.

WAR DIARY
of 151 FIELD COMPANY R.E.

INTELLIGENCE SUMMARY.

Volume VII page 7.

(Erase heading not required.)

Instructions regarding War Diaries and Intelligence Summaries are contained in F. S. Regs., Part II. and the Staff Manual respectively. Title pages will be prepared in manuscript.

Place	Date	Hour	Summary of Events and Information	Remarks and references to Appendices
GUESTREVILLE	22/6/16.		Out the same route marches as Nos 2 and 1 Sections respectively on the previous day. No. 1 & 2 Sections carried out demolitions and other work on the training ground. Fine warm weather, quite fine. Section in afternoon on R.E. work in offensive operations.	GWF
GUESTREVILLE	23/6/16		Whole company did drill before breakfast and after breakfast went up to training ground. Carried out demolition field fortification etc, remaining until 2.0 p.m. Weather fair, sunny and warm. Nothing of note during day.	GWF.
GUESTREVILLE	23/6/16		Paraded at 8.6 a.m. and went up to training ground drill. Joint did company drill and on arrival of the wagon, mounted section drill. Afterwards all sections carried out field fortification. Weather hot and clear all day. In afternoon heavy rain and thunderstorm. Received instructions in the evening from 115th Brigade for operations in the following day.	GWF
GUESTREVILLE	24/6/16		Paraded at 7.0 a.m. and marched to MONCHY BRETON to carry out co-operation scheme with 115th Brigade. Owing to the rapid advance and rapidity with which the practice was carried out, the company had no chance of instruction. Weather was very wet the majority of the day with heavy rainstorms.	GWF.
GUESTREVILLE	25/6/16		Received no orders for work and paraded at 9.0 a.m. At 12 noon received orders that the Divisional scheme was in progress and to come to out at once. Marched via CHELERS and the MONCHY BRETON ROAD to the manoeuvre area and found the whole scheme completed. Collected stores and returned to billets. Two men of the company, namely No. 67484 W/A/Z/n4A) P.D. Rogers and 62579 Sapper R. Milmington awarded military medals for service in the field. Weather fine, sunny and	

Army Form C. 2118.

WAR DIARY
of 151 F.D 6 R.E.
INTELLIGENCE SUMMARY.
(Erase heading not required.)

Volume VII page 8.

Instructions regarding War Diaries and Intelligence Summaries are contained in F.S. Regs., Part II. and the Staff Manual respectively. Title pages will be prepared in manuscript.

Place	Date	Hour	Summary of Events and Information	Remarks and references to Appendices
GUESTREVILLE	26/6/16	—	A hot summers day. Visitors of interest 2ot. At day finished off packing of wagons, etc ready to move off. Paraded at 4.0 p.m. and marched in column I with 17th Royal Welsh Fusiliers to BARLY by following roads AVERDOINGT, GOUY-EN-TERNOIS, HOUVIN HOUVIGNEUL, TANNEYTTE-MONT, REBREUVIETTE, BOUQUE-MAISON, a distance of over 20 miles. Company had but a march the whole in the morning, so in all marched about 26 miles in the day. Weather showery during the day and during the night marched to Vay Luang Jam. The roads were in comparatively soft and muddy condition. Arrived at BARLY about 2.45 a.m 27/6/16 and billeted.	SWF.
BARLY	27/6/16		Rested during day at BARLY. Weather was showery, but cleared later. Paraded at 9.0 p.m. and marched with the main body of the 115th Brigade to GEZAINCOURT (BRETEL) arriving about 1.0 a.m. via OUTREBOIS & HEM. Weather from hot & very marching, warm to being wet under foot. Men of the company tired out.	SWF
BRETEL (GEZAINCOURT)	28/6/16		Rested during day. Received orders to march at night to TOUTENCOURT, but these orders were cancelled and instructions issued to stand fast. Nothing of note occurred during day. Weather somewhat showery stormy at times, but generally fine and warm. One casualty, 1 sapper fell down a well, accidental.	SWF.
BRETEL (GEZAINCOURT)	29/6/16		Rested during day. Two drill parades, during day. Weather fine warm and summery. Visitors of note during day.	SWF.
BRETEL (GEZAINCOURT)	30/6/16		Letter during morning to the N.C.Os about concentration of transits. Men returning and grooming wagons. Received orders to march to TOUTENCOURT in the afternoon and evening. Paraded at 3.45 a.m. and marched via BEAUVAL,	SWF.

T2134. W1. W708—776. 500000. 4/15. Sir J.C. & S.

Army Form C. 2118.

WAR DIARY
of 151 FIELD COMPANY R.E.

INTELLIGENCE SUMMARY.
(Erase heading not required.)

Volume VII Page 9.

Place	Date	Hour	Summary of Events and Information	Remarks and references to Appendices
BEAUQUESNE and PUCHEVILLERS			until 115th Brigade. Huts for two hours before arrival at PUCHEVILLERS, to allow cleaning to dry. Weather fine warm and sunny with some slight showers. Inspected during day by Chief Engineer of II*nd Corps. No special remarks made at this inspection.	yes

1/7/16.

G.V. Fenton
Captain R.E.
O.C. 151 FLD Co R.E.

War Diary. Volume VII June 1916. Appendix I.

HANDING OVER REPORT OF THE 151st Field Company, Royal Engineers, on relief in the FAUQUISSART SECTION by 1/3 Field Company, South Midland Division.

1. **FRONT LINE.**

   WORKS IN PROGRESS.-
   (a) Cutting through parapet in front of mine shaft RED LAMP SALIENT. Nearly completed. Fixing some revetments, and fire steps to be done.
   (b) DUG-OUTS. Strong dug-outs are to be provided for Signallers in the Front Line and Garrison of the trenches in or near the Support Line. Two complete frames have been made in workshops, as drawing No. 71. Two more frames are in hand. Excavation completed for two dug-outs and work on others in hand.

Position of Dug-out.	For whom allotted.
N.14.a.3.4.	Temporarilly for Signallers. Permanent Coy H.Qrs.
N.14.a.3.6.	Signallers.
N.14.A.4.5.	Signallers.
N. 8.c.6.4.	Signallers.
N. 8.d.1.7.	Garrison in Front Line.
N. 8.c.5.3½.	Garrison in Support Line. (Room for two in this position.)

   (c) COMPANY HEADQUARTERS. There is another framework made up for strong Company H.Qrs in the workshops - Drawing No. 45.
   (d) MACHINE GUN EMPLACEMENTS. Dealt with in the Machine Gun Return. Drawing for No.33 M.G. Emplacement is No.47., and drawing has been made and carried to front line.
   (e) RESERVE STORE DEPOTS. These are being provided in the front line to contain

       50 boxes ammunition.) To be stored in
       100 boxes grenades.) three weather-proof
       10% boxes Very Lights.) shelters at each
       300 Iron Rations.) depot.
   Space to be cleared to hold
       200 Gallons water in petrol tins.
       100 Shovels.
       100 Picks.
       4000 Sandbags.
       300 Yards Portable Barbed Wire.
   Various odds and ends.

   Positions:-
     No.14 RED LAMP at Sally Port 11. Practically completed.
     No.15 NORTHUMBERLAND AVENUE, near ROCKET STATION.
     No.16 RIFLEMAN'S AVENUE, near M.G.No.8 and grave.
     No.17.SUTHERLAND AVENUE, near Drain 7.
     No.18 PICANTIN AVENUE, near Drain 6.
     No.19 PICANTINAVENUE, near Communication Trench.
     No.20 PICANTIN AVENUE, near No.33 M.G.Dug-out.
   (f) SAPS.-RHONDDA SAP.
       Sap has been driven out 250 yards into 'NO MAN'S LAND'. The Germans have filled in the end portion, but it will have to be reopened. The Australians are driving out two saps to join on the left. Steps should now be taken to improve the sap, which is only 4'6" cover.   Section

(2).

The work was postponed to allow Australians to carry out their work without disturbance and calling the enemy's attention. They have now started so the other sap can go on.

(g) WIRE IN FRONT LINE. Not normal R.E. duty, but should be watched. Has been strengthened considerably lately, but would still bear more. More system required in the Infantry work on this.

(h) SENTRY POSTS. One has been constructed in workshops, and is ready for erection. Position of sentry posts shown on plan No. 59.

(i) Number Plates for Bay 6 in front line are in Painters Shop, but have not been fixed at all.

2. TRENCH MORTAR EMPLACEMENTS.
(a) On right of ROTTEN ROW. This has been excavated, but knocked in by heavy artillery. It is doubtful if it is chance shooting or has been spotted. Type Plan 58, but needs modification.
(b) ON LEFT OF RIFLEMAN'S AVENUE. Excavation completed in Support Line. Framework being erected.

3. SUPPORT LINE.
(a) CHORD BEHIND RED LAMP SALIENT. This run's from RIFLEMAN'S AVENUE to FIREWORKS POST. It is to cut off the salient in case of it becoming untenable. It has been revetted throughout, but requires further earthwork. Requires heavily wiring in front. Not yet commenced.
(b) SUPPORT LINE GENERALLY. 38th DIVISION proposed to reclaim 50 yards each side of a communication trench first.

4. 300 YARDS RESERVE LINE.
(a) This has been done 6'6" high with firesteps 10 yards each side of a communication trench. Remainder to be 4'6" high. Position between BOND STREET and PICANTIN is most backward.
(b) Machine Gun Emplacement near ROTTEN ROW, Plan No. 73. Arc to right is a little indefinite. The details are attached to drawing.
(c) Machine Gun Emplacement in HOUSE NEAR PICANTIN AVENUE. Plan No.75. No remarks, except fires in front of wire.
(d) There is a Gap plan in the Brigade Office for the wire. The gaps should be checked, as I do not think they exist. I only just discovered the plan just before handing over. There are GAP boards in the Painters Shop.
(e) ATKINSONS POST. Pioneers were doing this, as well as ROTTEN ROW defences. Details are with C.R.E. of the post. The communication trench is to be defended by detached posts at end of spurs along the row of trees on the right of the communication trench.

5. COMMUNICATION TRENCHES.
(a) ROTTEN ROW. Constantly destroyed or damaged by shell fire.
(b) NORTHUMBERLAND AVENUE. Rapidly drying up. Very important trench if ROTTEN ROW or RIFLEMAN'S AVENUE are "barraged". Could be easily made fit for traffic with little work and is well concealed at present by cabbages, corn, etc. growing over it.

(3).

(c) RIFLEMAN'S AVENUE. Revetment and earthing up in hand.
(d) SUTHERLAND AVENUE & BURLINGTON ARCADE. Rapidly drying up, and can soon be re-opened.
(e) EDGEWARE ROAD. Being opened out as rapidly as possible
(f) PICCADILLY and GREAT NORTH ROAD. Opened throughout, but not much cover.

6. DRAINAGE. (Plan No. 30).
Division between FIELD COMPANIES and PIONEERS is RUE TILLELOY (exclusive to former). Field Companies in front, Pioneers behind, under C.R.E's orders. Each Field Coy in 38th Division has 40 Infantry attached for drainage, tramways and communication trenches. These are permanent, and are not altered except misconduct or casualties. The same party remains with each Field Company in inter-Division reliefs. Probably good to watch the drains during the summer, with a view to keeping open and any ~~during~~ *deepening* which can be carried out in dry weather.

7. TRAMWAYS.
(a) GREAT NORTHERN TRAM. to be extended on left of ditch, and hedge at present in front of RESERVE LINE and thence direct to Front Line at Artillery board 4. Requires some more crossing pla~~nes~~ *places* etc. Work at present hung up for steel rails.
(b) GREAT CENTRAL TRAM. to be extended to RED LAMP SALIENT Route along drain No. 11.
(c) RED CROSS truck to be always kept at railhead.
(d) WATER SIDINGS. Water Sidings to be constructed. They have been put in at BACQUEROT END, but no approaches made. The 38th Division scheme was to have four tank trucks on each line, two at railhead and two at rail base. To be changed every night first thing, and filled from water carts with drinking water.

8. POSTS.

A.1.   ) Front Line Posts. In fair condition, but extra
FLANK.   ) work can easily be done in them if labour and
FIREWORKS)   time available.
FOLLY.   Disused.
COPSE.   Very good little post. Field of fire requires
             clearing by judicious thinning of undergrowth.
JOCKS LODGE. Supposed strongly fortified house. Requires
             a lot of work.
HOUGOUMONT. No.B.10 M.G. Emplacement and dug-out. Plan
             No. 64. (See M.G.report).
DEAD END.   No.B.11 (Plan No.66) and B.12 (Plan No.67)
             No. 72.
             M.G.Emplacements and Dug-outs. (See M.G. report).
PICANTIN.   No. B.13 M.G. Emplacement (Plan No. 67) (See M.G.
             report).
             Officers dug-out for post *can* be started in the
old cellar.

9. BACQUEROT LINE - WIRING. In hand. Still needs further improvements. Plan of all existing wiring shown on plan No. 63. Plan No. 38, omitting 12a, is nearly right. Other plans are schemes got out which eventuated in the work being done as in 38.

(4).

10. **ADVANCED LEFT BATTALION H.QRS.** Position chosen M.18.d.10.8½. New dug-outs required. Protection against aircraft observation urgent. Plan No. 69.

11. **ROYAL ARTILLERY OBSERVATION POSTS.**
    (1) BRISTOL. (a) Provision of ROPE Exits (b) Provide iron ladders instead of wood, being safer and taking less room (c) Improve roof to left tower.
    (2) THE COTTAGE. Build outer tower round existing O.P. and strengthen roof.
    (3) SIEHE HOUSE. Continue at bursters and build brick tower behind.
    (4) TEA HOUSE. House wants strengthening and bursters, etc. Only a single brick tower. New double brick tower proposed on left of house.
    (5) THE FARM. Two new towers in hand. Plans all out of date owing to effects of German shell fire.
    (6) THE CONVENT. Nearly completed. Original proposed shewn in plan No. 81.
    (7) C.R.As HOUSE. House strutting up to be continued. Plan of new combined O.P. and Machine Gun Emplacement No. 74.
    (8) LOUNGE. H.24.b.4.9).)
    HOUSE to left of CONVENT)

12. **SCREENING RUE TILLELOY.** Much work requires to be done outside but affecting O.Ps. Best screen made of willows stuck in ground on chance of growing.

13. **EMERGENCY ROADS.** Boards have been painted, and sent to RED HOUSE for fixing. Roads want more marking out with taller stakes and sandbags. Plans from Brigade.

14. **WATER SUPPLY.**
    LAVENTIE. From well in Brewery. Can be considerably improved. Suggest (a) Petrol pump to tank in roof (b) Standpipe in road.

    FRONT LINE. Suggestion raised for artesian supply for front line. Understand experimental boring has been commenced on right. Details of boring apparatus in C.R.E's office.
    There are many pumps, which are in many cases broken in farms in RUE TILLELOY.

    RUE BACQUEROT. Wells in posts should be put in order. PICANTIN (1 well) DEAD END (1 well) HOUGOUMONT (2 wells).

10th June, 1916.

Capt, R.E.,
O.C. 151st Field Coy, R.E.

War Diary Volume VII ~~June~~ June 1916. Appendix II

EXTRACTS FROM

SPECIAL ORDER OF THE DAY

BY

MAJOR-GENERAL IVOR PHILIPPS, D.S.O.,

Commanding 38th (Welsh) Division.

Wednesday, 14th June, 1916.

The Major General Commanding has much pleasure in publishing the following letter from the Corps Commander and his reply thereto:-

XIth CORPS.

THE GENERAL OFFICER COMMANDING 38th DIVISION:-

On the departure of the 38th Division from the XIth Corps, I should be glad if you will convey to all ranks my appreciation of their work since they have been in France.

From the time of its first arrival the Division has done well, both as regards fighting and administrative work. It has carried out five successful raids into the enemy's trenches and has proved itself to possess a fine offensive spirit.

xxx xxx xxx xxx xxx xxx xxx xxx

The work of the Royal Engineers and Tunnelers, which has been of a most arduous nature, both in the front line and in the defences, communication trenches and drainage in rear, has been well carried out, and the exceptional ability and energy displayed by Colonel Atkinson, R.E. who has he now left the Division on promotion, has materially advanced the efficiency of the Division in trench warfare.

xxx xxx xxx xxx xxx xxx xxx xxx

Both I and my Staff regret that the Division is leaving the Corps, more especially considering the cordial relations and co-operation which have always existed between us. I am certain, however, that the Division will distinguish itself in its new surroundings, and will play a prominent part in defeating the enemy and winning the great victory which will bring the war to a successful conclusion.

(Signed) R.HAKING, Lieut-General,
Commanding XIth Corps.

12th June, 1916.

To Headquarters, XIth CORPS:-

On behalf of every Officer, Non-commissioned Officer and man in the 38th (Welsh) Division, I desire to thank the Corps Commander most sincerely for his kind appreciation of our work. I can assure him that his remarks are most gratifying to us all.

We are proud to have received such praise and all ranks will accept it as a valuable proof that in their desire to make themselves efficient soldiers of the King

(2).

they have not laboured in vain. It will also be a
stimulous to all ranks to continue their efforts
to qualify themselves to take their part in bringing the
war to a victorious conclusion.

May I be allowed to add our appreciation of and
thanks for the many kindnesses we have received from
the Corps Commander and the Corps Staff. We have
throughout our time in the Corps been helped to the
utmost, and requests made by us for advice or assistance
have always been met with a willingness and desire to
help, which has lightened our task and added much to
the pleasure of our work.

(Signed) IVOR PHILIPPS,
Major-General.
Commanding 38th (Welsh) Divn.

13/6/1916.

Vol 8

VOLUME VIII

WAR DIARY

OF

151st FIELD COMPANY ROYAL ENGINEERS

FOR

MONTH OF JULY 1916

Army Form C. 2118.

WAR DIARY
of 151 Field Company. R.E.
INTELLIGENCE SUMMARY.
(Erase heading not required.)

Volume VIII Page 1.

Place	Date	Hour	Summary of Events and Information	Remarks and references to Appendices
TOTENCOURT	1/7/16	—	Rested during day. Heavy battle proceeding along the SOMME. Division lining G.H.Q. Reserve. Lieut-Col KNOX. C.R.E. was thrown by his horse and taken to hospital. At 5.45 p.m. orders to prepare to move, but orders for 7th Field Company cancelled. 115th Infantry Brigade moving out. The other two field companies of the DIVISION moved into TOTENCOURT at night and C.R.E.'s Head Quarters with range TEMPORARY apparatus. Weather very hot all day, with little wind and strong sun.	GSF
TOTEN COURT.	2/7/16.	—	Rested during day. Battle still proceeding, but observers not very good. No action called for by 38th DIVISION. Weather fine, warm and sunny, but not so hot as previous day. Orders issued to be in readiness at night but no move ordered.	SENT
TOTEN COURT.	3/7/16.	—	Rested during day. Paraded at 8 a.m. to march to MÉRICOURT-L'ABBÉ via CORBAY FRANVILLERS and HEILLY arriving at 10 a.m. No billets only bivouac, all officers in a marquee. Marched with the other two Field Companies, followed by 19th (Pioneer) Welsh Regiment and Divisional ARTILLERY. Weather fine warm and sunny all day. Small storm in the evening turning to heavy rain after arrival in camp.	SENT
MÉRICOURT-L'ABBÉ	4/7/16.	—	Company rested during day. O.C. went up to MAMETZ to inspect line. Nothing of note occurred. Weather very wet all day and roads very muddy.	GSF
MÉRICOURT-L'ABBÉ	5/7/16.	—	Officer Commanding and 2 Section Officers proceeded to MINDEN POST near MAMETZ to take over from DURHAM FIELD COMPANY. R.E. Company paraded at 2.30 p.m. and marched via TREUX VILLE-SUR-ANCRE MÉAULTE FRICOURT and	GSF

T2131. Wt. W708—776. 500000. 4/15. Sir J. C. & S.

Army Form C. 2118.

WAR DIARY
of 151 FIELD COMPANY R.E.
INTELLIGENCE/SUMMARY.
(Erase heading not required.)

Volume VIII Page 2

Instructions regarding War Diaries and Intelligence Summaries are contained in F.S. Regs., Part II. and the Staff Manual respectively. Title pages will be prepared in manuscript.

Place	Date	Hour	Summary of Events and Information	Remarks and references to Appendices
MINDEN POST.	6/7/16		Arrived at MINDEN POST before dusk. Machine fire with small component of men. Rather cold. 2nd Lieut N A PATON attached to Brigade. Officer Commanding instructing him and coming around until 1.0 a.m. with G.O.C. 115th Brigade. On return received orders that the 115th Infantry Brigade intended to attack MAMETZ WOOD / EAST from to get in touch with G.O.C. of H.L.I. Brigade. Two sections ordered out to go with 11th South Wales Borderers to be ready to go forward to consolidate the function and make R.E. recommendations. They moved off at 6.30 a.m. and got into position in CATERPILLAR WOOD at 2.0 a.m. on morning 7/7/16. Weather fine day, rather wet cost at night. Remainder of Company meeting during at the LOOP.	2nd Lieut A PATON attached. GOC.
MINDEN POST.	7/7/16		At 3.30 a.m. received orders for the R.E. work in the attack. All sections were to be out in RESERVE at THE LOOP. 1 Company of 19th (Welsh) PIONEERS to be attached for work. Orders to be at THE LOOP at 7.0 a.m. and O.C. to return to G.O.C. 115th Brigade for instructions. Disposition at 8.10 a.m. Nos 1 & 2 Sections in RAVINE near CATERPILLAR WOOD. Nos 3 & 4 Sections in the LOOP. 16th WELSH and 11th S.W.B. attacked WOOD, but were held up by machine gun fire. Reinforced by 10th S.W.B. and 19th R.W.F. and at 4.0 p.m. G.O.C. 115th Brigade ordered up consolidating party as he intended to make strong attack at 5.30 a.m. Attack consisted and Brigade ordered to reconsolidate position on North side of RAVINE. Withdrew all sections and the remainder of the 19th (Pioneer) WELSH REGIMENT to the LOOP. at dark, and as no CATERPILLAR TRENCH was barraged. Weather very wet communication trenches muddy, underneath with wet mud. No orders received as to work, so O.C. returned to MINDEN POST to get	GOC.

T.2134. Wt. W.708—776. 500000. 4/15. Sir J.C.&S.

Army Form C. 2118.

WAR DIARY
of 151 FIELD COMPANY. R.E.
INTELLIGENCE SUMMARY.
(Erase heading not required.)

Volume VIII. Page 3.

Instructions regarding War Diaries and Intelligence Summaries are contained in F.S. Regs., Part II. and the Staff Manual respectively. Title pages will be prepared in manuscript.

Place	Date	Hour	Summary of Events and Information	Remarks and references to Appendices
MINDEN POST.	8/7/16		Orders arrived at 10.30 p.m. and Telephoned C.R.E. to inform him the men were tired out and ask for instructions. Orders received at midnight ordering consolidation of CATERPILLAR WOOD and MARLBOROUGH WOOD at dawn. Sent orders to Company for two sections to carry on work with company of PIONEERS, whilst two sections were withdrawn to MINDEN POST. Orders went astray and whole company returned MINDEN POST at 6 a.m. 8/7/16. Location of PIONEERS and Battn arrived. C.R.E. Sent information as to position. The only work therefore carried out during the day was the improvement of a trench across CATERPILLAR WOOD RAVINE to hold left flank and the preparation of the northern banks of the RAVINE for firing line.	Supp.
MINDEN POST.	8/7/16		All sections rested during day. The C.R.E. had given instructions that the consolidation of MARLBORO' WOOD was to be carried out by the company, assisted by the company of 19th Battn (PIONEERS) WELSH REGIMENT attached, during the night 8th/9th/7/16 in accordance with instructions given by the S.O.C. 114th Brigade. The orders given were as follows:- MARLBORO' WOOD was to be consolidated with machine gun emplacements and wire. MARLBORO' TRENCH running north of the wood towards FLAT-IRON COPSE was to be blocked by a bombing post 50 yds north of the Wood. Trench running North East from the wood about 50 yards from the MARLBORO' WOOD to be blocked by a Lewis gun position and the trench straightened beyond. Two machine gun emplacements to be prepared in CATERPILLAR WOOD to fire in a northern direction up the valley to the East of MAMETZ WOOD. In accordance with their instructions, Company paraded at 4.0 p.m. and proceeded to the LOOP, instructions being sent to the company of the 19th PIONEERS to railway-siding at the LOOP at 5.0 p.m. Just before starting for CATERPILLAR WOOD RAVINE, the O.C. of the PIONEER	

WAR DIARY
of 151 FIELD COMPANY R.E.
INTELLIGENCE SUMMARY.
(Erase heading not required.)

Army Form C. 2118.

Volume VIII page 4

Place	Date	Hour	Summary of Events and Information	Remarks and references to Appendices
MINDEN POST.	9/7/16		Company sent information that he had received orders from the Battalion Commander for the work. The scheme had therefore to be considerably curtailed. Nos 1 & 4 Sections under Lieut Jones (Lieut Freeth being sick) were detailed to carry out the wiring in front of the wood. No 3 Section the Lewis Gun stops and Lewis gun emplacement. No 2 Section under Sergeant I. M. Edwards behind the machine gun emplacements in CATERPILLAR WOOD and communication trenches between them and the Old German dug outs.	Cont.
MINDEN POST.	9/7/16	2.0 a.m	All sections have withdrawn from CHARLBORO' and CATERPILLAR WOODS to the LOOP and from there back to MINDEN POST during day. Consolidation of MARLBORO' WOOD was handed over to 11ᵗʰ SOUTH WALES BORDERERS. The company was placed at the disposal of 114ᵗʰ Brigade for fresh attack on MAMETZ WOOD. The O C proceeded to 114ᵗʰ Brigade H Q and thence to DIVISIONAL H.Q. together with the O C 19ᵗʰ (PIONEER) WELSH REGIMENT to receive preliminary instructions as to the arrangements. On his return to MINDEN POST the following disposition was made. No 1 Section of the 151 FLD Co under Sergeant J S Clark together with 1 company two 1 platoon of the 19ᵗʰ (PIONEER) WELSH REGT the whole under command of the O C of the PIONEER COMPANY were to follow and consolidate behind the attack on the right of the wood with through MAMETZ WOOD. There was to rendez-vous and form a dump near the junction of BEETLE ALLEY and WHITE TRENCH Nos 2, 3, and 4 Sections together with 1 company and the destined platoon of the other company of 19ᵗʰ (PIONEER) WELSH REGIMENT were to rendez-vous in CATERPILLAR WOOD RAVINE for the purpose of consolidating behind the right attack on the wood and making a communication trench between the RAVINE and the MAMETZ WOOD. O C 19ᵗʰ WELSH and O.C. Company made their Head Quarters at the CATERPILLAR WOOD RAVINE.	Cont.

Army Form C. 2118.

WAR DIARY
of 151 FIELD COMPANY, R.E.
INTELLIGENCE SUMMARY.
(Erase heading not required.)

Volume VIII page 5.

Place	Date	Hour	Summary of Events and Information	Remarks and references to Appendices
	9/7/16	10.0 p.m.	At POMMIERS REDOUBT. Divisional Brigade H.Q of 114th Infantry Brigade, final orders were issued. Field Company and PIONEERS were in their ordinary positions. LIAISON Officers were ordered to be found by 19th (PIONEER) WELSH REGT. to keep in touch with the front trenches attacking, so as to send back to inform R.E. when the attack was sufficiently progressed for the consolidating parties to be sent forward. The left LIAISON officer was in touch, but the right officer did not get in touch.	GMF
MAMETZ WOOD	10/7/16		Artillery bombardment and barrage timed to lift and move back at 4.15 a.m. after being very intense from 3.30 a.m. at which time the first waves of infantry were to be on the edge of the wood. At 4.45 a.m. Lieut. No 1 Section accompanied by M platoon of the 19th Welsh Regt. were sent forward to make a strong point near the centre end of the cross ride of the MAMETZ WOOD (near F).* At 5.15 a.m. the remainder of the section with another platoon of the 19th Welsh Regt went forward to the wood and commenced a strong point at the junction of the Southern cross ride and the main central ride through the wood, being reinforced later by 2 sections of the 124 FIELD COMPANY. On the right, enough to the known officer not having gained touch, all the consolidating parties in the CATERPILLAR WOOD were in the dark in to the progress of the action and at 6.40 a.m. only received instructions that the wood was clear up to O.Y.4 and to consolidate the front objective. This message had been taken to MINDEN POST in error and forwarded from there. Nos 2 and 3 Sections under Lieut CARROLL with two weak platoons of 19th WELSH Regiment were sent forward to consolidate by the construction of strong points near A.C. v W. On emerging from the RAVINE, they came under very rifle fire with from GERMAN Second LINE in trenches in MAMETZ WOOD and were obliged to make a detour through CATERPILLAR	* Map MAMETZ WOOD APPENDIX I

Army Form C. 2118.

WAR DIARY
of 151 FIELD COMPANY R.E
INTELLIGENCE/SUMMARY.

Volume VIII Page 6

(Erase heading not required.)

Place	Date	Hour	Summary of Events and Information	Remarks and references to Appendices
			WOOD itself and approach the MAMETZ WOOD from the south. The party sent to man W. (No 3 Section) were sent back by the infantry officer in charge as the Germans were not yet cleared and fell back and constructed the front near C. No 3 Section carried out front A. On completion of the works, the watching troops were causing many casualties, and so the works were complete. Nos 2 & 3 Sections with them attached PIONEERS were withdrawn down QUEEN'S NULLAH to MINDEN POST for further orders. At 2 o'm. the two redoubts constructed by No 1 Section were completed and the R.E and 19th (PIONEER) WELSH REGT were ordered to garrison them, at the same time detaching and SAP	
MAMETZ WOOD	10/7/16		improving. Work and garrison stemming to etc were carried on until 9.0 a.m. 11/7/16. Eventually at 11.0 a.m. all the No 1 Section and the company of 19th (PIONEER) WELSH REGT working with them were withdrawn to MINDEN POST to not	
POMMIERS REDOUBT	10/7/16		In evening O.C. 19th (PIONEER) WELSH REGT and O.C. 151 FIELD Co withdrew Head Quarters to POMMIERS REDOUBT. At 10.0 p.m. orders were sent to No 4 Section to withdraw until 19th PIONEERS to MINDEN POST. The 115th Brigade relieved 114th Brigade in the wood. Owing to fire from the German 2nd Line, very little progress had been made on the communication trench between the RAVINE and the WOOD, and owing to heavy shelling, several casualties had been caused among the R.E and many among the infantry garrison. It was therefore desirable to withdraw as many men as possible from this place as they were locked up there. The situation existing on the evening of 10/7/16 was therefore No 1 Section in MAMETZ WOOD, Nos 2 & 3 Sections in MINDEN POST, No 4 Section returning from CATERPILLAR WOOD RAVINE to MINDEN POST. But all messengers to No 4 Section went astray and they remained in the RAVINE.	

T/134. Wt. W708—776. 500000. 4/15. Sir J. C. & S.

Army Form C. 2118.

WAR DIARY
of 151 FIELD COMPANY R.E.
INTELLIGENCE SUMMARY

Volume VIII page 7.

(Erase heading not required.)

Instructions regarding War Diaries and Intelligence Summaries are contained in F. S. Regs., Part II. and the Staff Manual respectively. Title pages will be prepared in manuscript.

Place	Date	Hour	Summary of Events and Information	Remarks and references to Appendices
POMMIERS REDOUBT to MAMETZ WOOD	11/7/16	10.0 a.m.	Head-quarters of O.C. moved up to MAMETZ WOOD to H.Q. of 115th Brigade. Orders sent for Nos 2, 3 and 4 Sections to be moved from MINDEN POST to POMMIERS REDOUBT, to await orders. 10 h.m. G.O.C. 115th Brigade, who had been put in charge of all the forces in the wood, was ordered to attack and take the remainder of the wood, and that the work of the 151 (Field) Company was the preparation of strong points near S.T. and V. At the same time (received information from the) H.Q. of the company that No 4 Section had not returned on previous night and a note saying that they were in CATERPILLAR WOOD, both wounded and buried. Runners sent to the RAVINE and WOOD but unable to get in touch until No 4 Section, although they started out. At 8.30 p.m. the infantry were forwarded up for the advance to clear the north and west of the wood, but were disorganised by our own artillery firing into them. However after a delay, the advance was carried out, but not well extensive, and the consolidation was not required. At 10.0 p.m. S.O.C. 115th Brigade ordered the withdrawal of the R.E. as they were not going to be retained that night in MAMETZ WOOD. Consulting during the operations from 6/7/16 until 11/7/16 during the operations were 2 N.C.O's killed and 24 men wounded. LIEUT. T.C. FREEN slightly reported on sent to hospital from field strength on 8/7/16. At 8.30 a.m. Head-Quarters and No 1 Section paraded at MINDEN POST and marched via BRAY and arrived at Divisional H.Q. where the returns and times were handed at 12.0 m.m. Nos 2 + 3 Sections arrived took at MINDEN POST about 11.0 p.m. and paraded and marched via FRICOURT and MEAULTE to VILLE-SUR-ANCRE. No 4 Section arrived at MINDEN POST at 3.0 a.m.	
	12/7/16		and paraded at 9.0 a.m. and arrived at VILLE-SUR-ANCRE about 12.0 noon. No 1 + H.Q. paraded at their bivouac area 38th Divl H.Q. at 9.0 a.m. and marched via MORLANCOURT to VILLE-SUR-ANCRE arriving at 11.30 a.m. Our mounted men and	

Army Form C. 2118.

WAR DIARY
of 151 FIELD COMPANY R.E.
INTELLIGENCE SUMMARY
(Erase heading not required.)

Volume VIII Page 8.

Instructions regarding War Diaries and Intelligence Summaries are contained in F. S. Regs., Part II. and the Staff Manual respectively. Title pages will be prepared in manuscript.

Place	Date	Hour	Summary of Events and Information	Remarks and references to Appendices
			Vehicles fainted again at 2.0 p.m. and were attached to the DIVISIONAL TRAIN and moved to CARDONNETTE via RIBEMONT, LA HOUSSOYE, QUERRIEU & ALLONVILLE arriving about 10.30 p.m. Dismounted men and cyclists paraded at 5.0 p.m and proceeded to DERNANCOURT rly station where they were entrained.	GWF
	13/7/16		Train arrived at LONGPRÉ about 2.0 a.m. men detrained and marched to LONGUEVETTE, where the men had a few hours rest. Received orders to prepare to move at 11.0 a.m. in motor 'bus and proceeded to LONGPRÉ, when we waited until 7.0 h.m. Marching & the other two half companies of the Division. Moved off at 7.0 h.m. and proceeded via FLIXECOURT, VIGNACOURT, FLESSELLES to RUBEMPRÉ. Mounted portion of the company paraded at 6.30 a.m and proceeded to RUBEMPRÉ via RAINNEVILLE and PIERREBOT arriving at 17.0 noon.	GWF
RUBEMPRÉ	14/7/16		Paraded at 12.30 p.m. and the whole of the Divisional R.E. proceeded to COIGN, via PUCHEVILLERS, MARIEUX, AUTHIE and ST LEGER-LES-AUTHIE. On arrival at about 5.0 p.m were ordered to billets at COURCELLES-AU-BOIS, to take over the line from 2/1 Field Company, SOUTH MIDLAND DIVISION. The weather since last week during the day's clear and sunny.	GWF
COURCELLES-AU-BOIS	15/7/16		Getting settled during day. In a state of exhaustion, generally, and fit for no work. Officers were sent round to inspect the line with officers of 2/1 Field Company. In afternoon returned part of the line by O.C. 115th Brigade took over the night Brigade area. Weather fine all day. One of our aeroplanes was brought down by machine gun fire near HEBUTERNE and then fired on by artillery.	GWF

T.J134. Wt. W708 —776. 50000. 4/15. Sir J.C. & S.

Army Form C. 2118.

WAR DIARY
of 151 FIELD COMPANY. R.E
INTELLIGENCE/SUMMARY
(Erase heading not required.)

Volume VIII Page 9.

Instructions regarding War Diaries and Intelligence Summaries are contained in F. S. Regs., Part II. and the Staff Manual respectively. Title pages will be prepared in manuscript.

Place	Date	Hour	Summary of Events and Information	Remarks and references to Appendices
COURCELLES-AU-BOIS	15/7/16		All men again rested during day. Pumping plant at LA SIGNY FARM taken over from 2/. Field Company, who carried all work. Allotment of sections. No 1 Section Water Supply and Trench Tramways. No 2 Section, Russian Brigade area, No 3 Section, Workshops and No 4 Section front line area. With regard to the front line area, the matter of dividing will the work up preferred by the DIVISION and amplified by the 115th Brigade is appended. Officer commanding spent the day with the C.R.E. on preferred work and also report on the front situation. Weather fine & sunny, with a few showers of rain in the afternoon and evening.	Appendix IV Gost
COURCELLES-AU-BOIS	17/7/16		No 1 Section continued on water supply and Tramways. They took over the pumping machinery at LA SIGNY FARM, which was in very bad condition, and broke down during night. No 2 Section were employed on the communication Trenches in the Russian Brigade area. No 3 Section employed on workshops, but could not get the petrol engine working the circular saw to work. Work in accordance with original. No 4 Section employed in front line, chiefly in getting in communication trenches and support line through. Weather dull all day turning to rain at night.	Gost
COURCELLES-AU-BOIS	18/7/16		Sections continued on the same work as on previous days. Arrangements made with Officers commanding units to put with a string party on hand in future, but work did not happen at night owing to within - battalion reliefs. Petrol engine in the workshops still jibbing and considerable trouble with the engine at LA SIGNY FARM. No 4 Section in addition continued at various to fittings and trenches on the 2" water main supply. Weather sunny and misty all day. Turning to fine however in the evening. Nothing much of note during the day.	Gost

T.2134. Wt. W708—776. 500000. 4/15. Sir J. C. & S.

Army Form C. 2118.

WAR DIARY
of 151 (FIELD) COMPANY. R.E.
INTELLIGENCE SUMMARY
Volume VIII App 10

(Erase heading not required.)

Instructions regarding War Diaries and Intelligence Summaries are contained in F. S. Regs., Part II. and the Staff Manual respectively. Title pages will be prepared in manuscript.

Place	Date	Hour	Summary of Events and Information	Remarks and references to Appendices
COURCELLES-AU-BOIS	19/7/16		All sections continued at work as in previous days. Work progressed and fell in a faster leave on the first line. No 4 Section split up to sub to bascule different extension over the white works, day and night. No 2 Section continued working in the MUNCH Trench between the RED and ROSE LINES. No 3 Section continued at work in the slope, making by the engine dealing the wooden beam go. No 1 Section worked in the water supply and tramways, connecting up the 2" distribution system with the 4" NEBUTURNE supply. Also collecting and overhauling trestles and gauze on the tramways. The weather was fine and sunny, and very mg up the tunnion. Clouds flying low in the morning, but cleared later.	
COURCELLES-AU-BOIS	20/7/16		All sections continued at work as on previous days. No 1 Section continued work at water-supply and tramways. Very busy work repairing pump at LA SIGNY Farm which was put in proper working order during the night. NEBUTURNE supply still broken down. No. 2 Section on the tramways. No. 4 Section continued then work in the RUSSIAN Trench was on communication Trenches. No. 3 Section on the tramways. No 4 Section emptying in the posts in the front line. Wiring and cleaning of the ports in the front line system continued, but the work is slow. Weather fine and sunny, and changing western generally.	Goft
COURCELLES-AU-BOIS	21/7/16		All sections continued at work as on previous days. No 1 Section continued work at water-supply and tramways. No 2 Section on communication trenches up to the rd line. No 3 Section continued in waterline. No 4 Section carried on work at telling in front line ports. Weather fine warm and sunny, until very slight Scotch mist first half of night. Casualties 1 Sapper of No 4 Section killed.	Goft
COURCELLES-AU-BOIS	22/7/16		Work was continued in the same arrow as on previous days. No 2 Section also commenced work on the new Russian Gun Emplacements in the line. Work on the ports were delayed by water-controls on unholys. O recommencements been on with	Goft

Army Form C. 2118.

WAR DIARY
of 151 FIELD COMPANY. R.E.

INTELLIGENCE SUMMARY.

Volume VIII Page 11.

(Erase heading not required.)

Instructions regarding War Diaries and Intelligence Summaries are contained in F. S. Regs., Part II. and the Staff Manual respectively. Title pages will be prepared in manuscript.

Place	Date	Hour	Summary of Events and Information	Remarks and references to Appendices
COURCELLES-AU-BOIS.	23/7/16		with the exception of No 3 Section starting work on the Stokes mortar emplacements. Weather fine warm and sunny. The sections were employed as on previous days. No 1 Section also took on work on Club dug-outs. A resumsum? of this in the front line was ordered. No 3 section started on work for Trench mortar (Stokes gun) emplacements. Remainder of work as usual. Weather fine, but inclined to be lumpy with low flying clouds. Sections were given a half holiday, being Sunday	SAME ?
COURCELLES-AU-BOIS	24/7/16		The sections continued at work, as on previous days. No 1 Section started work on dug-outs, but not in the front line system. Water supply and drainage continually improved. No 2 Section continued at the machine gun emplacements. No 3 section continued at Stokes mortar emplacements, and No 4 Section on the front line system consisting the infantry. Weather fine and dry, but dull & lumpy generally. Nothing of note during day.	SAME
COURCELLES-AU-BOIS	25/7/16		All sections were employed in the front line system. No 4 Section took over the construction of the medium and heavy trench mortar emplacements from the 123 Field Company. HEBUTERNE water supply was put to work for the first day since we have been in the line by the R. Anglesea Royal Engineers Sup Company. The remainder of the work was of usual type. Weather fine all day, clear during the day, but generally lumpy.	SAME
COURCELLES AU SERRE ?	26/7/16		Sections all employed as previously. No 1 Section again overtaxed engineer at LA SIGNY FARM to get it in thorough working condition. No 2 Section had sufficient men to start on communication trenches again and got GREY and WARLEY trenches completed. No 3 Section continued at Stokes mortar emplacements. No 4 Section at Heavy	GAS

T.2134. Wt. W708—776. 500,000. 4/15. Sir J. C. & S.

Army Form C. 2118.

WAR DIARY
of 151 Field Company R.E.
INTELLIGENCE SUMMARY.

Volume VIII pages 1-4

(Erase heading not required.)

Place	Date	Hour	Summary of Events and Information	Remarks and references to Appendices
COURCELLES-AU-BOIS	27/7/16		Trench mortar emplacements. Weather dull most of the day and threatening rain. Cleared in the evening, but rained at night.	
			All sections were employed on work as usual. No 1 Section commenced work on the dug-outs in the support line. Wiring went on on the main front-line track. Nothing of note with the other sections. Officers of the 83rd Field Company arrived to take over the work in the line from this Company. Weather fine, generally, but clear and good for observation.	Egypt
COURCELLES-AU-BOIS	28/7/16		All sections employed in the morning only at usual work. Returned to camp at 12 0 noon and in the afternoon loaded all vehicles ready for moving in the morning. Handing over notes as attached in an attendix.	Appendix III
			Column Fenton on the evening O.M. in ambulance to hospital & followed by Major Long. Took over command. Weather fine, misty in morning but cleared at midday.	2 off
Courcelles au Bois	29.7.16		Left COURCELLES at 11.20 A.M. after handing over to 83rd Field Company the billets & marched to BUS-les-ARTOIS arriving at 12.30 p.m. where we bivouac for the night. Weather very fine.	
BUS-les-ARTOIS	30.7.16		Left Bus at 8 a.m. & proceeded via LOUVENCOURT, VAUCHELLES, MARIEUX, BEAUQUESNE to BEAUVAL arriving 1 p.m. where we billet for night. Weather very warm.	
BEAUVAL	31.7.16		Left BEAUVAL at 2 a.m. & marched to CANDAS, arriving 4.20 a.m. Entrained & left CANDAS at 7.37 a.m. for St OMER arriving at 3 o'clock after detraining we proceeded at 4 p.m. to march to	

Army Form C. 2118.

WAR DIARY

of 151ST FIELD COMPANY R.E.

~~INTELLIGENCE SUMMARY~~

(Erase heading not required.)

VOLUME VIII PAGE 13

Instructions regarding War Diaries and Intelligence Summaries are contained in F. S. Regs., Part II. and the Staff Manual respectively. Title pages will be prepared in manuscript.

Place	Date	Hour	Summary of Events and Information	Remarks and references to Appendices
Millain via Watten	18/6	8 P.M.	arriving 8 P.M. Weather everyfine chiefly very strong for marching	A/1

L. Lloyd. Young
Capt RE
O/C 151st Fd/Co/R.E.

NOTES ON MAMETZ WOOD OBTAINED BY PATROL, 2nd Battn,
ROYAL IRISH REGIMENT, ON NIGHT 3/4TH. JULY.

The wood was entered up to the East and West line passing X.24 central.

The wood is very dense with thick undergrowth in that part which was entered and movement for infantry is not easy. There is a trip wire at the edge of the wood which would not form a serious obstacle by day.

About 100 yards inside the southern face of the wood is a small shallow trench or dip.

There was no prepared work within the area traversed.

STRIP TRENCH is strongly wired and well traversed. Trees from the wood have fallen across the trench and make movement difficult.

WOOD TRENCH is well wired.

Position of machine guns at :-

    S.19.d.7.8   (certain).
    X.24.c.8.4   (suspected).
    X.23.b.5.8   (practically certain).
    ACID DROP COPSE   (certain).

The machine guns in ACID DROP COPSE FIRE DIRECTLY DOWN THE valley in S.S.E. direction.

NOTES ON MAMETZ WOOD OBTAINED FROM A FRENCHMAN;
THIS INFORMATION DATES FROM BEFORE THE WAR.

There is a path running from N. to S. at either side of which there are cut willows; the following trees are to be found :-

1. Oak 9 feet in girth.
2. Birch 2 feet in girth.
3. Beech (only a few of these) 8 feet in girth.
4. And some ash.

The average height of these trees is from 30 to 45 feet. On the N.E. border there is some strong undergrowth of hawthorn and briar. The long narrow strip running down from the wood at the S.W. end is a thicket of tall hornbeam 90 to 120 feet in width.

WAR DIARY JULY APPENDIX II

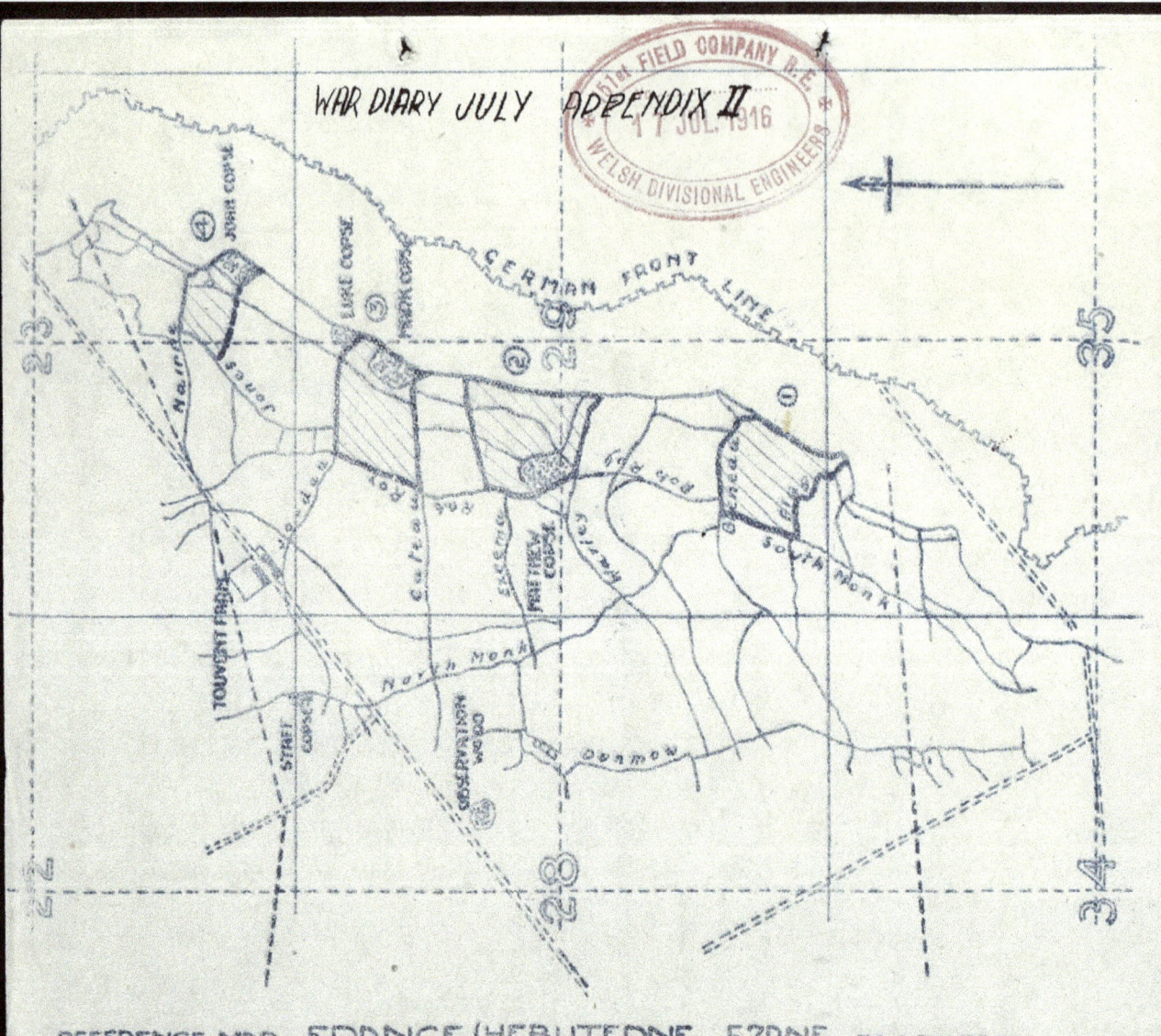

REFERENCE MAP FRANCE (HEBUTERNE 57D NE. 3 & 4 PARTS OF
SCALE 1:10,000

FOUR POSTS to be provided as shown above in Brigade Front Line System
1. FLAG K.29.I. BLENEAU
2. Southern ¾ of K.29 and its communication trenches
3. Northern ¾ of K.29
4. K.28.I. making a new communication trench at southern end

ORDER OF WORK

A........ Make Lewis Gun positions with small fire bays near corners or suitable places to fire in every direction.

B........ Wire all round posts

C........ Reclaim Front line portion of post straightening where necessary and possible and eliminate all salients and re-entrants

D........ Complete Communication Trenches with fire steps and stops for bombers to fire outwards from posts

E........ Complete Support Line to fire in both directions viz:- towards Front Line and bays to fire to rear

F........ Extra wiring to Communication Trenches and Support Line

G........ Connect wire between posts
   (a) Along Front Line
   (b) Along Support Line

H........ Clear and connect up posts by fire trench along front line straightening as before

I........ Connect up posts by Support Line in a similar manner to Front Line

WAR DIARY JULY APPENDIX III

HANDING OVER NOTES OF CENTRE SECTION

of the 38th Division front on relief by 20th Div.

151st (Field) Coy, R.E. to be relieved by 83rd
(Field) Coy, Royal Engrs.

GENERAL. Boundaries as shewn on hectograph sheet, and also 1/5,000 map prepared specially.
There are three front system of trenches, known as the RED LINE, BLUE LINE, and the YELLOW LINE (see hectograph map).
In 38th Division, all work in front of the BLUE LINE, including communication trenches therefrom, water supply, except as will be mentioned below, and tramways have been done by the Field Companies.
The Pioneer Battalion has been responsible for the BLUE LINE.

RED LINE. This has been worked at by the whole Brigade holding the Brigade front, and is gradually forming some semblance of a line in places, but much more work is required. A section of R.E. was detailed to help at first, but all help from the other Field Companies of the Division was withdrawn, when the Division took over a 3 Brigade Front, and re-distribution had to be made, and this section used for other work. Similarly, Infantry had to be obtained from the Brigade holding the front for working parties behind. The general scheme for preparing and reclaiming of the RED LINE was:-
FOUR POSTS to be provided in Brigade Front Line System, boundaries on four sides as follows:-
 1. BLENEAU, GREY, FRONT LINE and MONK.
 2. WARLEY, FRONT LINE, EXCEMA and ROB ROY.
 3. CATEAU, FRONT LINE, JORDON, ROB ROY.
 4. NAIRNE, FRONT LINE, New trench known as WESTERN VALLEY, JONES.

The order of work proposed was:-
(a) Make Lewis Gun positions, with small fire bays near corners, or suitable places to fire in every direction.
(b) Wire all round posts.
(c) Reclaim front line portion of post, straightening where necessary, and possible, and eliminate all salients and re-entrants.
(d) Complete Communication Trenches with fire steps, and stops for bombers, to fire outwards from posts.
(e) Complete Support Line to fire in both directions, viz:- towards Front Line, and bays to fire to rear.
(f) Extra wiring to Communication Trenches and Support Line.
(g) Connect wire between posts:-
 (1) Along Front Line.
 (2) Along Support Line.
(h) Clear and connect up posts by fire trench along Front Line, straightening as before.
(i) Connect up posts by Support Line in a similar manner to Front Line.

The actual work done is:-

(a) A certain number of Lewis Gun positions and defensive points have been provided.
(b) Reclaiming a considerable portion of the Front Line, burying bodies, etc.
(c) Wiring of the Front Line. A certain amount has been done to this, also a small quantity on the flanks.

(2).

A large quantity of material has been carried up to each post.

(d) Digging of the WESTERN VALLEY Trench.

(e) Reclaiming portion of the JONES, ROB ROY, SOUTH MONK Line. The most pressing need now is deepening of NAIRNE and WESTERN VALLEY Trenches, so as to allow a proper approach to JOHN COPSE.

Deepening and reclaiming JORDON and CATEAU between ROB ROY and the Front Line. Pressing on with the wiring all round the posts.

Two R.E. Officers commanding sections are detailed to report to the Os.C. Battalions in the front line to give them any assistance they might require in the work. The Battalion Commanders in the Front Line are entirely responsible for the work, both as regards its progress, method of carrying out, etc.

PRESENT DISTRIBUTION OF WORK OF R.E.:-

No. 1 Section:- Water Supply, Tramways, Deep Dug-outs, in Front and Support lines.

No. 2 Section:- Machine Gun Emplacements, dug-outs for same, and communication trenches between MONK - DUNMOW Line and Support Line.

No. 3 Section:- Stokes Mortar Emplacements, and advice to Left Sub-Section Battalion Commander for work in the front line.

No. 4 Section:- Medium and Heavy Trench Mortar Emplacements, and advice to Right Sub-Section Battn Commander for work in the front line.

WORK.

A map has been prepared shewing position of all existing trenches, work in hand, and proposed. Sufficient time has not elapsed since the collection of information to check it, but it is a start in the preparation of a complete plan.

MACHINE GUN EMPLACEMENTS.

Copy of the list of M.G. Emplacements, their positions and uses for the section, is attached.

DEEP DUG-OUTS.

A list of Deep Dug-outs, with their position and present state of the work, is also attached. The complete accuracy of this list is not vouched for, as no time has been available to carry this out.

COMMUNICATION TRENCHES.

To this section of the line there are two IN and two OUT Avenues. The IN Avenues are SOUTHERN and CENTRAL, and the OUT Avenues are RAILWAY and NORTHERN. These have not been labelled as such, and should be done. The forward communications are:- BLENEAU, GREY, WARLEY, EXCEMA, CATEAU, JORDON and NAIRNE. All these are passable up to the Front Line, with the exception of CATEAU, JORDON and NAIRNE, which are passable to the Support Line only, but are being pushed forward to the Front Line. WESTERN AVENUE leads from JONES to the Front Line, but does not go behind JONES at present, and is not deep enough for use by day.

Generally, all the above Communication Trenches

are in good order, and a good proportion trench-boarded, but if the trenches are to be used by Winter a considerable amount more trench-boarding and grading will be required.

FORWARD TUNNELS.

A report was handed to me regarding these, and a Mining Company is at present employed on them. I have had no opportunity to check this, but believe it is quite correct, with the exception of work done by the Mining Company of removing the damage reported since we came into the line.

STOKES MORTAR EMPLACEMENTS.

The following positions have been selected for Stokes Mortar Emplacements, and work has been started on the first four-named:-

K.29.c.4½.5.
K.29.c.3.6½.
K.29.a.8.4.
K.29.a.8½.7.
K.29.c.7.7½.

HEAVY and MEDIUM TRENCH MORTAR EMPLACEMENTS.

The positions of these have been selected by the C.R.A., and are as follows. Work has been started on the Heavy Emplacements on a design approved by C.R.A.:-
Heavy T.M. Emplacements K.23.d.9.4. K.29.c.5.7½.
Medium T.M. Emplacements K.23.d.1½.3½. K.29.a.9½.8.
    K.29.a.7½.3. K.29.c.6.9.

WATER SUPPLY.

There are three sources of supply to the area, viz:-
(1) The SUCRERIE, (2) LA SIGNY FARM, (3) HEBUTERNE SUPPLY.

(1) The SUCERIE. There are both a 4" and 2" supply from The SUCRERIE. The 2" supply enters the section on SACKVILLE STREET, and then goes on to OBSERVATION WOOD. At this point it is connected with a 2" supply from LA SIGNY. The 4" supply from this system is used generally to supply the old divisional area on the right. I am at present not aware under whose charge is the SCRERIE pumping plant.

(2) The LA SIGNY supply consists of a paraffin engine and three throw pump. This was handed over as cranky and unreliable, but has been worked on, the whole of the plant being overhauled, and is now fairly reliable. Engine Drivers have to be detailed from the Field Coy to work this, and live at LA SIGNY FARM. The pipes are now connected up to OBSERVATION WOOD, and STAFF COPSE, and are joined to the 4" HEBUTERNE supply, where the main crosses SACKVILLE STREET, and this supply has been found very valuable when the HEBUTERNE supply broke down.

A small party is required to keep the pipe line and tanks in good order, as they are continually bursting, or getting damaged by shell fire, thus needing very careful patrolling.

This LA SIGNY Pumping plant can be used either as a reserve, or to augment the HEBUTERNE Supply.

(3) The HEBUTERNE Supply is run by the Royal Anglesea Royal Engineers, and consists of a 4" main, running right through the area from LA SUCRERIE. This appears to be the most reliable source of supply in the area, but has only been working three days during our occupation of the line.

As stated before, it is connected to the LA SIGNY supply at SACKVILLE STREET.

A list of the storage, existing and proposed, is attached.

WATER SUPPLY - COURCELLES.

Two water supply tanks are at J.29.b.5.8. These do not affect the Field Company, with the exception of the maintenance of the pumps for filling the water carts, and baths.

TRAMWAYS.

There are two systems of tramways in the section; one running from COLINCAMPS to EUSTON in a communication trench, and is laid with iron rails; the other system runs from EUSTON to near by STAFF COPSE and to SACKVILLE STREET near LEGEND Trench, and is a wooden track.

A scheme was very recently asked for to connect the two systems at EUSTON, but nothing has up to date been done in the matter.

G.C.V. Fenton

Captain, R.E.,

O.C. 151st Field Company, R.E.

MACHINE GUN EMPLACEMENTS.

No. of Emplacement.	Position.	Object.	Condition.
1.	K.34.b.6½.8.	Fire on German 2nd and 3rd Lines front of SERRE Useful for overhead fire on cross roads & German trenches K.36.a.5.4. & enfilades fire K.35.b.9.4½. to K.36.b.3.2.	Open emplacement. Improved dug-out necessary.
2.	K.34.b.34.95. MAITLAND off BLENEAU.	Enfilades ground between 1st & 2nd German lines. Indirect fire on main road from SERRE. In case of attack enfilades strong points on left of section. Enfilades indirect fire from K.29.b.2.3. to K.29.b.8½.8.	Open emplacement. Well protected from front. Needs improved dug-outs near by. Suitable for covered empl. New firing platform completed.
3.	K.29.c.0.8. MONK STREET.	German Front Line K.29.d.2.7. to K.35.a.9.3. Indirect fire on SERRE.	Open emplacement. Very exposed. Dug-out too far from gun. New open empl. completed.
3a.	K.34.b.5½.8. EDEN.	Alternative position for No.3. Indirect fire on SERRE.	Open Empl. Good condition. New dug-out in hand.
4.	K.29.d.9½.9½. Jctn CAMPION and MONK.	In case of attack brings direct fire on German front line. K.29.b.3.5. to K.29.d.3.5.	Open empl. New empl. under construction, and new table being made.
5.	K.29.b.8½.1. S.Jctn EXCEMA and MONK.	Indirect fire on SERRE. Enfilades German trenches between SERRE and 2nd Line.	Open empl. New empl. under construction, and new table being made.
5a.	K.29.b.8.4. S.Jctn of JORDON and MONK.	Alternative position for No. 5 above.	Open emplacement - recently made.
6.xx	K.29.b.7½.9. Nr Jct with MONK & JORDON.	Overhead fire German trenches N and N.W. SERRE.	Open empl. Small deep dug-out, which needs enlarging. Position suitable for covered empl.
6a.	K.29.b.7.7.	Alternative position for No. 6 above.	Open emplacement - recently made.
7.	K.29.b.30.99. Near ROLLAND.	Fires up valley running to German lines. Overhead fire on SERRE. Fires on German front line K.29.b.	Covered empl. Well concealed, also dug-out below. Concrete roof, which requires strengthening. New firing table under construction.

MACHINE GUN EMPLACEMENTS.

(2).

No. of Emplacement.	Position.	Object.	Condition.
7a.	K.29.d.35.05. Near Jctn ROLLAND and NAIRNE.	Alternative position for Empl. No. 7. Field of fire same as for No. 7.	Open emplacement. Good condition. No dug-out, as position is near other empl.
8.	K.23.c.3.1. TOUVENT FARM.	Fires direction German front line K.29.b.1.1. K.23.d. 9.5. Useful in case of attack.	Open emplacement. Very exposed position. Small dug-out.
8x.	K.28.c.2.7½.		Concrete emplacement. Table Mounting.
8a.	do.		Concrete emplacement. Splinter proof head cover.
9.	K.27.b.99.05. HITTITE N.JCTN of HITTITE & CENTRAL AVENUE.		Concrete empl. Table Mounting.
10.	K.27.b.7.9.	Commands valley running E. with WAGRAM.	Concrete emplacement. Table Mounting. (Occupied.)
10a.	K.21.d.1.0. between NORTHERN AVENUE and WAGRAM.		Concrete emplacement. Table Mounting.

G.V. Fenter

Captain, R.E.,

O.C. 151st Field Company, R.E.

DEEP DUG-OUTS.

The following is a list of deep dug-outs said to have been constructed in the 31st Div. area, as handed over to 2/1 S.M. Fd Co, R.E. by the 223rd Fd Coy, R.E., and passed on to me.

	Position.	Map Reference.	Remarks.
1.	JONES.	K.23.d.9.4.	Two entrances commenced, 14 steps completed. Work in progress by 151 Fd Co.
2.	South of JORDON.	(not reconnoitred.)	
3.	North of EXCELA.	do.	
4.	HITTITE.	K.27.b.9.1.	Two entrances, but no dug-out.
5.	SACKVILLE STREET.	K.28.a.37.40.	Two entrances, and two dug-outs; sides not revetted.
6.	IN NORTHERN AVENUE.	K.27.b.8.7.	One complete.
	do.	do.	One complete, but not revetted.
7.	In DUNMOW between WARLEY and GREY.	K.28.d.53.40.	2 Entrances - completed by 151 Fd Co., R.E. Dug-out started.
7a.	In DUNMOW jst N. of FLAG & S. of WARLEY.	(No trace by 151 Fd Co., R.E.)	
8.	In LANDGUARD between WARLEY and GREY.	K.28.d.44.40.	2 Entrances. No dug-out.
9.	In MAITLAND.	K.28.d.25.35.	Two entrances, one fallen in. No dug-out.
10.	In LEOLND N. of FLAG.	K.34.b.30.95.	Double dug-out completed and revetted. Right Battn H.Q.
11.	Corner of FLAG & SACKVILLE STREET.	K.34.b.15.85.	Complete, but not revetted.
12.	In MONK N. of Jctn with BLENEAU.	K.29.c.30.48.	One entrance complete, and dug-out started. One entrance commenced.
13.	Between FERNY and DEZHENY.	(No trace).	
14.	Between JORDON and CATEAU.	K.28.D.8.4.	Entrance done, but fallen in. No dug-out.
15.	Nr New Cut from Jctn of ROLLAND to WRANGLE to join CABER & NAIRNE.	(No trace).	

In addition to the above the following new work on dug-outs were discovered by 2/1 S.M.FD CO., R.E.

16.	In SACKVILLE STREET just N. of GREY.		1 Entrance started for about 8 ft and a 2nd entrance started at jct of SACKVILLE STREET and GREY.
17.	In REST	K.28.d.d.43.63.	2 entrances completed by 151st Fd Coy, R.E. and dug-out started.
18.	In MONK between JORDON and NAIRNE, but nearer NAIRNE.		Work only just started, one entrance & four steps done.

(2).

The following dug-outs were found, and worked on by 151st Field Coy, R.E.

	POSITION.	MAP REFERENCE.	REMARKS.
21.	In NAIRNE near Jct to JONES TRENCH.	K.23.c.0.5.	One entrance commenced. 6 steps completed. Work in progress.
22.	In EXCEMA, between ROB ROY and Front Line.	K.29.a.6.4.	One entrance commenced.
23.	In MONK about 50 yards from Jctn to BLENEAU.	K.29.c.3.7.	Two wide entrances down 12 steps, and dug-outs commenced in each. The North one is used as a T.M. Bomb Store.
24.	In ROB ROY between EXCEMA and CATEAU.	K.29.a.5.4.	Two entrances about 20 steps each, with traverses half way down. No dug-out commenced.
25.	In ROB ROY between CATEAU & JORDON.	K.29.a.5.3.	One entrance about 16 steps, with traverse half way. No dug-out commenced.
26.	In CAMPION between NAIRNE & JORDON.	K.23.c.3.2.	One entrance about 6 ft deep, and excavations started for dug-out. (This should be made deeper.) Used by M.G. Company.

G.V. Foster
Capt, R.E.,
O.C. 151st Field Coy, R.E.

28th July, 1916.

FORWARD WATER SUPPLY.

DETAILS OF STORAGE.

"A" Main HEBUTERNE Supply. (4" main).		"C" LA SIGNY Supply.	
Details of Storage.	Position.	Details of Storage.	Position.
Existing.			
2 - 1600 gallon tanks	K.34.a.3½.3.	1 - 490 gall. tank.	K.27.d.9.5
Proposed.		4 - 100 gall. tanks barrels	K.28.c.3.4½
2 - 400 gallon tanks.	K.28.c.5.9.	4 - 180 gall. tanks	K.28.b.1.4½
2 - 400 " "	K.29.c.3.4.	5 - 50 " barrels	K.28.b.3.7.
1 - 400 " tank.	K.22.c.2½.3.	2 - 400 " tanks.	K.22.d.7.0.

"B" HEBUTERNE Local Supply.		"D" CHEAPSIDE-OBSERVATION WOOD (At present not in good order).	
Details of Storage. All tanks.	Position.	Details of Storage.	Position.
1 - 500 gallon)	K.15.b.3.9.	4 - 175 gall. barrel.	K.34.b.3.6½.
3 - 100 ")			
1 - 400 "	K.15.b.6.7.	4 - 100 " tank.	K.34.c.3.7½.
1 - 400 "	K.16.a.6.4.	4 - 100 " "	K.28.d.2½.4½
2 - 400 "	K.16.a.7.7.		
1 - 400 "	K.15.d.9.8.		
2 - 400 "	K.22.a.1.6.		
1 - 400 "	K.22.a.9.1.		
Proposed.			
1 - 400 gallon.	K.15.b.6.7.		

Original Vol 9

VOLUME VIII

WAR DIARY.

OF

151st Field Company Royal Engineers

For

Month of August 1916.

Army Form C. 2118.

WAR DIARY
or
INTELLIGENCE SUMMARY.
(Erase heading not required.)

Vol IX. page 1

Instructions regarding War Diaries and Intelligence Summaries are contained in F. S. Regs., Part II. and the Staff Manual respectively. Title pages will be prepared in manuscript.

Place	Date	Hour	Summary of Events and Information	Remarks and references to Appendices
Millain	1 Aug		Inspection of kit, foot cart & gas helmets, rested men & horses. Bathing in canal very hot.	249
"	2 Aug		Squad drill & light exercise for men. Awaiting orders for move to VOLKENICKHOVE, bathing, very hot.	249
"	3 Aug		Orders to move cancelled as 134 Fd.H/y R.E. had not evacuated billets. Later orders received for one section to be moved forward under 113 Brigade. This section started at 3.10 for Wormhoudt. Later orders received for the remainder of company to proceed to Wormhoudt. Left at 6.20 & arrived at WORMHOUDT at 11.15 A.M., where the remainder of section joined up.	24
Wormhoudt	4 Aug		Lt Jones & 2nd Lt Farvell left at 10.30 with their sections 3 & 4 for Ypres des Erport-to 2nd Division. The remainder remained at Wormhoudt awaiting orders. Rations for two sections forwarded. Very warm.	24
Wormhoudt	5 Aug		Captain Going proceeded to Nº 3.5.7 with HQ & transport via Herzeele & POPERINGHE, detraining tool carts & limbers of 4 sections under Corporal Davis to meet Lt Jones & Morgan R.E. at VLAMERTINGHE. Transport arrived at 10.30 P.M. Weather warm	24
Y p = S	6 Aug		Left transport at 6 a.m., found Lt Jones & Carroll with 3 & 4 section billeted at Ypres near canal. They were working under C.R.E. 2½ Division, & Special report of their work will be entered herely. Mr Morgan with 1st section were	

T.J 134. Wt. W 708—776. 500000. 4/15. Sir J. C. & S.

WAR DIARY or INTELLIGENCE SUMMARY

Army Form C. 2118.

Vol IX page 2

Place	Date	Hour	Summary of Events and Information	Remarks and references to Appendices
Ypres	7		Billeted in C 25 dug outs & were attached to 4th Division. Under instructions from C.R.E. moved on to join them, also with Lt Hogan spoke to Captain Martel O.C. 9th A Field Coy R.E. who arranged to meet us at 3am & show work. Weather warm	
			Was shewn work for sections, to make strong point & dug outs at Farm fence. This work is placed in charge of Lt Hogan who began work that night. Met C.E. who instructed me to arrange with Lt Thomas 218 A.T. Coy R.E.(?) to take over his duties in respect of L3, L0 & L4 defences. Shelling during day. Weather warm	
YPRES	8		Roll & section commenced work at fence Farm clearing foundation for 3 dug outs in positions agreed upon by O.C. 9th Fd Coy R.E. Planesville attached. Met Lt Thomas & went round with him L3, L0 & L4, the work is being carried on by the infantry at L0 & L4 strengthening parts of the redoubts commencing at certain points, found no plans of work is being done at L3. Weather fine & warm	

Army Form C. 2118.

WAR DIARY
or
INTELLIGENCE SUMMARY.
(Erase heading not required.)

Vol IX page 3

Place	Date	Hour	Summary of Events and Information	Remarks and references to Appendices
YPRES	9		Nos 1 & 2 sections carried out no work at night owing to the attack. Nos 3 & 4 sections had Sgts & L/Corpls L/Cpl & Williams, Bones hastly gassed during the attack & they have been sent to hospital. Own cookhouse there was some disturbance with Enem Rgt which lead to some replacements but we still got this may be gotover. Sapper Wymgares & another surveyed front line of L3 defence 2nd Lt Heaton Armstrong O.P. reported on work. Weather fine.	A/1
YPRES	10		Proceeded with Sapper Rees to survey L8 defence. Road to Poperinghe to Vlamertinge. Field Cashier. Found Dan away. Inspected house Ames & saw 2nd Lt Heaton Armstrong RE. Work carried on at Junco Farm. Body of woman found & some ma cellars with M Armstrong completed survey of L8. Nos 1 & 2 sections continued work. Weather fine.	A/1
	11			A/1
	12		Nos 1 & 2 continued work at Junco Farm. Weather fine.	A/1
	13		Took over L defence from 2nd Lt Thomas. Nos 1 & 2 sections continued their work.	A/1
	14		Two houses from Remount Nos 1 & 2 section continued work. Poperinghe Ryke or L. Often no complete. Weather breaking	A/1

T.2134. Wt. W708—776. 500000. 4/15. Sir J.C. & S.

WAR DIARY or INTELLIGENCE SUMMARY

Army Form C. 2118.

Place	Date	Hour	Summary of Events and Information	Remarks and references to Appendices
Ypres.	15 July		Work continued by 1 & 2 sections. Inspected 4 & 2 arranged with O.C. work to be carried out. Weather fine. Sapper Jones of C Co 6330 wounded in eye on No 4 section	O.S. Webb 13 Webb
Ypres	16 July		Work continued by 1 & 2 sections. Inspected 1 & 2 O.P. & arranged for work to be carried on with the O.C's of companies occupying the post. Arranged also to make H.Q at L.8 & to move in the same evening. C.R.E 30 Div inspected billets at Canal Bank. Met G.S.2 at L.4 & received instructions as to what work is to be carried out. Weather fine	4/
"	17 July		Work carried on by 1 & 2 sections. Arranged for erecting shelter on L.8 for platoon. Weather fine	4/
"	18 July		Work carried on by 1 & 2 sections. Arranged with C.E. 2nd corps. Weather stormy	4/
"	19 July		Work carried on by 1 & 2 sections. Weather stormy. Inspected new work on L defences.	4/
			Work of 3 & 4 Sections on N salient YPRES. This consists of reopening of fire trenches, communication trenches, dug-outs	4/

WAR DIARY
or
INTELLIGENCE SUMMARY.
(Erase heading not required.)

Army Form C. 2118.

Place	Date	Hour	Summary of Events and Information	Remarks and references to Appendices
YPRES	20		& drains between the rampart moat & Wells Cross Roads on the RAIL Salient. Work done. Trench widened 1170', French boards 216', Sandbags 7 parapet 244. Hurdle revetment 560', footpath built 290', drains cleared 205', drains scoured 70'. In G. Emplacement covered with bricks & sold hurdles revetted to 18th August	
	21		Took over from 9th Field Coy R.E. No 4 section rejoined Company & took over work on Canal Bank. No 3 rejoined company & proceeded to their billet at Jaux Lines. Work on Jauro Farm continued. Weather fine.	24
	22		Work continued & working parties arranged but altered in evening as R.E. have to concentrate on strong points. Weather fine. Gas alarm in Multin fine. No 3 section same to Canal Bank from Billets. Work continued.	24
	23		Inspected Highland Farm & Lancashire Farm. Drainage section arrived at Jauro Farm. C.R.E. arrived in evening & stayed night. Multin fine. C.R.E. inspected Highland Farm & approved plans, & also Lancashire Farm. Later L.S.I. & R.E. altered position at Lancashire Farm to Butts 12. Lt Jones & Farrell took over this work. Lt Weston Armstrong Highland Farm	24

Army Form C. 2118.

WAR DIARY
or
INTELLIGENCE SUMMARY.
(Erase heading not required.)

Instructions regarding War Diaries and Intelligence Summaries are contained in F.S. Regs., Part II. and the Staff Manual respectively. Title pages will be prepared in manuscript.

Place	Date	Hour	Summary of Events and Information	Remarks and references to Appendices
YPRES	23		Drainage kept commencing work at Willows. No 1 Section continue at Junco Farm. Weather fine.	24
	24		Sections work at these strongpoints. C.R.E. came round & inspected billets. Weather fine. Drainage continued work	24
	25.		Sections continue work at strongpoints. Drainage continued	24
	26		Inspected horse lines & arranged for many to A.20. Work continued drainage & strongpoints. Weather fine. C.R.E. called.	24
	27.		Horse transport moved to A.20. Billet taken over from 9th Field Co R.E. Work continued	24
	28		Inspected Junco Farm & Drainage with C.R.E. Work continued dull & showery	24
	29		Work continued weather bad. C.R.E. arrived on emergency	24
	30		C.R.E. inspected pts. Sections N Drainage carried on.	24
	31.		Drainage work clearing main drain & advising Infantry as to procedure. Weather fine, dull no rain	24

1/9/16

L Hopfour [signature]
O.C. 1st Field Co. R.E.

War Diary

151st Field Coy R.E.

September 1916.

Army Form C. 2118.

WAR DIARY
or
INTELLIGENCE SUMMARY.
(Erase heading not required.)

VOL IX Page 1

Instructions regarding War Diaries and Intelligence Summaries are contained in F.S. Regs., Part II. and the Staff Manual respectively. Title pages will be prepared in manuscript.

Place	Date	Hour	Summary of Events and Information	Remarks and references to Appendices
YPRES	1 Sept		Sections carried on work on strong fronts. Inspected Drainage system with Capt Mathews. C.R.E. called. Weather rather dull but dry.	A
"	2 Sept		Sections carried on work & Drainage work continued Weather still dry.	A1
"	3 "		Sections carried on work & Drainage. 2nd Lt A Paton R.E. reported unit. Weather generally dull, no rain	A1
"	4 "		Sections continued work & Drainage. Weather fine	A1
"	5 "		Sections continued work & Drainage. C.R.E. called & went round work. Sapper E Matthews wounded. Major N.H. Thomas reported & took over Command. Weather wet.	
"	6		Handed over to Major N.H. Thomas. C.R.E. called & took O.C. & myself round that of Drainage & Batta 10. & Highland Farm. Drainage party reported their Section Pte G.A. King 17 R.W.F wounded in action. Sections carried on their work. Weather fine.	A1
"	7		Sections carried on work at strong fronts. O.C. inspected canal Defences & that of Drainage with the Brigadier Commander & Lt Armstrong Marked out trench for infantry working party. Weather fine. Work interfered with by night attack.	A1

Army Form C. 2118.

WAR DIARY
or
INTELLIGENCE SUMMARY.
(Erase heading not required.)

Vol IX page 2

Place	Date	Hour	Summary of Events and Information	Remarks and references to Appendices
YPRES	8		Work continued by sections. Work interfered with especially at No 10 BUTTS by heavy bombardment. Defence line laid out on Canal Bank by 2/Lt Heaton Armstrong in conjunction with 114th Infantry Brigade. Weather fair.	App 6
	9.		Work continued by sections. No 3 section attached to No 1 for work at Turco Farm. No 4 section handed over to 123 Fd Coy, work on bridges, tramways & dumps. Weather fair.	Ref.
	10.		Work continued by sections. Handed over tramway to 19th Pioneer Batt. Weather fair	Ref
	11.		Work continued by sections. In addition screening was carried out at Burnt Farm for about 30 yds. Weather fair	Ref
	12.		Work continued by sections, also screening. Weather wet.	Ref
	13.		Work continued by sections, also screening. Enemy day bombardment. Weather fair.	Ref 6
	14.		Work carried by sections Screening	
	15.		Work at LA BELLE ALLIANCE Taken over from 123 Fd Co. & No 3 Sectn transferred. This work from TURCO FARM. Materials organised to take parts in all construction trenches and Rd to relate by Mt Bn & assembly trenches & accommodation, to infantry Batln (Mthr than Camy. Batln) supposed to be in......	
	16		Work continued by sections	

WAR DIARY
or
INTELLIGENCE SUMMARY.
(Erase heading not required.)

Army Form C. 2118.

Place	Date	Hour	Summary of Events and Information	Remarks and references to Appendices
	17th		No 2 Section under 2/Lieut Palin moved to ELVERDINGHE to work under C.E. VIII Corps.	Plus
			No 4 Section under Lt Jones took over work at HIGHLAND FARM in addition to No 12 Posts	
			Work continued by section making posts & tramway.	Plus
	18th		Work continued on string posts & tramway traction mt.	
			2/Lieut CARSETT proceeded on short leave to ENGLAND for 10 days. 2/Lieut ARMSTRONG taken on temporary command of No 3 section.	Plus
	19th		Work continued by section. Work commenced on Signal dugout at IRISH FARM. Further not-	Plus
	20th		-work continued on string posts & tramway. Scarcity of spoil from BURNT FARM Sap & Cupola tractor int.	Plus
	21st		Work continued on enlargement of recovery but delayed through lack of working parties. Mechanical	stop
	22		Work continued on enlargement of recovery but hampered by absence of working parties.	stop
			Major Thomas left for transport lines with a view of proceeding on leave on Sunday for 10 days. Weather fine.	stop
	23		Work continued. Weather fine	stop
	24		Work continued. " "	stop
	25		Work continued. " "	stop
	26		Work continued.	stop

WAR DIARY
or
INTELLIGENCE SUMMARY.
(Erase heading not required.)

Army Form C. 2118.

Place	Date	Hour	Summary of Events and Information	Remarks and references to Appendices
YPRES	27 28		Work continued. Weather fine. Work continued took over HILLTOP FARM work. Lt Morgan proceeded to 38" Divisional R.E. Park to relieve Lt Howells of 2nd Field Coy R.E. Work hampered by artillery fire & raiding parties. Weather fine	
	29.		Work continued but interfered with by artillery fire. 2nd Lt Carroll returned from leave. Sent information to O.P. re shaft on 17th west from A.20 central. Weather fine	
	30.		Work continued but work partially stopped by artillery fire. Result of information police found some of missing stores taken from A.20 central at the 2nd London R.E.S. Corporal Rogers returned from leave.	
	30/9/16			

J. Lloyd Jones
Capt R.E.
for O.C. 151 Field Coy R.E.

Secret   Confidential

Original

War Diary — October — 1916.

151 Field Coy. R.E. 38th (Welsh) Divn

31-10-1916.

Army Form C. 2118.

WAR DIARY
or
INTELLIGENCE SUMMARY.
(Erase heading not required.)

Instructions regarding War Diaries and Intelligence Summaries are contained in F. S. Regs., Part II. and the Staff Manual respectively. Title pages will be prepared in manuscript.

Place	Date	Hour	Summary of Events and Information	Remarks and references to Appendices
YPRES	Oct 1.		Work continued on strong points & screening but delayed owing to working parties being interfered with by reliefs. Weather fine	
	2.		Work continued on strong points but delayed by reliefs interfering with working parties. Weather fine	
	3.		Work interfered with by Brigade reliefs. Weather bad.	
	4.		Work continued on strong points. Corporal Wells went on leave.	
	5.		Weather wet - Major Rhodes returned from leave & assumed Command	
	6.		Work continued on string points. Weather dull	
	7.		Work continued on string points. Weather changeable - some rain	
	8.		Sections continued work on string points. 2 lieut Armeling attached to Major out supervision on Acting Adjutant. Weather dry	
	9.		No 4 Section took over Capt work at ELVERDINGHE from No 2 section. 2nd Lieut took over work at No 12 Busses & NIGHTENOUD FARM. Sections Continued work on string points. 2 Lieut McPATON proceeded to ENGLAND on seven days leave. Weather indifferent, some rain	

T2134. Wt. W708—776. 500000. 4/15. Sir J. C. & S.

Army Form C. 2118.

WAR DIARY
or
INTELLIGENCE SUMMARY.
(Erase heading not required.)

Instructions regarding War Diaries and Intelligence Summaries are contained in F.S. Regs., Part II. and the Staff Manual respectively. Title pages will be prepared in manuscript.

Place	Date	Hour	Summary of Events and Information	Remarks and references to Appendices
	10		Work continued by S Party. Present Infantry working party of 2 Officers, 113 OR obtained from 115" Bde in lieu of daily working party hitherto furnished	
	11		Daywork continued at 12 BUTTS + HILLTOP. Nowork at 12 BUTTS TURCO FARM at night owing to Construction drains. Work discontinued at HIGHLAND FARM for the present, owing to shortage of working parties not	
	12		Work continued by Section working parties. Weather changeable. Somewhat warmer.	
	13		Work continued as usual. Weather changeable. Some showers.	
	14		Work continued on string bonds. Walking platoons to & from Hautville.	
	15		Work continued daytime. Somewhere.	
	16		Work continued on string bonds. Work at TURCO FARM interfered with by bombardment. Weather fine. Kingdom brightpt.	
	17		Section Continued with ee usual. Weather changeable. Some showers at night interfered with work.	
	18		Section Continued work as usual. HILLTOP & LA BELLE ALLIANCE night parties were given a rest Captain L. GORME proceeded between & returns on return leave. Nowork at Turcos night 18/19 owing to sleep in the weather showery	
	19		Work continued by Sections: work hampered by heavy rain	
	20		Work continued as usual. Weather fine. TURCO FARM shelled during morning.	
	21		Work continued as usual TURCO FARM shelled at 9.30 A.M	

Army Form C. 2118.

WAR DIARY
or
INTELLIGENCE SUMMARY.
(Erase heading not required.)

Place	Date	Hour	Summary of Events and Information	Remarks and references to Appendices
	22d		No work on TURCO FARM & N°12 POSTS on night 22/23 owing to "Enemy" Artillery barrage. Work continued on new at HILLTOP, LAPEREHE ALLIANCE & IRISH FARM. Weather clear, frosty - wind considerable.	
	23rd		Work on strong points continued. Weather cold. Lieut 2/Lieut N.A. PATON returned from leave.	
	24"		Work continued as usual. Weather still damp, clear & bright.	
	25"		Continued work in progress. Weather temperate, fine & bright.	
	26"		Work continued as usual. Nothing to report. Steady rain during morning, fine later.	
	27"		Section's continued work on strong points. Weather wet.	
	28"		Work in progress continues. Weather dull on morning, rain evening.	
	29"		No work on ELVERDINGHE DEFENCES. HILLTOP & LAPEREHE ALLIANCE owing to inter-division relief of N°3 B-r-A between N°3 & many sub-Brigade. Capt LLOYD-GEORGE proceeded on leave. Weather showery.	
	30"		Work on strong points continued. 2/Lt HEATON-ARMSTRONG proceeded on leave to Ireland.	
			Weather mild. Heavy showers & fine breaks. Stormy wind.	
	31"		Work on strong points continued. Weather some heavy showers, brighter.	

J. Wilson Major
OC 151st Co R.E.
1/11/16.

T2134. Wt. W708—776. 500000. 4/15. Sir J. C. & S.

Vol 12

SECRET.

ORIGINAL

WAR DIARY - NOVR 1916

151st (FIELD) COMPANY, ROYAL ENGINEERS.

38th (WELSH) DIVISION

30-11-1916

Army Form C. 2118.

WAR DIARY
or
INTELLIGENCE SUMMARY.
(Erase heading not required.)

Instructions regarding War Diaries and Intelligence Summaries are contained in F. S. Regs., Part II. and the Staff Manual respectively. Title pages will be prepared in manuscript.

Place	Date	Hour	Summary of Events and Information	Remarks and references to Appendices
YPRES	Nov 1st		Work Continued on ELVERDINGHE DEFENCES, TURCO FARM, No 12 BUTTS, IRISH FARM, HILLTOP & LA BELLE ALLIANCE. Weather dry fine.	
	Nov 2nd		Sections continued work on strong points &c. Rain during day, then clear night.	
	Nov 3rd		Work continued by sections. Day quiet, fine, somewhere. Weather fine.	
	Nov 4th		Work on big point-continued. Several instructional	
	Nov 5th		Work continued as usual. Weather fine, sharp winds, bit.	
	Nov 6th		Work continued as before. Instructional going on as shown.	
	Nov 7th		Work continued on strong points. No1 Section Commenced work on bird railway from SPATH FARM (looking U/P from AUSTERLITZ - LANCASHIRE FARM LINE) to CLIFFORD TOWERS; work on TURCO FARM at Kruppe & Sprouse & trench-huts in attempts during Gehenna of railway. Very heavy rain all day.	
	Nov 8th		Sections continued work on strong points and railway. Work at 12 BUTTS handed over to Infantry. ang. Sept/se. badly. Forty-four wounded slaves	
	Nov 9th		Work on railway strong points continued. Weather fine, cold.	
	Nov 10th		Work continued by sections.	
			2/Lieut HEATON-ARMSTRONG returned from leave.	

Army Form C. 2118.

WAR DIARY
or
INTELLIGENCE SUMMARY.
(Erase heading not required.)

Instructions regarding War Diaries and Intelligence Summaries are contained in F. S. Regs., Part II. and the Staff Manual respectively. Title pages will be prepared in manuscript.

Place	Date	Hour	Summary of Events and Information	Remarks and references to Appendices
YPRES	Nov 11th		Continued work on trench. Left work party on bivouac bivouac ready to halt shelling on ridges 10/11"	
	Nov 12th		working fort part.	
	Nov 13th		Work continued by Detachm. working from dugouts. Detachments carried work on Canadian dugout, replacing existing punch I by firewood planking fitted.	
	Nov 14th		Continued work making firestep. Trenches from clear bodies & dirt cleaned up.	
	Nov 15th		Work continued. Working party. Weather fine, cold.	
	Nov 16th		Work continued. Working party. Weather from very cold.	
	Nov 17th		Work continued. Thy rations. Weather very cold. Snow hard frost.	
	Nov 18th		Work continued at EVERDINGHE. New work on shaping punch toolbox ready to road on H.C. in most on ridges 17/18.	
	Nov 19th		Snow in morning. Work continued at trench. Supply dugout at TRASH FARM completed. India Culvert being put in.	
	Nov 20th		Weather followed work out. Work from trench.	
	Nov 21st		Work on shaping punch item laid making culverts. Weather clear & frost.	
	Nov 22nd		Between trench work complete. Drain in morning, from clear cold.	

WAR DIARY or INTELLIGENCE SUMMARY

Army Form C. 2118.

Place	Date	Hour	Summary of Events and Information	Remarks and references to Appendices
YPRES	Nov 23		Section carried on usual work. Weather fine.	
	Nov 24		Ditto. Weather overcast, improved.	
	Nov 25		Ditto. Weather dull but mild.	
	Nov 26		No 1 section patrolled No 3 section & ELVERDINGHE DEFENCES. Work continued on string point which railway line through to CLIFFORD TOWERS on night 26/27. Weather dull & now rain.	
	Nov 27		Work carried on as usual. Weather dull & rain.	
	Nov 28		Ditto. Weather dull & foggy.	
	Nov 29		Ditto. Weather mostly between showers.	
	Nov 30		Orders received for 197 Field Company to hand over to 225 Field Coy & proceed to HOUTKERQUE under 39th Brit. Section relieved for ELVERDINGHE & No 2,3 & 4 sections from CAVAL BANK on evening of 30th inst. & Company concentrated at brick fields at A 28 central.	

1/12/16.

R.W. [Thomasmoore?]
OC 197 Field Coy R.E.

SECRET

ORIGINAL

WAR DIARY   DECEMBER 1916

151ST FIELD COMPANY   ROYAL ENGINEERS

38TH (WELSH) DIVISION

31-12-16

Army Form C. 2118.

WAR DIARY
or
INTELLIGENCE SUMMARY.
(Erase heading not required.)

Vol XIII Page 1

Instructions regarding War Diaries and Intelligence Summaries are contained in F. S. Regs., Part II. and the Staff Manual respectively. Title pages will be prepared in manuscript.

Place	Date	Hour	Summary of Events and Information	Remarks and references to Appendices
POPERINGHE	1 Dec		No 1 section under 2nd Lt HEATON ARMSTRONG proceeded by motor lorries to Houlle to arrange billets. Later the transport proceeded under Capt Carey by road, via WORMHOUDT, BOLLEZEELE to VOLKERINCKHOVE. The 205th Field Coy R E arrived & took over the billets & work from the company. Weather fine	
HOULLE	2 Dec		The transport arrived at Houlle at 12.30 p.m having left VOLKERINCKHOVE at 11 a.m. No 2 & 4 sections under Major THOMAS left the horse lines at A 28 central by motor lorries at 9 a.m & arrived at Houlle at 1.30 p.m & took up billets at the Mallery & various house adjacent. Weather cloudy & cold but fine	
"	3 Dec		Major THOMAS proceeded with the Acting C R E 39 Division to inspect sites of proposed rifle ranges at Q 9 a & Q 16 & reference sheet 27 A SE. Weather cold & cloudy	
"	4 Dec		Work commenced setting out Butts & firing points at Q 7 a. Weather fine	
"	5 Dec		Work continued at Q 7 a. The 19th Welsh Pioneers arrive at Houlle. Weather fine	
"	6 Dec		Work continued at Q 7 a. The 19th Welsh Pioneers reported & commenced work under instruction from Major THOMAS. Nos 3 & 4 sections under 2/Lt Jones & Carroll proceeded to set out work at Q 16 & Weather cold & dull	

Army Form C. 2118.

WAR DIARY
or
INTELLIGENCE SUMMARY. Vol XIII page 2
(Erase heading not required.)

Place	Date	Hour	Summary of Events and Information	Remarks and references to Appendices
Houttre	7 Dec		Weather Fair. Work continued on range. 11th Royal Sussex reported & commenced work. A loading & unloading party being detailed to be stationed at St Omer for purpose of loading trucks.	24
"	8 Dec		Work continued on range. Weather fine.	24
"	9 Dec		Work continued on ranges. Weather fair.	24
"	10 Dec		Work continued on ranges. C E 2nd (Army) inspected work. Weather fair.	24
"	11 Dec		Work continued on ranges. Lt S O Jones proceeded on leave. Weather fair.	24
"	12 Dec		Work continued on ranges. Work rather hampered by material not arriving on order.	24
"	13 Dec		Reviewed for use. Weather fair.	24
"	14 Dec		Work continued on ranges. Weather fair. 11th Royal Sussex have orders to proceed elsewhere & 13th Welsh Regt arrive.	24
"	15 Dec		Work continued on ranges. 13th Welsh commence work 1 coy at Q?a & 3 coys at Q 14 b. Weather fair.	24
"	16 Dec		Work continued on ranges	24
"	17 Dec		Work continued on range	24

Army Form C. 2118.

WAR DIARY
or
INTELLIGENCE SUMMARY.

(Erase heading not required.)

Vol XIII Page 3

Instructions regarding War Diaries and Intelligence Summaries are contained in F. S. Regs., Part II. and the Staff Manual respectively. Title pages will be prepared in manuscript.

Place	Date	Hour	Summary of Events and Information	Remarks and references to Appendices
Houlle	1916 Dec			
	18		Work continued on ranges. Arrangements made for carrying out work for bayonet courses at NORTBECOURT, MORINGHEN & MENTQUE. 1 officer & 30 men of 13th Welsh under supervision of R.E. of 101st EASTERLING being detailed	21/
	19		Work continued on ranges	21/
	20		Work continued on ranges	21/
	21		Work continued on ranges	21/
	22		Work continued on ranges. The Army Commander inspected the work & expressed his appreciation of what had been done, &c.	21/
	23		Work continued on ranges. Q1a being completed at the Butts & fence put up so as to allow fence to commence on the 24th. Weather dull, hazy & damp.	21/
	24		Work continued at ranges. Fence commences on Q1a range. Weather dull.	21/
	25		Xmas day. The company rested. Photographed. Weather dull & cold.	21/
	26		Work carried on at ranges. 2nd Lt Armstrong proceeded to formulate to prepare plans for another range. Weather dull. Lt Powell R.E. arrived.	21/
	27		Work carried on at ranges. Lt Powell left for School of Musketry Telgues where arrangements are to be made for all work of R.E. outside ranges are left Canada. Weather bad.	1/

T2134. Wt. W708—776. 500000. 4/15. Sir J. C. & S.

WAR DIARY
or
INTELLIGENCE SUMMARY.
(*Erase heading not required.*)

Army Form C. 2118.

Vol XIII page 4

Place	Date	Hour	Summary of Events and Information	Remarks and references to Appendices
HOWE	1916 Dec 29		Work continued at ranges. 2nd Lt ARMSTRONG with party proceeded to W2 & a Rifle Factory for a near range. Weather very cold, rain in evening	24
	30		Work continued at ranges. Weather boisterous, rain.	#1
			Work continued on houses - at ranges B making bridging or heavy gate papers, during A wd md Complete, Instr dull, some men & staff going. troops & weed still at A wd into trenches.	
	31		Work continued as range. Instr bridging	

R Thomas Wayne
OC 157 R2 Type

1.1.17

APPENDIX.

151st Field Company, R.E.

HANDING OVER NOTES.
on relief of 151 Fd Coy. R.E. by 225 Fd Coy. R.E.

1. HILL TOP FARM. (Sheet 28.N.W.2 ST JULIEN - C.21.d.1.8).

   (a) Work completed.-

   Covered trench B.E. completed, with the exception of small rise in the floor near entrance B has to be lowered and properly graded with the remainder of the trench, also about six boxes have to be fixed in the roof, so as to enable men to travel through the covered way without the aid of a lamp in the day-time.

   (b) Work in Progress.-

   Trench E.F. revetted and trench-boarded: parapet and parados levelled and turfed over. Fire-steps required. Trench has been graded to drain through covered way.
   Trench E.D. revetted and trenchboarded. Parapets and parados partly levelled, but work should be carried on to complete the parapets and parados, also turfing of same. Firesteps required. This trench has also been graded so as to drain through covered way.

   (c) Work Proposed.-

   Trench D.C., B.A. A section has been taken of this trench with regard to the drainage of same into the main drain at point A.
   It is proposed, and work has been started at A, for the trench A-B, C-D. to be graded on a rise from point A at 1/500, as shewn on the section.
   Trench E.F. is to be extended to meet the covered way, midway between B.E. on completion of other trench.

   M.G.Emplacements--- It is proposed that open Machine Gun emplacements are to be made at a point fixed by the Brigade about 15 yards east of trench E.F., also near Signallers dugout about 30 yards east of point D.

   M.G.Emplacement No.1--- It is proposed that this M.G. Emplacement should be made into a double concrete M.G. Emplacement, but this work has been postponed until the trenches are completed: also space to be left in roof for periscope O.P.

   Wiring---- Low wire entanglements put up around points B.F.D., but new wire is required north of trench D.C. and west of trench C.B. the low wire entanglements require strengthening.

   The Mining Company are at present driving galleries from dugouts to enter the trench near M.G.Emplacement No. 1 and between point E.F.

   At present the strong point is held by three Machine Guns at point X.Y.Z. The machine guns at X and Y never fire, and are kept for an attack.

(2) LA BELLE ALLIANCE (Sheet 28 N.W.2 ST JULIEN - C.21.c.8.7).

(a) <u>Work completed</u>:-

Drains opened between points A.B.C, C.D, B.E.

Fire trench F.E. re-opened out, and graded for drainage: parapets and parados, also fire steps to be completed.

(b) <u>Work proposed</u>:-

Trench C.D. has to be re-opened and properly graded, so as to increase depth of the present trench.

Trench B.K. has to be re-opened into a fire-trench to fire west.

Wiring to be completed, and positions of M.G. Emplacements and Dugout to be fixed after the completion of the fire trench.

NOTES:- (LA BELLE ALLIANCE and HILL TOP).

<u>Material</u>.-

The following material is on hand at HILL TOP FARM:-

20 Hurdles.
20 "A" Frames.
30 Revetting Panels.
4 Bundles Corrugated Iron sheets.

<u>LA BELLE ALLIANCE.</u>

20 Hurdles.
20 "A" Frames.
40 Pickets.
10 Coils three-strand wire.

All stores are indented for to the 123rd Field Coy, R.E. 24 hours in advance, and drawn from RAILWAY COTTAGE DUMP, and taken up on tram-line to HILL TOP FARM and LA BELLE ALLIANCE, as the case may be.

3. TURCO FARM. (Sheet 28 N.W.2 ST JULIEN - C.15.c.2.4.

Material.

Due to great difficulty of taking up material for the work from BOUNDARY ROAD DUMP a new railway has been built branching off from the LANCASHIRE FARM line.

Material for this work will therefore come from the C.R.Es Yard by lorry, and be unloaded at AUSTERLITZ DUMP, from where it will be trammed across Bridge No.6 to CLIFFORD TOWERS near the farm, and the present terminus of the railway. Material will be carried from the railhead at CLIFFORD TOWERS straight into the TURCO FARM STRONG POINT.

Work-General Remarks- The strong point at TURCO FARM is considered by the Staff to be one of the most important out of all the strong points in construction in this Divisional Area.

The number of men employed on it is one section of R.E., with an Infantry working party of 30 men.

Work at present should be concentrated on the following points:-

(a) Work completed.

The only work actually completed on this point is the Double Elephant dugout near M.G.Emplacement No.3.

(b) Work in progress.

No.1 M.G.Emplacement--Second roof is in progress, about half of it being completed. About ten more rails will have to be taken up to complete the roof.

No.2 M.G.Emplacement--Second roof is in progress, about half of it being completed. There are enough rails at site to finish the roof.

The Machine Gunners want to occupy this emplacement as soon as possible.

The old walls outside the emplacement will have to be xxxxxx broken through for the loopholes and carefully camouflaged.

No.3 M.G.Emplacement.--Second roof has not been started yet, and no rails have been taken up so far. The 1' air space in this emplacement is not being put in, due to the fear of the emplacement being too high, and the chance of observation by the enemy. It is proposed to put only a 4" air space, then a course of rails (touching) and then debris; the 4" air space to be got by the top course of rails resting on a rail wall plate.

(c) Work Proposed--

It is proposed, after the completion of M.G. Emplacements Nos 1,2 and 3, to concentrate on a small portion of the concrete trench on each side of each emplacement. Each emplacement would therefore be a strong point on its own. It was proposed to only do such a length of trench that would allow the construction of four loopholes on each side of each emplacement.

The excavation for the concrete trench between Nos 1 and 2 M.G.Emplacements has been completed, and at present full of water. Most of this water can be drained into the moat and two channels were being made for this on the last night my men were on the work.

3. **TURCO FARM** (continued).

        The concrete trench between the double elephant dugout and M.G.Emplacement No. 3 is already completed in parts, and two or three more loopholes have still to be done.

        Work has been started on the small trench from the door of M.G.Emplacement No. 3 to one of the old cellars of the farm. This cellar is in a very good condition, and it was proposed to use it as a jumping off point for an elaborate system of deep dugouts. The Tunnelling Coy have taken borings for this work, and it has been found that good clay is only twelve feet below the surface.

No. 12 BUTTS.

Deep Dugout. 12 bunks to be erected and both sumps to be kept pumped dry. The water accumulates to a depth of three feet in six hours.

Burster layer of concrete slabs to be laid on top of dugout.

Front Trench. To be lowered to depth in progress and shallow communications trench to be deepened to suit. North and West Fire Trenches to be completed, and additional traverse cut in North Trench.

At junction of above trenches a communication trench to be cut to Lancashire Dugouts, utilising the existing drain.

Various dugouts have to be constructed as per drawing, also dugouts for S.A.A. Water Storage, also two latrines.

The pickets have been fixed for wiring round the Butts, and there is a plentiful supply of material at LANCASHIRE FARM, consisting of revetting hurdles, "A" frames, Screw Pickets, Cement, Sand and Timber.

CANAL BANK IMPROVEMENT SCHEME.

Accommodation commences at dugouts Nos 41 and 42. These are not very satisfactory, particularly 42, 43 and 44 to be pulled down and steel shelters to be erected with concrete front.

Two shelters in course of erection between 44 and 45. One is proposed to be a cookhouse for the Coy.

Dugout 45 to stand as existing.

The present cookhouse to be pulled down and steel shelter erected with concrete front.

46 to remain is existing.

Officers Quarters-- The kitchen to be pulled down and a new one erected, and the officers dugout which is collapsing at present to have the front pulled down, and a concrete face.

Across the bridge the dugouts to have concrete fronts. This work has been commenced, and several almost completed.

The small one marked "O.C." to be pulled down, and a half elephant erected with further excavation.

After these improvements have been completed, revet strongly the YPRELEE BANK. For this purpose frames and 5' and over are not permissable.

A company of Infantry 100 strong is attached, and are billeted in canal tunnel dugouts, but they have to move, and accommodation erected for them on canal bank - time given one week.

The cookhouse made of sandbags was intended on completion to be handed over to the Infantry attached. The latrine in front of cookhouse to be completed with concrete floor with corrugated sides, roof of corrugated iron with 1' fall.

Ablution benches on one side of cookhouse used by Infantry, and those of the other side by R.E.

Latrines immediately in front of dugout 54 used by attached Infantry.

Doors required to be fixed to cycle shed, and proposed bath-house.

RATIONS.

Rations are brought up to the Canal Bank from the Transport Lines after dark nightly.

The water cart is brought up from the Transport Lines nightly, and the water emptied into the "Drinking Water Tank" on the bank.

MATERIALS.

Indents for material for work are sent to the Officer i/c 38th Divisional R.E. Park to be delivered either by railway trucks to RAILWAY COTTAGE DUMP, or AUSTERLITZ DUMP, or are brought down to Canal Bank and even taken to BOUNDARY ROAD by our own transport.

REFUSE.

All refuse is collected and placed in sacks and sent back nightly to the Transport Lines for incinerating

MEDICAL.

The Medical Officer sees all sick men at 8.30.a.m. at the Dressing Station about 50 yards the other side of Bridge 6.

GUM BOOTS.

The loan of gum boots and shovels, etc. can be obtained on indent from the RED HART ESTAMINET EMERGENCY DUMP.

LIST OF ARTICLES HANDED OVER

BY 151st Field Coy, R.E.

TO 225th Field Coy, R.E.

on relief - 1st Dec. 16.

CANAL BANK.

1 Company Office.

1 Draughtsman's Office.

1 Cycle Shed.

1 Stores Shed.

1 Bath-house.

1 Dugout for Shoemaker.

1 Water Tank.

2 Ablution Benches and 12 Ablution Bowles (opposite C.S.M's Dugout for use of R.E.

2 Ablution benches and 3 Ablution Bowls near R.E. Cookhouse, for use of R.E.

3 Ablution Benches and 7 Ablution Bowls near R.E. Cookhouse, for use of Infantry attached.

1 Latrine under ~~xxxxxxxxxx~~ reconstruction opposite R.E. Cookhouse.
1   do.   do.   for use of Infantry.
1 Latrine for use of R.E. near Bath-house.

7 Stoves and 8 Braziers in office and Dugout.

4 Stoves in Officers Dugouts.

1 Cookhouse containing 1 meat safe near CSM's dugout.
1   "   "   2 "   "   , stand & 1 table opposite dugout No. 54.

48 Barrels Cement.
 8½ Steel shelters.
16 Baby Elephants.
 1 Box Bolts and Nuts.
 3 Wheelbarrows.
 1 Hand-barrow.
 1¼ Casks Lime.

LIST OF PLANS AND DRAWINGS
handed over by
151st Field Company, R. E.
to the
226th Field Company, R. E.
on relief 1/12/1916.

TURCO FARM DEFENCES.

General Block Plan	3 plans various dates & scales.
Detail of Building in North Front,	4 plans.
" " " " East Front	3 plans.
" " " " South Front	1 plan.
Various Details of M.G.Es.	2 plans.

No. 12 Butts.

General Plan.	2 plans.
Detail of M.G. Emplacement	1 plan.

Highland FARM.

General plan of site	1 plan.
Detail of work on No. 1 Building	1 plan.
" of work on No. 2 "	1 plan.

Hill Top Farm.

General plan of site	2 plans.
Levelling of Coney Street.	2 sheets

LA BELLE ALLIANCE.

Site plan (early drawing)	1 sheet.
Corrected site plan 28/11/16.	3 copies.
Proposed alterations to Officers Mess Kitchen	1 sheet.
Details of oven for new Men's cookhouse	1 sheet.
Trench Map "ST JULIEN" Ed.3-E.	8 copies.
Large scale plan of Divisional Area	2 sheets.
Plans and particulars of L.2, L.4 and L.3 Posts.	2 sheets.

Various odd drawings received from other companies in previous occupation.

Present and old drawings of ELVERDINGHE DEFENCES.

SECRET

ORIGNAL

WAR DIARY – JANUARY – 1917

151ST FIELD COMPANY   ROYAL ENGINEERS

38TH (WELSH) DIVISION

31-1-17

Army Form C. 2118.

WAR DIARY
or
INTELLIGENCE SUMMARY.
(Erase heading not required.)

Vol XIV page 1

Instructions regarding War Diaries and Intelligence Summaries are contained in F. S. Regs., Part II. and the Staff Manual respectively. Title pages will be prepared in manuscript.

Place	Date	Hour	Summary of Events and Information	Remarks and references to Appendices
Houlle	1917			
	1 Jan		Weather fine, wind high. Work on Butts carried on. No 1 & 4 sections B range 27a & No 3 on A range 21 4 b	
	2 Jan		Weather fine, wind high, rain in evening. Work carried on as on previous day.	
	3 Jan		Weather fine. Wind stormy. Work carried on as usual. C.S.M. Thomas left to take up his new duties as Sergeant Military Foreman of Works with 12 Somewhere Labour Batt.	
	4 Jan		Weather fine. Work carried on as usual. Two companies of Pioneers left Houlle for Cornette in order to commence work on new Range. Range broke out in stables two horses affected.	
	5 Jan		Weather fine. Work carried on as usual. 2nd Lt Heaton Armstrong R.E. proceeded to CORNETTE range to shew Pioneers the work required.	
	6 Jan		Weather fine but cold. Work carried on as usual. No 67385 L/Corporal H HOWES awarded D.C.M. Gazette 1st January. Remainder of Pioneers left Houlle for billets near work at CORNETTE range.	
	7 Jan		Weather fine, & cold. Work continued on ranges.	
	8 Jan		Weather Stormy, sleet & rain. Work continued on ranges	
	9 Jan		Weather bad, rain. Work continued on ranges. No work, part explanatory.	

WAR DIARY or INTELLIGENCE SUMMARY

Army Form C. 2118.

Vol XIV Page 2

Place	Date	Hour	Summary of Events and Information	Remarks and references to Appendices
Houlle	10 Jan		Weather bad snow. Work continued as usual.	
	11 Jan		Weather bad cold. Work continued. Officer from 2/ Wet Lancs R.E. arrived to take over.	
Houlle	12		Weather bad. Sections proceeded to St Momelin under Captain Lloyd-Gory & entrained for Poperinghe. Marched them to FERME CARLOER to take over work in sector & billets from 124 Field Company R.E. The Transport proceeded by road under 2nd Lt Carroll N.E. to HOUTKERQUE.	
Elverdinghe	13		Weather bad. Morning officers with sergeants inspected line. Evening No.3 sections went over communication trenches under guidance of sergeants. Transport under 2nd Lt Carroll arrived.	
	14		Weather cold. 1st Lt Carroll left Company to join 112 Fd. Company R.E. No 4 section worked on front line No.2 & 3 on communication trenches. No. 1. in clearing up billets.	
	15		Weather fine. Corps Commander inspected line. Work continued.	
	16		Weather cold. 115 Brigade took over new line. Arranged working parties with Brigadier.	

Army Form C. 2118.

Vol XIV. Page 3

WAR DIARY
or
INTELLIGENCE SUMMARY.
(Erase heading not required.)

Instructions regarding War Diaries and Intelligence Summaries are contained in F.S. Regs., Part II. and the Staff Manual respectively. Title pages will be prepared in manuscript.

Place	Date	Hour	Summary of Events and Information	Remarks and references to Appendices
Fluerbaix	17		Weather cold. C.R.E. inspected line. Work continued. No 1 section working on sufflant line & tramways. 1st TROOP R.E. ordered to inspected work of field companies in the line. Infantry attached for work arrived	
B1862 8	18		Weather cold & muddy. No 2 excavating & preparing dug out for J.M.E. No 1 on sufflat line. No 3 Communication trenches. No 4 Frontline	
"	19		Weather cold. Work continued by sections	
"	20		Weather cold. Work continued by sections. 2nd Lt P H ANDREWS R.E. reported for duty from Base. 2nd Lt F H Mogan R.E. transferred to 124 Field Coy R.E. Stables to be erected for horses on site chosen by Coy.	
"	21		Weather cold, beginning of heavy frost. Work continued by sections.	
"	22		Weather cold. Work continued by sections. 2nd Lt Barber T reported for duty on transfer from 124 Field Coy R.E.	
"	23.		Foot continued. Ground very hard & work of sections impeded. 1 horse died from accident	
"	24		"	
"	25		"	Pte Smith 16th Welsh

Army Form C. 2118.

WAR DIARY
or
INTELLIGENCE SUMMARY.
(Erase heading not required.)

Instructions regarding War Diaries and Intelligence Summaries are contained in F.S. Regs., Part II. and the Staff Manual respectively. Title pages will be prepared in manuscript.

Place	Date	Hour	Summary of Events and Information	Remarks and references to Appendices
C186.2.0	26		accidentally shot, removed to hospital seriously wounded	
			Frost continued. 2t. Scraf left for England on completion of duty. C.R.E inspected	
	27		billets. Work continued. 5 sections on accurany of alarm about the tunnel	
	28		sap to be got to front line had to be stayed.	
			Frost continued. Yser frozen hard. Preparations pushed on for defence	
	29		Frost continued. Yser frozen hard. Work of sections continued	
			Frost continued. Yser frozen hard. Work of sections continued with Enemy	
			aeroplanes right & left.	
	30		Frost continued. Work of sections continued	
	31		Frost continued snow. Work of section continued	

31/1/17

J. McGorony
Capt. R.E.
for O.C 1st S.T Field Cy R.E.

Vol 15

SECRET

(ORIGINAL)
WAR DIARY   FEBRUARY 1917

151st Field Company Royal Engineers

38TH (Welsh) Division

28-2-1917

SECRET

ORIGINAL

WAR DIARY   FEBRUARY 1917

151ST Field Company Royal Engineers

38TH (Welsh) Division

28-2-1917

Army Form C. 2118.

WAR DIARY
or
INTELLIGENCE SUMMARY.
(Erase heading not required.)

Vol XXV page 1

Instructions regarding War Diaries and Intelligence Summaries are contained in F. S. Regs., Part II. and the Staff Manual respectively. Title pages will be prepared in manuscript.

Place	Date	Hour	Summary of Events and Information	Remarks and references to Appendices
GARDEN FARM	Feb 1		Weather frost continued. Work continued with owing to bombardment of enemy front line	
	2		Work continued by sections	
	3		" " " "	
	4		" " " "	
	5		" " " "	
	6		" " " "	
	7		" " " "	11 2Lt Paton RE went on leave
	8		6.16.G. " " " "	Heavy bombardment of neighbouring
	9		Weather frost continued. Work continued by sections	
	10		" " " "	
	11		" " " "	
	12		" thawing of slowly "	
	13		" " " "	
	14		" " " "	
	15		" thawing of slowly but freezing at night. Bombardment of neighbouring billet	

T2134. Wt. W708-776. 500000. 4/15. Sir J. C. & S.

Army Form C. 2118.

Vol XV page 2

WAR DIARY
or
INTELLIGENCE SUMMARY.
(Erase heading not required.)

Place	Date	Hour	Summary of Events and Information	Remarks and references to Appendices
CARDEN Farm	26.16		the 11th S.W.B. take refuge in our billets for the night	
	18		Weather continues the same. Major McMutrie R.E. arrives & takes over command. Capt MATTHEWS therefore on arrival.	
	19		Capt MATTHEWS proceeded to Eng School at Camp J for a course of instruction 116 S.10.13. vacates billet	
	20		Considerable trouble with tramway the road being in bad state. Called at Brigade H.Q. No IV Section commenced work on extension of tramway to front line.	
	21		Vacated horse lines at Cardoen Farm & occupied those at A 28 central which were in very dirty dilapidated condition. Mr Paton returned to duty from leave having been held up for 3 days. No 8498 Pioneer A moore killed by maneuver fa in front line during night	
	22		Visited work on M.G. emplacements with Major Bone O.C. 115 M.G.Coy. Queen Moore buried this day. Visited F.L. Battn. H.Q. Battn. Relief took place night working parties & Ros later	

WAR DIARY
or
INTELLIGENCE SUMMARY.
(Erase heading not required.)

Army Form C. 2118.

Place	Date	Hour	Summary of Events and Information	Remarks and references to Appendices
Laudun	1917 July 23		C.R.E. went round the Sector	
	24		Capt Lloyd Going proceeded to J.B.D. Staples. Col Pryce Jones visited the camps.	
	27		Testing the light pontoon bridge from Rue F.C.Ts strafed at night	
	28		Tramway stopped in morning afternoon emergency	
	2		Party at night to repair & Barn off bombed by C.R.?	

J.M.Murtrie
Capt. R.E.
O.C. 151st Field Coy R.E.

Vol 16

SECRET.

War Diary (Original)
for March 1917.

151st Field Coy, Royal Engineers.

Army Form C. 2118.

WAR DIARY
or
INTELLIGENCE SUMMARY.
(Erase heading not required.)

Volume XVI Page 1

Place	Date	Hour	Summary of Events and Information	Remarks and references to Appendices
Cordoen Farm	March 1		Lieut Knox affected by new device said not to be mange	
	2		Coy granted holiday from midday	
	3		Work restarted at midday	
	4		Working area visited by C.R.E. C.E. & Genl Egerton B.G. G.S.Corps.	
	5		Snow fell again with a frost during night	
	6		Frost in morning but thawed later. Coy very short of materials to work with.	
	7		No IV Sectn. started putting in French Doors	
	8		Motor Cyclists to Conger Lein to Font Line commenced Brig. Genl Stickie left Bde No I Sectn started on Southbanty Trench.	
	9		Coy received motor bicycle	
	10		Experimenting with mats in front to walking over mud	
	11		Visited Belgian Engineer Battalion now been trestying experiments Belgian C.R.E. came over to see our efforts	
	12		Played Belgians Soccer Lost 3-4	
	16		Major Genl Blackader & Brig Gen + C.R.E. visited line	
	18		Started loosing trenchboards in Cardiff St.	

WAR DIARY
or
INTELLIGENCE SUMMARY.
(Erase heading not required.)

Army Form C. 2118.

Place	Date	Hour	Summary of Events and Information	Remarks and references to Appendices
	1917 Mar.			
	19		Coy Holiday	
	21		C.R.E. visited billets & inspected bridging experiments	
	22		No IV Sec. Started work on Support Line. also T. Heads Sap. No III Sec. Started new Tube.	
	24		Summer time adopted at 11.0 p.m	
	25		Sunday C of E., N.C., & R.C. services held by Armstrong went to gas School	
	29		2nd Major ? slightly wounded in Pont ?? by Armstrong rejoined the Coy.	
	30		Mr Ellis rejoined the 11th Fd B.	

31st 3.17.

J. M. Whee Capt RE
OC 1st Field Coy.

SECRET.

ORIGINAL.
War Diary - April 1917.

151st Field Company, Royal Engineers
38th (Welsh) Division

30/4/1917.

Army Form C. 2118.

WAR DIARY
or
INTELLIGENCE SUMMARY.
(Erase heading not required.)

Instructions regarding War Diaries and Intelligence Summaries are contained in F.S. Regs., Part II. and the Staff Manual respectively. Title pages will be prepared in manuscript.

Place	Date	Hour	Summary of Events and Information	Remarks and references to Appendices
Suffeya	1917 April 2		Corps Commander visited the front line work & expressed himself as being extremely pleased with progress made. Cy. Orders. Divn. Gen. mates Iulles witnessed some practice with mugging expedients which gave satisfaction, some amusement	
	3		Spent snow blizzard. Coy. Heastay commenced at midday	
	4		Lt. Gatern went to Hospital	
	5		- Driver received as reinforcement	
	6		Started to put in holts in both h hoes. Ry Bridge together	
	8		2nd Lt. Benfees 10th RWF's reported to relief 2nd Lt. Bellamy 10th SWB	
	9		to alter duty. Trench & Support line handed over to 19th Welsh Pioneers. No 4 Section started work on making light	
	10		Pontoons & No 1 Section commenced 2 new safes in front line. G.O.C. G.S.O.I. Brig. Gen. Price Davis & Mushels for Bairsboorow	
	11th		2nd Lt. Penfield proceeded to hospital. Fractures at Billet. 5 reinforcements received	
	13th		P4. M.G. mounting put in by No 2 Section 5x reinforcement receive	

WAR DIARY
or
INTELLIGENCE SUMMARY.
(Erase heading not required.)

Army Form C. 2118.

Place	Date	Hour	Summary of Events and Information	Remarks and references to Appendices
In the field	April 1917 15		No 4 Sec. commenced supervision of new Regt Aid Post shelters at Boesinghe & also T.M. Platform by the Church	
	18		No 4 Section practised pontoon(light) by Bridge 1 on the canal successfully.	
	19		Report to Brig. Gen. on progress A.A.P.s & advanced stores. Half the Coy bathed. Half day off (Relief) Pay.	
	20		Morning no work owing to relief. Half Coy Bathed.	
	21		Nos 3 & 4 Sections started the Infantry putting in forward Sakem ammunition dumps. Lt Jaton returned to duty from home front.	
	23		No 4 Sec. had demonstration of light pontoon bridge with Infantry at Bridge 3. G.O.C. & 3 Brig. Genl present very successful.	
	30		Mr Andrews started reconnaissance for bridge sites over same front. No 2 Sec. Stokes M.G. dug out at Iseuben St.	

WAR DIARY
or
INTELLIGENCE SUMMARY

Army Form C. 2118.

Place	Date	Hour	Summary of Events and Information	Remarks and references to Appendices
In the field	1917 April 26		No 2 Sec started to excavate for concrete dug out at Doctors to. Send a party of men required to 113 Inf. Bde. 67318 Sapper Griffiths W. wounded not sevre.	
	27			
	29th		No 30 proceeded to Gas School for a 4 days course of instruction	
	30		See Corpl Wynne Jones proceeded to Regeurny as Cadet to qualify for a Commission in T.F.R.E. Brig Gen Minshull Ford came to inspect method of crossing water by mats	

30/4/1/1917

J M McRae
Major R.E.
O.C. 1st Field Coy

Secret

Original

War Diary – May, 1917.

151st Field Coy, Royal Engineers.

38th (Welsh) Division.

31-5-1917.

Army Form C. 2118.

WAR DIARY
or
INTELLIGENCE SUMMARY.
(Erase heading not required.)

Instructions regarding War Diaries and Intelligence Summaries are contained in F. S. Regs., Part II. and the Staff Manual respectively. Title pages will be prepared in manuscript.

Place	Date	Hour	Summary of Events and Information	Remarks and references to Appendices
In the field	1917 May 1		The 115 Infy. Bnde. was relieved by 114th Infy. Bnde. Draft of 1 driver & 1 Sapper received. Coy. took afternoon off to coincide with Bnde. relief.	
	2		Morning off Bnde relief. Gas alarm received at 10 pm by horns etc. & again at 10.15. The alarm was a false one in each case.	
	3		See Capt. Bregg's Supt. Holden went to Divisional School for a course of instruction.	
			Gas alarm was received from Belgian front at 11.30 pm but it proved to be a false alarm.	
	4		No. 1 Section took over work on Support line from the 19th Battn. Welsh Regt. Lt. Griffen went to Divisional School for a course of instruction in Cookery.	
	6		Received services for C of E. N.C.F. & R.C. religions.	
	7		Brig Gen. Marden CMG inspected the attached Infantry	
	8		Sapr. Clegg sent to Hospital slightly wounded by shell in Cardiff.	

WAR DIARY
or
INTELLIGENCE SUMMARY.
(Erase heading not required.)

Army Form C. 2118.

Place	Date	Hour	Summary of Events and Information	Remarks and references to Appendices
In the field	9		Driver Hutton transferred to 133rd Field Coy. R.E.	
	11		Capt. Coley wounded by shell in Village & went to hospital.	
			No 4 Sec. commenced work on shelter at Ironware Cut for Machine Gun Coy.	
	12		Horses fed out and on open standings.	
	13		Orders to move on 15th not received.	
	14		Major Paton proceeded with advance party of 12 to arrange billets at Poperinghe. Major M°Murtrie Watten. Capt. proceeded to 46 CCS for dental treatment. All plans for work in Poeringhe Sector were handed over to 19th Pioneer Battn Welsh Regt.	
	15		The whole Coy proceeded to Poperinghe entraining at Poperinghe. The transport travelled by road under Lt Jones halting for one night at Poperinghe Capel.	
	16			
	17		Engineer training for whole Coy.	

Army Form C. 2118.

WAR DIARY
or
INTELLIGENCE SUMMARY.
(Erase heading not required.)

Instructions regarding War Diaries and Intelligence Summaries are contained in F. S. Regs., Part II. and the Staff Manual respectively. Title pages will be prepared in manuscript.

Place	Date	Hour	Summary of Events and Information	Remarks and references to Appendices
In the field	1917 May 18		The whole Coy engaged in Engineer Training	
	19		" " " " " "	
	20		" " " " " "	2nd Lieut Deaton Armstrong proceeded to England on leave
	21		" " " " " "	
	22		" " " " " "	
	23		" " " " " "	
	24		" " " " " "	
	25		" " " " " "	
	26		Transport proceeded to Cardoen Farm by road under 2nd Lieut Andrews halting for 1 night at Jaggers Coppel at Boulbec & advanced party of 8 proceeded by road to the Canal Bank. Main mounture returned to duty	
	27		& proceeded to Canal Bank. 2nd Lieut Omer returned from the remainder of Coy entrained at Bavincourt & marched to Canal Bank taking over billets from 123rd Field Coy R.E. All plans work in connection taking over work at C.R.E.s Yard.	
	28		10/7 Section proceeded to Havelines work in connection	

WAR DIARY
or
INTELLIGENCE SUMMARY.
(Erase heading not required.)

Army Form C. 2118.

Place	Date	Hour	Summary of Events and Information	Remarks and references to Appendices
In the field	1917 May 29		Farm Section taken over from 133rd Field Coy. R.E. Coy transport took over horse lines from 133rd Field Coy R.E. No 2 Section carried on work on St. Hts. Heavy French Mortar emplacements & Mugger Trice Coy H.Q.s & extension of Divisional Baths No 3 Section to moved Bridge 5 & started on the causeway & repairs on stores of Bridge 6B & Chokes bridge demolition stores. No 4 Section commenced grading of French Headway have to Butt 10 carrying dug outs by bridge 4 & excavating & erecting new dug outs at Bridge 13. False gas alarm at night.	

31/5/17

Wm White Major R.E.
O.C. 151 [?] Field Coy

Vol 19

Secret

Original

War Diary - June 1917

151st Field Coy, Royal Engineers

38th (Welsh) Division

30/6/1917.

Army Form C. 2118.

WAR DIARY
or
INTELLIGENCE SUMMARY.
(Erase heading not required.)

Instructions regarding War Diaries and Intelligence Summaries are contained in F.S. Regs., Part II. and the Staff Manual respectively. Title pages will be prepared in manuscript.

Place	Date	Hour	Summary of Events and Information	Remarks and references to Appendices
In the field	1917 June 3		Gas shell bombardment at 11.50 p.m. One Sapper was affected for one day. Extension of Stapton C.T. started by No 4 Section	
	4		Lt. Rather admitted to hospital for dental treatment	
	5		New C.T. in north of 23 Post to new front line started by No 4 Section	
	6		2nd Corpl Harris & Lce Corpl Humphreys proceeded to Divnl School. Pte Thomas W. attd. wounded by shell at Ely Cottage during Repair Parties attached to Pride in charge of trades.	
	7		2nd Lt. E.A. Clough reported for duty. Corporal Withoning J.S. went on leave (10 days)	
	9		67993 Pioneer Armoun R + 140689 Sapr Wilson S + 22286 Pte. Davis W. attd. Killed in action at 3.45 am in front line being extension + 167174 Sapr. Ridgway a wounded all by shell fire. The Division transferred to 14th Corps.	
	11		2nd Lt. P.H. Andrews wounded in action by hand grenade during a German raid + sent to hospital.	

Army Form C. 2118.

WAR DIARY
or
INTELLIGENCE SUMMARY.
(Erase heading not required.)

Place	Date	Hour	Summary of Events and Information	Remarks and references to Appendices
In the field	1917 June 12		508.12 Pte. Nix R. att'd. killed by shell at Rly Cottage dump. Sergt. Stanier proceeded to England on leave. Commenced extension of Coursdon trench by No 3 Section. Sapr. Hunt B. 446963 + Sap. McCarthy W.C. 446969 joined the Company for duty.	
	14.		2nd Lieut Heaton-Armstrong returned from leave to England. Sergt. D.B. Evans returned from leave to England.	
	15		2nd Corpl Harris + Lce Corpl. Humphries returned from Div. School. Work stopped on Ealing Extension C.T., Matruba Cswy. H.2. + Causeway by Bridge 5.	
	16		The Company left dug outs on East Canal bank + moved to dug outs on West Canalbank between 5 + 6 bridge. Work commenced on new Causeway at bridge 6 W. by No 3 Section. also new Coursdon trench by No 3 Section + new dug outs on West Canal bank by	

WAR DIARY
or
INTELLIGENCE SUMMARY.
(Erase heading not required.)

Army Form C. 2118.

Place	Date	Hour	Summary of Events and Information	Remarks and references to Appendices
On the field	1917 June 17		Work prestration on Ealing Endeavour & New Front line from post 28 by No 4 Section	
	18		67462 Sap Woults W.D. + 62761 Pioneer Wilkens D. proceeded to rest camp at Dunkerque	
	19		67385 Capt. Howes E.W. proceeded to England on leave	
	20		2/2 Lt. D.L. Morgan joined the Coy for duty. 36521 Por. Farrell G.H. attd. wounded in action	
	21.		Great difficulty in obtaining material & getting it carried up. Tramway constantly knocked out.	
	23.		107173 Sap. Cardo W. + 13956 Put. Moose J. attd. wounded by shell on panel bank	
	24.		67814 Corpl Williams J.E., 62813 Sap Turnidoe A. 44696 Sap. Bone J. 62750 Sap. Thomas L. 3 3894 Put. Davis A. 16149 Put McLelen 36152 Pte. Goodwin H. wounded by Shellfire Ho1. Clough wounded 67521 Sap. Arthur S. to hospital from effects of gas shell.	
	25		36552 Pte. Greenfield H. 36396 Pte. Hurley J., 50707 Pte Hughes A.	

Army Form C. 2118.

WAR DIARY
or
INTELLIGENCE SUMMARY.
(Erase heading not required.)

Instructions regarding War Diaries and Intelligence Summaries are contained in F. S. Regs., Part II. and the Staff Manual respectively. Title pages will be prepared in manuscript.

Place	Date	Hour	Summary of Events and Information	Remarks and references to Appendices
In the field	1917 June 25		21009 Pte. Bethel S. (died) wounded in action 28934 Pte Allan W. 40233 Pte Purdy J. 29726 Pte Sageman J wounded at duty	
	26.		Glencoe Cottage tramway repaired in daylight.	
	28		50195 Pte Morgan W.F. wounded.	
			"Looker" 497 Field Coy taken over the Coy work. All work was handed over to 493 Field Coy R.E. + the Coy left the area. Transport preceded by road + the remainder of Coy by rail from Asylum Ypres.	
	29.		Coy arrived at Proven + proceeded in afternoon to Stew Road + went into camp at E.15.d.6.0. Bivouac for the night.	
	30.		Commenced work on Road bridge for 7 ton lorries + on alterations to road + rail bridge for all traffic. Party cutting timber for bridging. Dress + erected tents. Day very wet.	

J.M.H. White Major R.E.
O.C. 161 Field Coy

Secret.

Original
War Diary – July, 1917.

151st Field Company, Royal Engineers.

38th (Welsh) Division.

31/7/1917.

WAR DIARY
or
INTELLIGENCE SUMMARY.

(Erase heading not required.)

Army Form C. 2118.

Place	Date	Hour	Summary of Events and Information	Remarks and references to Appendices
In the field	1917 Nov 1		No 2 Section working on Road Bridge No 3 Section working on Corduroy road bridge remainder of Coy drilling doing rifle exercises	
	2		Blacksmiths & road building No 1 Section of No 2 Section	
	3		Bridge on road suddenly suspended waiting for girders	
			Covered Wilow road bridge.	
	4	6.25	Lee Cpl Doub proceeded to England on leave	
	5		No 3 Section cutting timber for piles for bridge	
			Cinders & decking put in for ordinary road bridge	
	6		Corduroy road bridge completed	
	7		Company doing training exc't No 2 Section on New Bridge	
	8	6.25	Sapt Arthur S proceeded to England on leave	
			Proceeded to England in order to be course of structural with a view to accepting a commission	
			in the Infantry / Hung girder decking for widening drawbridge julin	
	9	10.30	Capt Murray returned from leave Road bridge completed.	

Army Form C. 2118.

WAR DIARY
or
INTELLIGENCE SUMMARY.
(Erase heading not required.)

Place	Date	Hour	Summary of Events and Information	Remarks and references to Appendices
In the field	1917 July 10		A Carter A.I. returned to Coy from sick leave. Leaving superintendent to be established. 20 for Pk Bruce to it 10/8/1 Reinforcement from base. ii I Section commenced work on making new huts for Brit Head Quarters at Proven.	
	11		All Sappers paid of duty Marines trekked at hospital but no change of clothes. All lectures in company part 4 allst. Infantry worked on erection of Nissen huts at Central Camp Proven. Eng[ines] completed.	
	12		Whole Coy except a party of NO II Sec finishing the road bridge worked on Central Camp. Road bridge completed. Reinforcement +4 8639 SAp.	
	13		Marro 3. mms from the base	
	14		Capt Rugden 6715 proceeded to England on leave Work on Central Camp Proven completed 23 Nissen huts 4 Cot RE houses & Latrines	
	15		No 4 Section commenced work on Photography Hut	

T2134. Wt. W708-776. 500000. 4/15. Sir J.C.&S.

WAR DIARY
or
INTELLIGENCE SUMMARY.

(Erase heading not required.)

Army Form C. 2118.

Place	Date	Hour	Summary of Events and Information	Remarks and references to Appendices
Suakatra	1917 July 16		No. 14 Squadron R.F.C. Rec. some delay for material 63677 Sap. Zilio to proceeded to England on leave	
	17		5729 Sgt. Williams S. proceeded to England on leave	
	18		63691 Cpl. M.S. Gamble W. proceeded to England for Cadet Course with a view to Commission in Infantry. Mounted Section carried out competition in dressing & harnessing & saving to 6 horse team.	
	19		Whole Coy. with all animals did a 55 mile march in the dark with respirators on.	
	20		Lt. Bellamy left the Coy to report to R.F.C. CRO's Conference Proceedings 6715 Lee Cpl. Henderson left to Yousef Brown 6yrs W. Clegg G. 6609 Sgt. Aley J. 63714 Probie P.C. G. 6538 Dr Page G. proceeded to England on leave. 6 photos on R.E. Photographic Hut Completed	

WAR DIARY or INTELLIGENCE SUMMARY

Army Form C. 2118.

Place	Date	Hour	Summary of Events and Information	Remarks and references to Appendices
In Reserve	July 1917 20		No 1 Section constructed public latrine at Proven for Town Major. Orders received to proceed to Canal Bank & relieve the 23rd Field Coy. C.R.E.'s conference held at Reninghelst attended by O.C.	
	21		Company proceeded by road to Canal Bank at C.19.c.3.4. to relieve the 160th Field Coy resting at Cardoen Fm on the way. Mr Barbor & 8 N.C.O.s went as advanced party to Canal Bank. Transport proceeded to G Camp. 27832 Pte Miles J. #45619 & 22951 Pte Greenall E. 115 SWB wounded on the way up to Canal.	
	22		2/Lt Barber A.J. wounded in foot by shrapnel in Corridor. Section No II Section commenced work on Tramways No II Sect on Cachus pontoon bridge & Sects on L A Pontoon bridge & ADS at White French No IV Sects preparing sites for light pontoon bridges. Shell fire heavy over the whole area especially	

Army Form C. 2118.

WAR DIARY
or
INTELLIGENCE SUMMARY.
(Erase heading not required.)

Instructions regarding War Diaries and Intelligence Summaries are contained in F. S. Regs., Part II. and the Staff Manual respectively. Title pages will be prepared in manuscript.

Place	Date	Hour	Summary of Events and Information	Remarks and references to Appendices
Sn Ruffles	1917 July 22		at night. Gas shells intermitted from 11pm to 4am. Shelves were worn for about 4 hours. Sapr Arthur was affected by gas slightly.	
	23		N° 7 Sectn Commenced work on fishing picks in Invalere & Johns and Roats. N° 7 did some work on Balaclava Trench. Gas was put in intermittently at night in form of shells. Respirators worn for about an hour. Sproyt 40306 Pte Ballin y J5266 Pte Harris S416y Pte Frazier MG all affected by gas went to hospital. 4403 Pte Thomas J wounded at Belmont dump by shell fire. Shelters, heavy & gas at night. Respirators worn for about 2 hours altogether.	6737 Spr Barwell J 10572 Spr Oakley R removed by KetleWeel Casino Bridge
	24		2nd/1st Batts. 11th Suffolks reported for attachment to this Coy in charge of Infy.	
	25		Section continued work on Advanced Survey Stations Repairs and improvements to trenches	

WAR DIARY
or
INTELLIGENCE SUMMARY

Army Form C. 2118.

Place	Date	Hour	Summary of Events and Information	Remarks and references to Appendices
	26		Major J. Robertson killed in action. Capt J. Fraser assumed command of the Company. One attached Infantry killed in action.	
	27		Work on behalf Horse Batts. H.Q. taken over by 19.F (Pioneer) Batln held Regt. N°2 Section took over maintenance of bridges 6W, 6Y, 6Z & 6D. Remainder of Sections carried on usual work. One attached infantry wounded.	
	28		Lieut H.E. Doyle R.E. joined from 123 F.C.R.E. and took over command of N°4 Section. N°2 Section employed on keeping clear YPRES BOESINGHE Road & repairing work for launching light pontoon bridges across the YSER Canal. N°3 Section repairing damage done to bridges by hostile shell fire. N°4 Section carrying light portion and superstructure and preparing position for launching. N°1 Section employed on upkeep of tramways.	

WAR DIARY or INTELLIGENCE SUMMARY.

Army Form C. 2118.

Place	Date	Hour	Summary of Events and Information	Remarks and references to Appendices
	29		No 3 Section repairing damage done to bridges by hostile shell fire. No 4 Section employed on preparing boats for launching. Light pontoon bridge across YSER CANAL and repairing damaged pontoons. No 2 Section preparing site for Curtis Pontoon Bridge. No 1 Section maneuvers of trestles, and trestling joints.	
	30		Transport Lines moved to Advanced position at B20a54. No 4 Section preparing pontoons and superstructure for light bridges. No 1 Section Clearance of tramways and bridge. No 3 Section repairing damage done to tramways Curtis bridge by shell fire. 9.30 p.m. – 12 midnight new pontoon bridge constructed 100 yards south of 65 bridge across the YSER Canal by No 3 Section & 20 attached Infantry. Lieut N.A. PATON, Sapper & 2 attached Infantry wounded.	

WAR DIARY
or
INTELLIGENCE SUMMARY.
(Erase heading not required.)

Army Form C. 2118.

Place	Date	Hour	Summary of Events and Information	Remarks and references to Appendices
	31		Six light pontoon bridges constructed across the YSER Canal by No 4 Section completed at 12.30 a.m. CACTUS PONTOON Bridge constructed by No 2 Section with 20 attached Infantry and 2 Platoons from 11th Batt K.R.R. No 1 Section employed on Maintenance of trenches and bridges. 1 R.E. and 1 attached Infantry wounded.	

D O Jones
Capt. R.E.
t/b OC 15th F.C.R.E.
31/7/17

Vol 21

SECRET.

ORIGINAL

WAR DIARY - AUGUST.

151st FIELD COMPANY - ROYAL ENGINEERS

38th (WELSH) DIVISION

WAR DIARY
or
INTELLIGENCE SUMMARY.

(Erase heading not required.)

Army Form C. 2118.

Officer Commanding 151st Field Company R.E.

Page 1

Instructions regarding War Diaries and Intelligence Summaries are contained in F.S. Regs., Part II. and the Staff Manual respectively. Title pages will be prepared in manuscript.

Place	Date	Hour	Summary of Events and Information	Remarks and references to Appendices
	1917			
Canal Bank (Essex Farm)	1/9/17		Repairs to Chapse Cottage and Dinden Castle tramline, and the extension of track from runway causeway with 1 Battalion of the 59th Division	
	2/9/17		Consolidation of strong points on the Green line. 1 Killed 5 wounded 2 since died of wounds.	
	3/9/17		Construction of track from the Boroughs YPRES Road to BARD Causeway. Lieut Roberts joined the Company from the 538 FCRE(T)	
	4/9/17		Construction of track from BARD Causeway to HUDDLESTON ROAD. Major W.R.Champlin joined the Coy and assumed command.	
	5/9/17		Repairs to HUDDLESTON ROAD. Handed over work on HUDDLESTON Road to 96th FCRE	
	6/9/17		Entrained at ELVERDINGHE for PROVEN F10 35.2. Transport proceeded by road to same camp.	

WAR DIARY or INTELLIGENCE SUMMARY

Army Form C. 2118.

Page 2

Place	Date	Hour	Summary of Events and Information	Remarks and references to Appendices
PROVEN F.10,V,5,2 Sheet 27 N.E.	7/8/17		Kit inspection and overhauling equipment & transport.	
	8/1/17		Baths at Divisional Baths, Crothoe	
	9 Aug.		Unit attended de-lousing station near Poperinghe. One Section working at Div. H.Q. camp, Proven. No.1 Section work to Hedges for road on rifle range.	
	10 Aug.		Work on Div. H.Q. camp & Hedges for rifle range. Also making 100 pairs of grids for pack saddles	
	12 Aug.		" " "	
			A sample sent to C.R.E.	
	14 Aug.		Work continued as above. No 3 Section sent to Corps Park, Ondank to make Aprons & Artillery bridges. Attacker 2/Lr dog drill a mule.	
	16 Aug		Altr 2/Lr Speed on 30 yards range (115 Bale) . Work as above	
	17 Aug		The Company entrained at Proven & moved to Canal Bank C.19C.2.6. Jo Kron for 84 Fld Coy. Transport moved by road from Proven. The	
Canal Bank Sheet 28 N.W.	18 Aug		Company worked on Green line in front of Jargeneed during the right. Two Section wiring and two Section digging O.T. a right flank ALOUETTE FARM. Altr 2/Lr carried up wire from IRON CROSS Shee it was though 5 mules	

Army Form C. 2118.

WAR DIARY or INTELLIGENCE SUMMARY.

(Erase heading not required.)

Page 3

Place	Date	Hour	Summary of Events and Information	Remarks and references to Appendices
Canal Bank	19th Aug.		Work on Green Line continued as yesterday. Parts of 50 metres from Bde. Carried out wiring stores to STEENBEEK on IRON CROSS - LANGEMARCK RD.	
	20th		Work as before, except these sections a wiring and one on dugouts. Strong point at U.29.B.4.8. (Sheet LANGEMARCK 1/10,000). 50 metres from Div. and 8 of our own enemy up wire.	
	21st		Work on Green Line. Very little work was done owing to shelling on approaches and on Green line itself. Mule transport as before.	
	22nd		No work. Capt. D.O. JONES wounded in right leg at 21st inst.	
	23rd		Three Sections and h.q. began work on C.T. from Canal bank along old German tramway cutting towards IRON CROSS and LANGEMARCK. Draining, levelling & duckboarding. One section trying a Green line. Z and 1, 4 began with duckboards to PILKEM Rd. Mules as before being 30 from Div.	
Details from Room C.19.a.0.7 House from B.23.d.3,4	24th 25th		Work as above. Moved billets N. along Canal Bank, to C.19.a.0.7. Sheet 28 N.W. Continued from end of tramway cutting down old German C.T. towards LANGEMARCK. 2 miles from Div. 2 miles laid duckboards up tramway for the new C.T.	

Army Form C. 2118.

WAR DIARY
or
INTELLIGENCE SUMMARY.
(Erase heading not required.)

Page 4

Instructions regarding War Diaries and Intelligence Summaries are contained in F.S. Regs., Part II. and the Staff Manual respectively. Title pages will be prepared in manuscript.

Place	Date	Hour	Summary of Events and Information	Remarks and references to Appendices
Canal Bank	1917 26th Aug.		3 Sections working on duckboard track from Candle trench, Pilchem Rd, to Steenbeek. 1 Section working on Green line. Duckboards taken up to lt. "INGS" by tramway.	
	27th	"	Work as above. Duckboard track reached Steenbeek. Lt. is only nightly limit. No truck close to Green line owing to heavy shelling. Sectors now march to reach the site.	
	28th	"	Continued work as above. About 150 yds of track laid East of Steenbeek.	
	29th	"	3 Sections duckboards between Steenbeek & Langemarck. 750 yards by 2 Sections. Clearing track & laying duckboards between Pilchem Rd. & Candle trench. No wiring.	
	30th	"	Continued as above. 300 yds duckboards laid into Langemarck by one section and 700 yds duckboards laid between Pilchem Rd. & Candle trench. One section with 9 OR. wiring party (30 OR). Further light duckboards up into Langemarck at night owing to heavy shelling East of Steenbeek.	
	31st	"	Continued with duckboard track, this is practically finished from Pilchem Rd. to Langemarck. Took 400 duckboards into Langemarck at night. Began laid a new track from Iron Cross to Reitres Farm.	

Army Form C. 2118.

WAR DIARY
or
INTELLIGENCE SUMMARY.
(Erase heading not required.)

Page 5

Place	Date	Hour	Summary of Events and Information	Remarks and references to Appendices
Canal Bank	1/8/17 to 31/8/17		Casualties during month R.E. 2 OR killed, 1 Officer & 15 OR wounded. 1 Officer & 12 OR went to Hospl sick attached Infy., 7 OR killed, 6 OR wounded. 2 OR went to Hospl sick. Reinforcements 40 men joined from Base & 8 returned from Hospital leave, 36 OR R.E. and 3 OR AMC Infy given leave to U.K.	
	1/9/17			

W. P. Henryson
Major R.E. (M)
Officer Commanding.
151st Field Company R.E.

ORIGINAL WAR DIARY

UNIT :- 151st FIELD Coy. R.E.
(38) Welsh Division

(SEPTEMBER)

Army Form C. 2118.

WAR DIARY
or
INTELLIGENCE SUMMARY.
(Erase heading not required.)

September 1917 Page I

Place	Date	Hour	Summary of Events and Information	Remarks and references to Appendices
Canal Bank C.19.A.0.7. Sheet 28 NW	1917 1st Sept.		Working on duckboard tracks between MALAKOFF FARM and HUDDLESTONE CROSS ROADS. also North of DAVIES ST. from CORK HOUSE to STEENBECK.	
	2nd "		Duckboard track South of LANGEMARCK was continued 400 yds. Eastwards of What place up to Green line (night work) but no other two tracks has advanced as about commenced new Northing across canal from Colonso Farm to connect up duckboard tracks. C.R.S. was wounded this evening.	
	3rd "		Work on tracks continued. Track along BRIELEN Rd. completed to Railway Bank East of Steenbeck. On Malakoff track one section with 10 Infty has laid 1600 yds of duckboard track on pickets etc. in 3 days. very little shelling required, but good deal of carrying from the roads. Work on Malakoff track continued. Started work on gap joining Bde & B's	
	4th "		dug-outs in forward area. Bridge & causeway near Colonso Farm were heavily shelled in the afternoon. Cactus pontoon bridge damaged.	
	5th "		Repaired Cactus pontoon bridge. Completed Inf. pont Bridge at Colenso Farm. Duckboard track completed between Magenta Cross & Huddlestone Cross Rds.	

WAR DIARY or INTELLIGENCE SUMMARY

Army Form C. 2118.

Page 2

Place	Date	Hour	Summary of Events and Information	Remarks and references to Appendices
	1917			
Canal Bank	5th Sept		Pontoon Bridge at 6A dismantled & stores collected.	
	6, 7, 8		Work on duckboard tracks continued. Taped out wire on support line west of Steenbeek.	
	9th		The Coy. was relieved by 96 Field Coy by 9 am. Billets taken over by 84th Field Coy also. Transport lorries. The Coy moved to PROVEN area by tram from Elverdinghe. Transport moved by road to same area. Location E.17.d.5.3 Sheet no 27.	
PROVEN	10th, 11th		Kit inspection & drill in mornings.	
March	12th		The Coy marched with 115 Bde. S road to EECKE area, location Q.13.c.2.1 Sheet no 27, accompanied by transport.	
	13th		The Coy marched as above to MORBECQUE AREA. Location on MERVILLE Rd. near LE TIR ANGLAIS.	
	14th		The Coy marched to ESTAIRES area, location farm north of LYS, 1½ mile from (west) LA GORGUE	
	15th		The Coy marched to NIEPPE area, location on STEENWERKE – NIEPPE Rd.	

WAR DIARY
or
INTELLIGENCE SUMMARY.
(Erase heading not required.)

Army Form C. 2118.

Page 3

Place	Date	Hour	Summary of Events and Information	Remarks and references to Appendices
	Sept. 1917			
	16th		1½ miles East of STEENWERCK. The Coy relieved the 502nd Field Coy R.E. (57th Division) in ARMENTIERES. Maps, plans, work in hand & billets were taken over.	
ARMENTIERES	17th		HQ & 2 Sections (1 & 2) went to RUE SADI CARNOT, Armentieres. Sections 3 & 4 went to HOUPLINES. Transport went to TROIS TILLEULS. Map reference Sheet 36 N.W. HQ Armentieres C, 25, c, 4, 4. 2 Sections Houplines C, 21, d, 4, 2. Transport (J. Spinetta) B, 28, b, 2, 5. HQ work on INGLIS Bridge near bridge P, making approaches & bridge, also work on billets, gas proofing etc. Houplines work on BUTERNE Avenue near cross cut, also on billets.	
	18th		Inglis bridge completed approaches for field artillery.	
	20th		Sections in Houplines began work clearing drains.	
	25th		No 1 Section overhauling demolition arrangements Bridges L, G, K. Work on drains continued. Inglis bridge completed for traffic up to 6" Howitzers inclusive.	

WAR DIARY or INTELLIGENCE SUMMARY

Army Form C. 2118.
Page 4

Place	Date	Hour	Summary of Events and Information	Remarks and references to Appendices
	Sept 1917			
ARMENTIERES	26		Inniskilling Avenue, began cleaning & revetting trench.	
	27		Headquarters bath, Started excavation to execute dug out.	
	28-30		Continued work on Drains, Inniskilling Avenue, Conects dug out & demolition of Lodge.	
			Casualties during month.	
			2/Lt CUNDALL joined from Base 6/9/17	
			Capt. W.A. Evans " " 123 Field Coy 7/9/17	
			2nd Roberts returned from Hospital 19/9/17.	
			2/Lt Watts 11SWB replaced by 2/Lt D.J. Jones 11S.W.B. 24/9/17	
			Casualties in action Killed – 3 O.R. R.E (Sgt. Evans)	
			Wounded – 5 O.R. R.E.	
			To Hospital Sick, 15 O.R. R.E, 4 O.R. attached Infantry.	
			Joined unit from Base, 14 O.R. R.E.	
			Gone to U.K. 38 O.R. R.E. 20 O.R attached Infantry.	

W.M.Montgomerie Major R.E.
Officer Commanding,
151st Field Company R. E.

Army Form C. 2118.

WAR DIARY
or
INTELLIGENCE SUMMARY.
(Erase heading not required.)

Instructions regarding War Diaries and Intelligence Summaries are contained in F.S. Regs., Part II. and the Staff Manual respectively. Title pages will be prepared in manuscript.

151 Field Coy R.E.

Vol 23

Place	Date	Hour	Summary of Events and Information	Remarks and references to Appendices
October 1917 ARMENTIERES	1st		Pontoon same as before. No 1 Section under 2/Lt Roberts, at R.E. Park, BAC-ST-MAUR. Started Billets for one Section near FOCKERBER DUMP. Working on Irish Avenue between Subsidiary Line & Second Support Line. also Started work on Cambridge avenue in front of S. Support Line.	
	2nd		Started executing plan, dug out in Headquarters walk.	
	7th		Dugout in Signals Cable Junction begun, excavation & materials prepared	
	8th		Started work in Subsidiary Line. Forming parados & improving generally. Four Infantry parties on two hour work relief, 8 hrs a day, and more relieved by a fresh four parties who work remaining 4 hrs.	
	13th		Headquarters work dugout, walls completed.	
	15th		Started gun pits for Bde R.F.A.	
	18th		2nd Lt. J Roberts accidentally injured. Evacuated to Hospital 24/10/17.	
	21		2nd Lt. Morgan in command at WRB Major McLaughlin proceeding to 1st Army Sig School for a fortnight	

Army Form C. 2118.

151 Field Coy RE

WAR DIARY
or
INTELLIGENCE SUMMARY.
(Erase heading not required.)

Instructions regarding War Diaries and Intelligence Summaries are contained in F. S. Regs., Part II. and the Staff Manual respectively. Title pages will be prepared in manuscript.

Place	Date	Hour	Summary of Events and Information	Remarks and references to Appendices
October 1917	21		Commanders conference	
	24		Headquarters work dugout roof complete	
	26		No 3 gun pit completed	
	28		Fochties O.P. finished. Major Ostroftsky R.E. proceed on leave	
	30		Brentwood O.P. finished	
			Casualties during month.	
			2 Lt. Roberts R.E. admitted to hospital 21/10/17.	
			Casualties in action	
			1 O.R. R.E. killed. 2 O.R. R.E. wounded, 2 O.R. R.E. accidental wounds	
			To Hospital sick	
			1 O.R. R.E. 6 O.R. attached infantry	
			11 O.R.,R.E.	
			Joined unit from Base 11 O.R. R.E.	
			Strike off U.K. 11 O.R.R.E. 1 Officer R.E. & 18 O.R. attached Infy	

W.T. [signature] Capt 6 R.E.

Vol 24

Confidential.
War Diary
of
151st Field Co. R.E.
From 1st Nov. 1917 to 30th Nov. 1917.

Army Form C. 2118.

WAR DIARY
or
INTELLIGENCE SUMMARY.
(Erase heading not required.)

November 1917
Page 1.

Instructions regarding War Diaries and Intelligence
Summaries are contained in F. S. Regs., Part II.
and the Staff Manual respectively. Title pages
will be prepared in manuscript.

Place	Date	Hour	Summary of Events and Information	Remarks and references to Appendices
	November 1917			
Armentières 3 Sector	3		Commenced camouflage for execution of new H.T.M.B at Buttercup Farm. Inst at C.28.C.7.3. Sheet 36 N.W.	
	5		Lt. G.S. Horton Cmdg returned from 1st Army Gas School, Boulogne.	
	6		Commenced training outline in demolition of dugouts in view of proposed raid on the enemy trenches.	
	8	1/24 A.M	2 N.C.O's & 18 Sappers assisted 300 men of 10th S.W.B. in a raid on enemy trenches at l.11.a 4.3. to l.5.c.2.6. Sheet 36 N.W. They demolished 3 concrete dugouts in front line & 1 in the support line. 6 charges used was a 30 lbs Mobile Charge with 3 minute fuze. Owing to an early withdrawal the other dugouts were not demolished. One Sapper missing believed killed. Twelve prisoners captured & one 40 Germans killed.	
	9th		Circuits dug out to Signals cable junction completed. Maj Hodgetyll returned from leave.	
	10–17		Begun defensive posts off Edwards chain. Hedgerow well. bench being repaired & levelled. R.A.P. Spine Farm begun. Cavalry & Irish avenues repairs continued.	

WAR DIARY
or
INTELLIGENCE SUMMARY

Army Form C. 2118.

November 1917 Page 2

Place	Date	Hour	Summary of Events and Information	Remarks and references to Appendices
Nov. 1917				
Aolfre	18th–24th		Irish avenue, repairs completed up to Everards drain. Coverings over northern drain between Pots 6 & 7 begun. Japan area drain, begun deepening & regrading. 250 Portugese troops on working party on Subsidiary line to the west from 21st Nov.	
	25th–30th		Work continued as above. Pots 5 & 6 drain, begun re-grading. Iron Subsidiary line, commenced formation of Reserve dumps at Irvings & Jocketes in case of advance. Casualties during month: 1 RE missing believed killed (in raid on 8th Nov) 4 RE wounded, 1 returned to duty. 8 RE 2 attacked happy to Hospital sick. 10 RE arrived from Base as reinforcements. Home 2 to Mot. voly. station; Leave 2 Officers & 1 O.R. granted leave to U.K.	

30/11/17

W Murphy
Officer Commanding,
161st Field Company R.E.

CONFIDENTIAL.

War Diary of

151st. Field Company R. E.

From 1-12-17 To 31-12-17.

Army Form C. 2118.

WAR DIARY
or
INTELLIGENCE SUMMARY.

Officer Commanding,
151st Field Company R.E.

December 1917   Page 1

Place	Date	Hour	Summary of Events and Information	Remarks and references to Appendices
Armentières	December 1917			
	1st		HQ'd, 1 Section in ARMENTIERES, 2 Sections at HOUPLINES, 1 Section at BAC-ST-MAUR on trench area work.	
	1st to 8th		Work continued as usual. Began new trench for Cambridge Avenue from Post 24 to Post 6.	
	3rd		No 4 Section returned from employment under CRE 2nd went to HOUPLINES. Party No 3 Section went to FICKERBER trench area.	
	11th		Handed over Right Battalion Sub-Sector to 124 Field Coy R.E.	
	11th to 20th		No 1 Section at Houplines employed on Cambridge Avenue. No 3 Section at Houplines, employed on drainage in Left Sub Sector. No 2 Section at Armentieres employed on Subsidiary Line. No 4 Section at Armentieres employed behind Subsidiary line and on billets at Houplines.	
	20th		The Coy and Transport marched to NOUVEAU MONDE. Work and billets handed over to 9th Australian Field Coy R.E. Pumping Plant at Subsector was taken over from 124 Field Coy and work in whole Brigade Sector was handed over to 9th Aust. Field Coy.	

WAR DIARY
or
INTELLIGENCE SUMMARY.

Army Form C. 2118.
Page 2

Place	Date	Hour	Summary of Events and Information	Remarks and references to Appendices
	December 1917			
NOUVEAU MONDE	21st	9.22	Men working in Tillel & horse lines, doing repairs.	
	22nd		Reconnoitred Fleurbaix defences with C.R.E. & G.S.O. 2, also D.M.G.O. 24th	
	23rd	20°	Working 2 Sections at Fleurbaix, cutting loopholes in existing emplacements.	
	25th		No work.	
	26th		Took Officers & NCOs round Fleurbaix reconnoitred work.	
	27th		Three Sections working in Fleurbaix, began work on three M.G. Emplacements on South side of village.	
	30th		Started concrete floors of two emplacements during period of thaw.	
	31st		Reconnoitred defences of Fleurbaix with G.S.O. 1 Today. Selected sites for Infantry Posts & wire. Arranged work for C Coy Pioneers, 176 M.G. Coy & XV Corps Cyclist Battn	
			Casualties during month. Killed in action 1 O.R. R.E. Sick to Hospital 2 O.R.R.E. Transferred to Tank Corps 10 O.R. R.E. Leave to U.K. 2 Off. & 12 O.R. R.E. Reinforcements from Base 16 O.R. R.E. Officers 2/Lt Cundall returned to England, 2/Lt Carolin joined.	

31/12/17

J.M. Murdoch Major R.E.
Officer Commanding
181st Field Company

CONFIDENTIAL.

War Diary.

151st Field Coy, R.E.

From 1st January to 31st January 1918.

Army Form C. 2118.

WAR DIARY
or
INTELLIGENCE SUMMARY.
(Erase heading not required.)

Officer Commanding, 151st Field Company R.E.
January 1918. Sheet 1

Place	Date	Hour	Summary of Events and Information	Remarks and references to Appendices
January 1918			**151st Field Company R.E.**	
	1st		HQrs, three Sections and Mounted Section at NOUVEAU MONDE. One Section at near R.E. Park, at LA BOUDRELLE. Work continued on Corps Defence Line, Flemtrin Sector, the Coy was employed on erecting and preparatory work for five machine gun emplacements. Following units working under supervision of this Coy were employed on the work as follows: "C" Coy 19 held Pioneers making good Infantry Posts in Flemtrin defences; 176th M.G. Coy and Detachment XV Corps Cyclist Bn (80 OR) daily, also 10th S.W.B. (240 OR) on two days a week, were employed erecting wire.	
	3rd		2 & 4 Section rejoined the Coy from R.E. Park.	
	6th		Mounted Section moved to standings near BAC ST. MAUR.	
	13th		Concreting which had been delayed by frost, was carried on in two M.G. Emplacements which were in closed buildings, fires being used to prevent freezing. All temporary iron for 3 emplacements was delivered from Mourcel troco in Flemtrin.	
	14th		O.C. 70th Field Coy went over Flemtrin defences.	
	15th		Went over Corps Line with O.C. 70th Field Coy. South of Armentières.	

WAR DIARY
or
INTELLIGENCE SUMMARY.
(Erase heading not required.)

Army Form C. 2118.

January 1918 Sheet 2

Place	Date	Hour	Summary of Events and Information	Remarks and references to Appendices
January 1918	16th		The Coy moved to ARMENTIERES. Billets at B.29.a.5.0 Horse lines at B.30.d.0.3. Sheet 36. Work on Fleurbaix Defences was handed over to 70th Field Coy, while we took over from them work on Corps Defence Line from Armentieres to L'armee.	
	17th		Began work on two M.G. Shelters, also reclaiming old trenches and shooting selected posts and wiring around these posts.	
	28th		Began concreting body of first M.G. Shelter. All nosework & shuttering having been placed in position, concreting was carried on continuously by 6 hour shifts. Began 6.0 am 28th & finished 1.0 am on 30th inst. Started laying out front line of trenches for Defence Zone.	
	31st		Casualties during month. To Hospital Sick. 7 OR RE, 6 OR attached Infantry. Reinforcements joined — 3 OR RE. 6 OR attached Infy. Leave to UK. 2 Officers 16 OR. Commanded to prison 1 OR RE, 1 OR Infy. Officers Lt Dance 11th SW.B rejoined his Battalion. Lt G. Callen to UK to join Cadet School. Horses 1 Destroyed (Sick) 5 evacuated (mange) 2 Remounts received	

31/1/18

W.W. Hamilton Major RE
Officer Commanding
161st Field Company R.E.

WAR DIARY
or
INTELLIGENCE SUMMARY.
(Erase heading not required.)

Army Form C. 2118.

151 Field Coy. R.E. Sheet 1

Place	Date	Hour	Summary of Events and Information	Remarks and references to Appendices
February 1918	1st to 12th		HQrs and 4 Sections at ARMENTIERES, B.30.d.0.3, Mounted Section at B.29.a.5.0. Sheet 36. Work was continued on the XV Corps Defence Line on Battle Zone, from the Southern boundary of ARMENTIERES to the Southern boundary of 57th Division area. Work was continued on 3 Concrete Shelters, each for two M.G. detachments. Materials were also collected for a point d'Appui Shelter. Trenches in the Battle Zone were worked on, the lines of trenches being subtracted 3'×1' continuously, and selected points were dug to full depth. Trenches were intersected, the sides being sloped about 1:1. Working parties of 100 to 300 infantry from 57th Division were employed on this trench work, daily.	
	13th		The Coy. relieved the 502 (Wessex) Field Coy R.E. in the WEZ MACQUART SECTOR. HQrs & 3 Sections were billetted at H.18.c.9.2. one Section at LA ROLANDERIE FARM H.11.c.5.5, and Mounted Section at B.28.b.2.5. The work being done on the Corps Defence Line was handed over to 502nd Field Coy.	

Army Form C. 2118.

Sheet 2

WAR DIARY
or
INTELLIGENCE SUMMARY.

(Erase heading not required.)

1st Field Coy. R.E.

Place	Date	Hour	Summary of Events and Information	Remarks and references to Appendices
February 1918	13th & 28th		No 1 Section with 25 attached Infy under Lt. ARMSTRONG R.E. was placed under the orders of G.O.C. 115 Infy Bde. for work in the forward area. Remainder of the Coy. was employed under C.R.E. 38th Divn mainly on Concrete Battle HQrs in the Battle Zone.	
	23rd		Work was begun by working parts of 17th R.W.F. on trenches in the Battle Zone, posts being dug at selected points in the front line of trenches. The Battn was given a task for the period of 6½ days between reliefs.	
			Note on concreting. On heavy concrete work, where shuttering and most of the reinforcement had been placed in position, it was found best to employ large parties on putting in the concrete, working 4 hour shifts. Each party did 2 shifts one day and one shift the next day, alternately. In one case 83 cubic yards of concrete were put in in 700 man hours or .12 cubic yards per man hour. In this way the best use is made of the hours of daylight without over fatiguing the men.	

Army Form C. 2118.

WAR DIARY
or
INTELLIGENCE SUMMARY.
(Erase heading not required.)

151st Field Coy. R.E.   Sheet 3

Place	Date	Hour	Summary of Events and Information	Remarks and references to Appendices
February 1918				
	28th		Casualties during month	
			To Hospital, Sick . 6 O.R. R.E., 4 O.R. Inf².	
			Reinforcements from Base 2 O.R. R.E.	
			Leave to U.K. 16 O.R. R.E. 2 O.R. Inf².	
			Horses Evacuated to M.V.S. (suspected skin disease) 2.	
			Remounts received 6.	
			W.P.Mclerough	
			Major R.E.(SR)	
			28/2/18	
			Officer Commanding,	
			151st Field Company R.E.	

Army Form C. 2118.

Sheet 1.

151st Field Coy. R.E.

Vol 28

WAR DIARY
or
INTELLIGENCE SUMMARY.
(Erase heading not required.)

Instructions regarding War Diaries and Intelligence Summaries are contained in F. S. Regs., Part II. and the Staff Manual respectively. Title pages will be prepared in manuscript.

Place	Date	Hour	Summary of Events and Information	Remarks and references to Appendices
March 1918.	3rd		Two Sappers attached to a party of 17th R.I.F. took part in a raid on 1.22.a.5.1. that35.NW. blew up a concrete dugout with a 30lb. mobile charge.	
			General Arnaud Distinguished Service Certificate	
			awarded the 30th Survival Distinguished Service Certificate.	
	16		Major the Lord H.R.E. proceeding on leave D.U.K.	
	17		Brigade Battle Headquarters at Sandy Farm I.1.d.6.4. completed Sheet 36. N.W.	
	20		Headquarters + 3 Sections / Mounted Section moved to La Haye Farm B.28.d.7.9. Sheet 36.	
	28	3.30 AM	Lewis gun Sappers with a party of 180 Infantry took part in a raid on I.21.d.1.8. Sheet 36 NW. Two concrete dugouts are sniper cupola demolished with 30lb. mobile charge of Ammonal.	
	31		Company moved to Busseboom I.8.c.2.1. Sheet 36 A.	
			Casualties during month	
1st to	31		To Hospital - 1 Officer + 3 OR. R.E. + 2 OR. Infy.	
			Wounds - 1 —	
			" (wounds not at duty)+ 1 S./Str. accidentally wounded	
			Ground - 1 Other " accidentally drowned.	
			Leave to U.K. - 1 Off.+ 40 OR R.E. + 8 OR. Infy.	

21/3/18

M.T.Armonji R.E.
O/C 151 Field Coy R.E.

38th Div.
V.Corps.

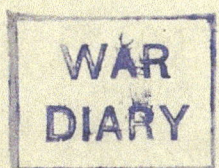

151st FIELD COMPANY, R.E.

A P R I L

1 9 1 8

Army Form C. 2118

WAR DIARY
or
INTELLIGENCE SUMMARY.   Sheet 1.   151st Field Coy R.E.

(Erase heading not required.)

Vol 2 ef

Place	Date	Hour	Summary of Events and Information	Remarks and references to Appendices
	APRIL 1918			
BOESEGHEM	1st	5.0 p.m.	Entrained at STEENBECK for DOULLENS. Arrived 4.0 A.m. 2nd inst.	
	2nd		Marched to VILLERS BOCAGE and then to CONTAY, marched all night.	
	3rd		Bivouacked near VARENNES	
VARENNES	4th		Working on trenches East of ENGLEBELMER with Infantry party from 115 Infy. Brigade.	
WARLOY BAILLON	5th to 10th		Company moved to WARLOY BAILLON. Continued work on ENGLEBELMER — BOUZINCOURT Line, digging platoon posts on front + support lines. No Infantry working parties were provided.	
SENLIS	11th		Relieved the 69th Field Coy R.E. and went into bivouac at SENLIS, transport lines remained at WARLOY. The Coy. was placed under the orders of 114th Infantry Brigade for work in Rt Sub Sector opposite ALBERT. Shelled out of bivouac in evening, dug in new position 500 yds. north west of SENLIS.	
	12th		Working on HQrs of Right, Left & Reserve Battalion, 114 Bde.	
HENENCOURT	13th		Moved to new bivouac under banks north of HENENCOURT. Began work on new Brigade HQrs on same banks.	

Army Form C. 2118

WAR DIARY
or
INTELLIGENCE SUMMARY

Sheet 2, 151 Field Coy R.E.

(Erase heading not required.)

Instructions regarding War Diaries and Intelligence Summaries are contained in F. S. Regs., Part II. and the Staff Manual respectively. Title pages will be prepared in manuscript.

Place	Date	Hour	Summary of Events and Information	Remarks and references to Appendices
	April 1918			
HENENCOURT & CONTAY	15th		Battle Surplus and Rear HQrs (2 Officers & 16 R.E. & 16 Infty) sent to Transport Lines. Transport Lines moved to CONTAY.	
	14th to 23rd		Work continued on Brigade and Battalion HQs, also with Infantry working parties of 250 men each night on Support and Reserve Lines in Right Brigade Sector.	
TOUTENCOURT	24th		The Coy. including transport moved to camp at TOUTENCOURT being relieved by 2nd Australian Divl Engineers.	
HENENCOURT & CONTAY	25th		Divisional relief cancelled, Coy moved back to bivouacs at HENENCOURT and Transport to CONTAY.	
	26th		Work continued on Brigade & Battalion HQs in Right Bde. Sector.	
TOUTENCOURT	27th		The Coy. including transport moved back to camp at TOUTENCOURT being relieved by 2nd Australian Divl Engineers.	
do.	28th		Training of Sappers & Attached Infantry Begun. Musketry, aim testing & pontooning; also first round of Football competition. All men's aim was tested today.	
	29th		Training Programme continued – Rapid loading & fire control.	

Army Form C. 2118.

WAR DIARY
or
~~INTELLIGENCE SUMMARY.~~
(Erase heading not required.)

Sheet 3. 151st Field Coy. R.E.

Place	Date	Hour	Summary of Events and Information	Remarks and references to Appendices
TOUTENCOURT	April 1918 29th		Men proficient in aiming fired on the range as follows:— 5 rounds grouping, 5 rounds rapid shooting 5 secs exposure. Miniature target at 25 yards. Men not proficient instructed in use of rifle & aiming. Football competition continued.	
	30th		Continued instruction of men not proficient. Inter-section competition on rifle range, snap shooting by teams at named targets, 5 secs exposure at 50 yards. 5 rounds per man. The great majority of Sappers & Sapants are proficient in handling their rifle, loading and aiming. More practice in trigger pressing is required. About 10% require instruction in aiming & use of rifle. The short training programme was completed today.	
			Casualties during the month Killed 1 OR R.E., 1 OR Infy. Wounded 4 OR Attd. Infantry. Sick to Hospital H. Armstrong, 2/Lt D.L. Morgan (gassed), 10 OR R.E., 4 OR Attd Infy. 2 horses to M.V.S. Reinforcements 1 Offr & 18 OR R.E. from Base. Both R.E. and attached Infantry up to strength at end of month.	W.P.M. Daughly. Major RE. O.C. 151st Field Coy R.E.

Vol 30

151st Field Coy R.E.

War Diary, for month of May

WAR DIARY or ~~INTELLIGENCE SUMMARY~~. Sheet 1, 151 Field Coy R.E.

Army Form C. 2118.

Place	Date	Hour	Summary of Events and Information	Remarks and references to Appendices
V.2,d and HARPONVILLE.	May 1918 1st		The Coy. relieved the 205 Field Coy R.E. in left subsector of MARTINSART - BOUZINCOURT Sector. Sections & Forward HQ³ to V.2,d, Sheet 57D. Transport lines & Rear HQ² to HARPONVILLE. No. 1 & 4 Sections worked under orders of the C.R.E. on the Purple System N of trenches North of BOUZINCOURT. No 2 & 3 Sections were placed under the orders of 114 Infantry Brigade for work on the Tunnel System. The Sections under C.R.E. were chiefly employed digging & wiring the front line of the Purple System to the north of BOUZINCOURT. Infantry working parties from 119 Bde. Reserve Battalion worked each night. The R.E. Sections were chiefly wiring the work being done in the early	
do.	2nd-8th		morning before visibility was too good. Sections under 114 Infy. Bde. were employed making or digouts. One Section made 4 French Elephant dugouts with 6ft. of Chalk cover for double Battalion HQ² behind MARTINSART. The other Section constructed two tunnelled dugouts with 15ft. of cover for the same HQ². Also other miscellaneous work.	

WAR DIARY
or
INTELLIGENCE SUMMARY.
(Erase heading not required.)

Army Form C. 2118.

Officer Commanding 154 Field Company R.E.

Sheet 2

Place	Date	Hour	Summary of Events and Information	Remarks and references to Appendices
	May 1918			
V.2.d & HARPONVILLE	9th		A party of 1 N.C.O. and 12 Sappers with 40 bangalore torpedoes were placed under the orders of O.C. 15 Welsh Regt for the attack on AVELUY wood on 10th May. Owing to failure of the attack no torpedoes were used.	
	10th		The three Field Coys were placed under orders of O.C. 19th Welsh Regt (Pioneers) to act as Divisional Reserve in case of attack.	
	10th-16th		Continued work as already detailed.	
V.5.a & HARPONVILLE	17th		The Coy. & H.Qrs. moved to V.5.a. Central taking over camp from Reserve Battn of 113 Infantry Brigade. As camp had been shelled the night before, Sections were spread out as much as possible.	
	18th		Heavy gas shelling of battery areas east of our camp began 10.0 p.m. and we respirators for short time. It as shelling did not reach camp & wind was blowing from a flank there were taken off. Shelling continued for several hours.	
	19th		Gas shelling of battery areas again began about 10.0 p.m. and continued most of the night. Slight smell of gas (yellow cross) in the camp all night and especially in the early morning. This was too long lasting	

Army Form C. 2118.

Officer Commanding,
151st Field Company R.E.

Sheet 3.

WAR DIARY
or
INTELLIGENCE SUMMARY.
(Erase heading not required.)

Instructions regarding War Diaries and Intelligence Summaries are contained in F.S. Regs., Part II. and the Staff Manual respectively. Title pages will be prepared in manuscript.

Place	Date	Hour	Summary of Events and Information	Remarks and references to Appendices
V.5,a and HARPONVILLE.	19th		to wear respirators and too widely distributed. troops were at first leaving the camp altogether turning reasonable. hovel near MARTINSART Chateau was cleaned by use of gun cotton & cutting down small trees, 90 trees in all were felled and about 500 lbs of gun cotton used. Time did not permit of towing the trees to place internal charges. They were cut by untamped charges fired on the surface. The Coy was relieved by 203 Field Coy R.E., 35 Div. Relievers unit moved dinners back to old position at V.2.d, before occupying them. This unit and Transport moved to Stegens camp at TOUTENCOURT.	
TOUTENCOURT.	20th			
	21st-29th		Carried out training programme, including ½ to 1 hr. close order drill daily, 2 hrs musketry & range practice and 2 hrs. repair of equipment + transport. Mounted Section did close order drill + musketry.	
	27th		The Coy with Transport paraded with 115 Infantry Brigade for inspection by G.O.C. V Corps.	
	30th		Musketry Competitions arranged by C.R.E. were carried out. also.	

WAR DIARY
or
INTELLIGENCE SUMMARY

Army Form C. 2118.

151st Field Company
Officer Commanding
Sheet 34

Place	Date	Hour	Summary of Events and Information	Remarks and references to Appendices
	May 1918			
TOUTENCOURT	30th		Competition in riding & changing horses.	
	31st		Continued training. All Sections and mounted Section were put through gas test chamber by Gas Officer 114 Bde. There were no defective respirators.	
			Casualties during month. 2nd Lt. PICKING wounded (shell). 2nd Lt. DENNING to Hospital sick. reported at end of month.	
			Killed in action 3 O.R.R.E. (2 missing) Wounded 1 O.R.R.E. 20 R. Infantry attached. Wounded (gas) 6 O.R.R.E. 20 R. Infantry attached 1 O.R.R.E. To Hospital sick 6 O.R.R.E. 2 O.R. Inf. To Base Medically unfit 4 O.R.R.E. Leave to U.K. 2 O.R.R.E. 1 O.R. attached Infantry. Reinforcements 16 O.R. R.E. joined from Base depot. 1 Officer joined Attached Infantry rejoined their Battalions on 24/5/18	
			Note. Casualties from gas were sent to Hospital up to 31st May on more than 10 days since leaving the camp at V.S.A. 20 men had been exposed to gas since 20th May.	

W.P. Shaugh
Major R.E.
O.C. 151 Field Co. R.E.

31/5/18

Secret.

Original War Diary.
June 1917

151 Field Company R.E.
38 (Welsh) Division

1.7.18

Army Form C. 2118.

WAR DIARY
or
INTELLIGENCE SUMMARY. 1st Sheet. 151st Fld Coy R.E.
(Erase heading not required.)

JUNE/1918.

Place	Date	Hour	Summary of Events and Information	Remarks and references to Appendices
Intrenchmt. P.30.d.9.3. 9 Coy tops	June 5/6		Coy tops relieved the 248th Fld Coy R.E., 63rd Division & men to billets at P.30.d.9.3 Sheet 57 D S.E. No. 2 Section in reserve & men to Section move to new billet at 0.30.a.8.6. Sheet 57 D S.W. No. 4 L.to. took over work on tunnelled dug-out. Q.26.c.3.6. Sheet 57.D.S.E. working in her relief of 1 N.C.O. & O.R. and this section on demolition of wells & station. Maintaining a permanent party of 1 N.C.O. & 3. O.R. billets at Q.28.a.8.8. Sheet 57D S.E. Nos 1 & 3 Sections were working on the strongpoints from Q.27.c.4.9 to Q.21.d.3.9. Coy (Cos) was ploud underneath of Reserve Brigade (114) in case of attack.	
	11.		No. 3 Section moved into billets near the No. 3 coml into reserve. One of heavy shelling (Incl. drifting) of Coy billets & wire ones from P.30.d.9.3. to P.26.d. 18. Saunders orders B.19 - Which in case of attack.	
P26.d.7.8 9 Coy tops	15			
	15		Coy tops Coded work on intrenchments line to 123rd Fld Coy R.E. 9 No. 1	

Army Form C. 2118.

WAR DIARY
or
INTELLIGENCE SUMMARY.
(Erase heading not required.)

151st 2/1st Fd. Cy. R.E. Sheet 2.

Place	Date	Hour	Summary of Events and Information	Remarks and references to Appendices
	June 15		Section took over tunnelled dugout at Q.26.b.6.7. (Sheet 57 D S.E.) & strengthened walls & roofs at Bickleroi & Foncerville. Unsuperior RA dugout & mining. No 2 Section took over tunnelled dugouts from 10th Fd. Cy. R.E. at G.31.b.9.8 Sheet 57 D.S.E. & elevations of nuclei & craters near Noeuxville (Maintenance of RA dugouts & mining in War area	
	20		Batt. H.Q. dugout in Q.26.b.6.7 (Sheet 57 D S.E) completed	
	22		" " Q.26.c.6.9 " completed	
			Casualties during month.	
			Maj. W.R. McLaughlin R.E. to Hospital 11/6/18; 2nd Lt Bowdler R.E. 2ty 93rd Fld Cy. R.E. 5/6/18; 2nd Lt A.D.O. McKenzie from Base 18/6/18. 2nd Lt Donald Gassed - 3, Sick to Hospital - 17. Reinforcements 13. O.R.; Leave 1 officer & 1. O.R.	
			Note:- Work during month greatly delayed owing to epidemic of P.U.O. affecting two sections strength 30%	

W. A. Brown R.E.
O.C. 151st 2/1st Fd. Cy. R.E.

90R 32

War Diary. July 1918.
151 Field Coy R.E.

Army Form C. 2118.

Page 1

151st Field Company R.E.

WAR DIARY
or
INTELLIGENCE SUMMARY.
(Erase heading not required.)

Place	Date	Hour	Summary of Events and Information	Remarks and references to Appendices
Sheet 57d Div HQ & 4 Section P26 d 78 Recon HQ House Lines Q 20 c 37 CLAIRFAYE	July 1916 1st		Company working on deep dug outs for Batt. HQ R.F.A. M.G. and T.M. each find labour for their administrative Sapper Supervision, some being found by the Company. 13 Sections working on other three shifts for 24 hours	
	4th		O/C Capt G.W.M.BORN R.E.(T) proceeds and took over the Company from Capt N.A.EVANS, R.E.(TEMP) authority Jnd. Own A1/1565. A.G's N.A.G.55/2837 d/28/6/16. III Corps A12/205/18 d 24/6/16	
	5th		O/C round near HQ Riles Battalions and looking into detail of Brigade and Workshops	
	6		O/C and Capt EVANS R.E. round the FORCEVILLE wells examining munitions	
	7		O/C round and inspecting the work on deep dug outs	
	8	Noon	Conference at M.G. Batt HQ a/C.R.E. C.O.M.G. Batt and Corp M.G. officer V Corp informed MOIR hill layer it was settled that CO.M.G. Batt and O/C 151 Fd.Cy R.E. chose ligale side in 5 MoirHill layer to Division area	
	8	4 P.M.	O/C with V Corp M.G. Officer to ROSEL V Corp R.E. park to see MOIR hill boxes order.	
	9		C.O.M.G. Batt. O/C 151 Fd.Cy and Corp M.G. officer V Corp R.E. park to see type MoirHill boxes, Commenced work on 2 MoirHill sidings and arranging Canoufleur for 6 MoirHill boxes being found by M.G. Batt Sappers from 1 M.G. driving Q17 a 60 one at P.30 a 91 and Q32 c49 labour and one R.E.A. dug out completed Q17 a 60. One at P.30 c 91 and Q 32 c 49. Labour sapping from 1 M.G. driving P & Tunneling and 1 Batt HQ finished	
	10			
	14		Ordering all reports made to Z and officers I/126 Fd.Coy (21st Divn) shown around the park or 15"m	
	16		Field Canoufle.	
	17		OC round MoirHill Boxes and Dug outs and afternoon attention OC Canoufler at CRE office. To discuss training programme to equalise Divisional first tab ensuring ordering & have work in the North Divisional Sech. 63rd Divisional R.E., Southern Div. Sech is 17 Divn R.E. Returning copy & policy to mess 5 AM 19/7	
	18	enough	Having over statements made and work shown to representatives of the company then Batt. Orders for company. 3 P.M. Th 4/C.R.E. 38th 2 Division went round with O/C 151 Fd.Cy R.E. Arrived to the	
	19		HEADQUILLE FORCEVILLE Sectn of th BROWN LINE (Copt LINE) on which Div advancing R.E. and Our Batts Infantry was taken to command 204 under C.R.E. 38th Divn represent C.E. IX Corp O/C and T.M. Div inf were round with a/C.R.E. 17 Divn and IX Corp Camouflage officer satisfied Siteg at N7 c 36 and Y17 a 86 for 2 M.G. machinii emplacement at each OPE; I/C.R.E. 17 Divn anxious for 1 Sech of 151 Fd.Cy to finish at rock emplacement and the third trenches with the 2 M.G. old Batt. Commence at Q 32 c 49. 51st Hutton and Dannois R.E. with this section command	
	20th		to a Coast of V8 c 66, this use the work at SENLIS and BOUZINCOURT L' Dulba will have section continue work on the 2 MoirHill beyond Q32 c49. All labour being	

T2134. W. W708-776. 500000. 4/15. Sir J.C. & S.

Army Form C.2118.

PAGE 2

151st Field Company R.E.

WAR DIARY or INTELLIGENCE SUMMARY
(Erase heading not required.)

Place	Date	Hour	Summary of Events and Information	Remarks and references to Appendices
	JULY 1918			
Shel 57d	20th		All labour being supplied from 2 Companies Infantry detailed by 38th Division. The Division being notified the men were constantly changed for training and the working parties were not satisfactory. Some leave & wash 2 hours from work.	
HQ P26d75	21		O.C. to detachment at V8a66 thence C.R.E. 17th Div. for particulars re Monolithic post at C.R.E.'s office. Saw C.E. V Corps and discussed the question of accommodation and forward O.C. round Monolith sites with C.R.E. and later a/C.R.E. 17 Division officer.	
Detchmt V8a66	23		for further particulars and borrowing details. Saw adjutant C.E. V Corps re the Hoser Emm.	
Hoser Emm O30a37	24		raised the question of obstacles, accommodation. 151 Fd Coy R.E. were in command when plan submitted V Corps M.G.O. called by appointment & settled the question of Lostile area	
	26		accommodation, gun crews and stores at DOWN LINE with Lt. REYNOLDS and Cols. & attachment V8a66	
	29		O.C. "I" BUTLER round MOIR PILLBOX MARTINSART VALLEY, and the MONOLITHS, BOUZINCOURT & SCHLIS all working parties formed by 38 Division Cas. & INOON.	
	30		North 54N & 92 Nov. Chronomat "artillery" signs in 17 Div Front. 9 AM provided sleep rations C.R.E. 17 at Callen 10AM in Cy HQ 17 Brigade First working parties for MOIR & MONOLITHS. From MIR 308 Silver man MOIR Pill Boy until "L" HUTTON & C.R.E. 17 Div 6 V6 & 3.2 and made down to Camefery.	
	31		9FM on all work & 123 Fd C.R.E. Corps meet to Billiet in TOOTENCOURT. 9Pm 5th. HQ. Detachment and Moir Section moving separately. The bulk of the Moir line over battle	
TOOTENCOURT U1			Sunken with Capt Evans & McKenzie had already moved 26b coming to somewhere Dyneny away. HQ & MH Section at the billet O30a37.	
			Casualties.	
			Capt G.W.M. BORNS R.E.) from 288 ATC, RE with Command France 4.5 unit	
			"Lt. Reynolds by Diss Rail Camp 18Mar from Base 27 O.R. 28 ATC Pte IOR. 234 Fd Cy R.E. IOR.	
			Lt. 234 Fd Cy R.E. I.O.R. LEAVE 2.O.R. Hospital (Shell Wound) 2 Sick 4	
			Killer in action 1 (Shell) (Cas)	
			Horses 2 Evacuated	
			The Epidemic of P.U.O. (Influenza) very prevalent at the beginning of the month died down to Nil on or about 14th	
			A couple of cases of Suspected Dysentery (mainly Dhobi) 2 proven dysentery occurred in the Hoser Enem	
			etc. removed from CLAIRFAYE a sick man on a Fd Ambulance.	
			Weather fine except for small storms but has hills in the month.	

G.W.Burns Capt R.E. (T)
O.C. 151st Fd Cy R.E.

3/8/18

WR 33

151st Field Coy. R.E.
WAR DIARY.
August 1st to 31st 1918.

Army Form C. 2118.

WAR DIARY
or
INTELLIGENCE SUMMARY.
(Erase heading not required.)

PAGE 1

151 ST FIELD COMPANY R E

Place	Date	Hour	Summary of Events and Information	Remarks and references to Appendices
	AUGUST 1918			
SHEET 57D U.I.	1		TOUTENCOURT Village was Bombed the night July 31/Aug 1. One section billets shaken and all men taken through gas. 2nd Cpl Crossing Rfm. Shakes. All men moved to Bivouacs with Woods out of Village.	
	2		Continued Training. Physical Drill, Squad + Section Drill, Rifle Exercises, Musketry but Bayonet fixed. N.C.O. tournament.	
	3		Training during difficult during Warm odd weather. Training had to work in c/o	
	4		Tarpaulines and divested by rain. Lectures by Coys Commanders. M.O. some Rifle practice at Range (V17a62) including field exercise shooting.	
	5		O.C. proceeded to SENLIS (V17a62) to take over from O3 w/ field Cy RE the taking over was received difficult in that owing to misalignment a line approximately the Railway with the ANCRE Valley all Work Programme was cancelled and the new Programme was got out. Police control of Toutencourt handing over points on W side of ANCRE Valley	
SHEET 57D V17a62	6		Company moved to TOUTENCOURT to All HQ 147 Sudn V17a82 Rea HQ Wood end at HARPONVILLE 1 Sudn alth 114 Bae 2 Sudn working on a/c R.E. wiring supporteries and mur pill box W.8 a 26 115 Bae sudn on front line work 114 Bae Sudn Rubble tri (railway) and accommodation 60 US Engineers attached to maintain division among it action reconnt. Work	
	7		Balts 8 sph q 110th and thong him. C.R.E returned from Sick leave Culler and orders for parade too bad instant for dismantling. That night to certain a Rondy much as ANCRE in AVELUY Reconnaissance about there being already demolished	
	8			
	9		Owing to no African programme 8 units Longth Spisses work. 114.2 Bargue sudn were employer to assist 2 Sudn were working for Winch Walking from AUTHOVILLE - AVELUY and being Retring ours dismantering all canopy AUTHOVILLE - AVELUY audience all officer and next night	
	12		on Thur Brigade Holding the line	
	13			
	14	9AM	O.C. to U.S. Battn review MESNIL - NESLE of AVELUY had harang covering party for reconnaissance of AUTHUVILLE Canneron Spent afternoon in AVELUY was from AUTHUVILLE but could not from a road	
	15		U.S Patrol cancelled 2 Platoon of 112 Bae duce cross AUTHOVILLE Canning at AUTHUVILLE O.C. 112 Denney 113 was discontemp foundered Cawing of Timber Salvo from SENLIS All available subspan working forwd bridges of AUTHUVILLE start night with a Company Se at attacks congines of 113 Bae Mfg cf crossing at AUTHUVILLE start night with a Company Lt Denney 6 R.E. with Eagle Bridge got the Intents Patrol across the Ponders but in Infile water. 25 men detailed for the further fatals tight is along the mountstreet	
			O.C. 147 ATCY RE Office commences Cleaning approach to B pocking road AVELUY L/ Bubler 1 Sudn commences taking in posts in AVELUY and AUTHUILLE Canopy CONTINUED	

T2134. Wt. W708—776. 500000. 4/15. Sir J. C. & S.

Army Form C. 2118.

WAR DIARY
or
INTELLIGENCE SUMMARY.
(Erase heading not required.)

PAGE 2

Place	Date	Hour	Summary of Events and Information	Remarks and references to Appendices
SHEET 57D V18 a 82	16		OC made reconnaissance & marches South of AVELUY to find track & locality spot of Teams. From slope North AUELUY spot was likely to exhibit them crossing the R. HULLER made reconnaissance on Sth of R. Bank, found a cream Capt. Evan RE of 151st Field Coy RE approach improved, terminated 123 W. Field Coy RE. His Section prepared repairing approach to BROOKER I Post. OC with C.O. M.G. Batt. Silver MOIR FILED W.6 a 26 with Commence on same that night. Guns from to 147 A TCH, RE at W.6 a 26 with Commenced on same that night. Guns from to 147 A TCH, RE. Truck reconnaissance of AVELUY Causeway. 2 Section cleaning Brocken Path approach	
	18.		and making good behind it. Causeway No.11 of AVELUY Causeway.	
	20.		Burning OE's conduct. Causeway at AUTHUILLE & 147 A TCH, RE Seen to reconnoitre and & provide wide boats. Transport Bridge in W 28 b. OC went with a C.R.E. t CR.E 18 Div. who arranged for 92nd Field to help & Machine 157 Field. Made a reconnaissance with single Bank. Found with troops ammunition. No Aeroplane photographs were available, and only partial outfits of war aeroplane photographs taken afternoon & late evening. Enemy troops CONDUIT AVELUY GROTHVILING and sundry mortar were not useful. Contruor club of CRE at HQ 123 Field R.E were forgotten. Part patrols of 114th Brigade held at 6 in evening in advance mode.	
	21	9 pm	All demanded Bridging Equipment packed by 8 pm and MARTINPORT trees OE and all left Bridgeing ground to AVELUY Sending W19 a 25.	
	22.		Improving infantry Causeway N. S of AVELUY pulling extras from tonnelle trees hardware.	
	23.		Reconnaissance of 2 possible bridges in Q350 and W6 b mining & any me OC reconned same to learned Ghromack 9 am Lellius CRE. Improvised down plan the Command Colt Conference 3.30 PM H.Q. 121st Field Reg. during conference OC received new from L'Butler who had been all day making Reconnaissance. Can't find on BROOKER I PATH new & 3 Section deposited at once (CAPM). Its forth writing made H McKimm lifted wreck over for Infantry. All bridge at W 26 & 85. At 12 there sent this ordinate informed the Company at BROOKER PATH – the Hot Dinners all night and next day without interval at BROOKER'S PATH. 30 Tanmilla and 30 Tanmiser reported Gone 7AM respectively 24th inst. Trucks on approach four Bridges and	
	24		approach ready for First Transport 4 p.m. 24th inst when the Sapper's were withdrawn except a party of 10 OR left in case of breakdown. Transport 253 & 3 Division crossed down the night 24/25 without mishap. Sappers returned on the morning 25th to improve approach and made a crew in the bridge. C.E. Corps never approved the lateral lettering.	
SHEET 57D W10 d 22	25			
	27		Mixed camp Adv. Hq. to H10 d. 22. Rear HQ. from 2am to HQ d 77	

CONTINUED

Army Form C. 2118.
PAGE III

WAR DIARY or INTELLIGENCE SUMMARY
(Erase heading not required.)

Instructions regarding War Diaries and Intelligence Summaries are contained in F.S. Regs., Part II. and the Staff Manual respectively. Title pages will be prepared in manuscript.

Place	Date	Hour	Summary of Events and Information	Remarks and references to Appendices
SHEET 57 D W10d.22	27. 28.		Work on bridge and approach maintenance and improvement continued. 100/OR of 153 Fd Cy. Reported for work at B Rocher Pass. Champ approach. Duke never started and work never upon the BOISELLE–CONTALMAISON ROAD	
	30.		Received orders to take over AUTHUILLE Crossing from 123rd Field Cy RE, and continue improving approach and maintain the bridge. (Pontoon & Trestle)	
	31.		Work on BOISELLE CONTALMAISON Road taken over the BAD Pts Road. No. 2 Section AUTHUILLE Crossing taken over; work plan made; reconnaissance of Forbay and approach to sect; submitted to CRE. Work on Drainage Bridge Sally approach to ROCHERS Pass continued. Weather through AUGUST fine but hot; a men occasionally ill slightly.	
			CASUALTIES	
			T. Hospital Sick 2 Howden (blw) 2 Accidentally Injured 2 (MO Section) Transfer To 123rd Field Cy RE 5 OR. To 124th Field Cy RE 5 OR. Reinforcement from Base 11 OR. (8 ♂ two NCO.) Courses RE training school Rouen On 7th month 3 week 1 Officer 1 OR (Cpl) 5th Corps Gas School on 11th inst for 14 days 1 Officer 3 OR 5th Corps RE Park instructional Course Sunday on 13th inst 2 OR (Still away) Horses Evacuated NIL Return 1 Rider (Depoin) Rider to 6 weeks	

3/9/18

G M Denny MAJOR, R.E.
O.C. 151ST FIELD COMPANY R.E.

SHEET 1.

Army Form C. 2118.

WAR DIARY
or
INTELLIGENCE SUMMARY.
(Erase heading not required.)

151st Field Company R.E.
Sept. 1918.

Vol 34

Place	Date	Hour	Summary of Events and Information	Remarks and references to Appendices
	Sept 1918			
Sheet 57D W10.d.22.	1		OC and CRE at BROOKERS PASS and went with him to the AUTHUILLE Crossing to explain purpose of new bridge & superimpose existing Pontoon. Three men from CRE approved Friday for Lorries of 12"x 5" x 22' R. JOISTS; work put in hand at once.	
Sheet 57C T.13.c.15.	2,3		Approach to BIRDER'S PASS complete, work on bridge and approach at AUTHUILLE	
	4	9AM	Company moved to GUINCHY. Commenced work on plankroad GUINCHY LONGEVAL	
	5	8.15AM	All company working on GUINCHY LONGEVAL plank road	
V.8.c.88.			Same received from C.R.E "Report with whole company and 2 Pontoons to OC. 123 Fd Coy RE at V8c8 at once". OC 151st Fd. RE got instruct. will OC.123rd Fd Coy RE arrange with 2 men 8 Lan mechanic	
	6		necessary reconnaissance. Company went 8PM with guide from 123 Fd. Co. RE medium pontoon bridge over the Canal du Nord at MANNANCOURT at site chosen by 123 Fd. Co. RE. bridge approach very bad. The bridge completed 4 AM company had 16 gas casualties. Working under another company very unsatisfactorily, they would not take the least men over, and would not take over responsibility and this was all time to make reconnaissance 2) Bill for casualties	
S.10.d. 55.	6		Company returned to new camp at S.10d. West of LONGEVAL Battersupsaple (16 OR) under transport Officer	
	7		working of HuDo Pond at WATERLOT FARM. (S.15.a.9.) Whole all company working	
	8		OC. and 3 Subaltern Officers working recommencing 1) HUTS and SAILLY SAILLISEL 2) TRAMWAY and BEAUCOURT. Our Sub. Officer will be detailed. Details drunk shortly under CRE.	
O.7.c.	9	9am	Moved to Hut Supply.	
	10		Company moved to VILLERS au FLOS. O/C all employed repairing and excel's huts N.18 & 55 4 Section Officers will the Section in hut (Wash Section) and is afterwards) OC met with Deputy CRE at site and Chief signal at YTRES Station.	
P.32.c.rd	11	6AM	Company her transport to ETRICOURT new Bn HQ. take with old camp 77 Fd Co. RE moved to P32 C'rd leaving Baths, Suttle. 16 OR at Bn receptor camp 417.32 c.rd. T.O.7.c. Scratch and carried her campat N.18 & 78.	
	12	8AM	On knocking off work at Bn HQ, all ranks proceeded to new camp at P.17.32 cr'd.	
	12	6PM	Our Officers 2 Sections at Bn HQ. Our Officer 2 Section CRE HQ. DC and on Officer reconnoitre FINS GOUZEACOURT Line as our fruitless W8.15-90. (Recons)	
	13	8AM	In the evening 2 Section men killed in EQUANCOURT V.4 d.16. under an Officer	
	14	8AM	Our Officer 2 Section in Baths. Our Officer 2 Section in FINS GOUZEACOURT road. Sub officer men Rocques	
	15	9am	CRE and OC and went with them along the road FINS GOUZEACOURT and Tramway W2 d to W5a. 2 Section in Front. 1 Section in Bath supply.	

CONTINUED

Sheet 2

Army Form C. 2118.

151st Field Company R.E.
Sept. 1918.

WAR DIARY
or
INTELLIGENCE SUMMARY
(Erase heading not required.)

Place	Date	Hour	Summary of Events and Information	Remarks and references to Appendices
Sheet 57c.				
P32 d.c.	16		2 Sections EN: GOUZEAUCOURT ROAD. 1 Section WATER. 1 Section with 1 Platoon Pioneers.	
	17		Decauvilleshack OC all around all work, called CRE, & Co pioneers	
	19	8AM	3 Sections & 1 Platoon pioneers road repair commenced GOUZEAUCOURT to HOOK on Strong point Q36A and Q35 central. 4 Section Saps. On platoon pioneers started	
			8 AM. Light and transport by 3 AM. Left Camp 5 AM. ex cept 2 Section. 8 AM. one section 1 & Company Reading OC. called CRE ny NCO's promotion as many 1 tt Company NCO's were made. 1 &	
	20		Reinforcements subaltern NCW's were sent from Reserve making Company much under strength.	
	22		Sections supplied with 9 gunnders Rifle, S.B.R. inspection Hacking & repairing Wagons,	
	23		B'n Office with 2 Sgts (on acount) on sapper & F&CM Bowlby.	
	24		2 Sections under 1 officer Damaged Cinema 2 Sections Monty Bastion TRACKS Badoux	
	26	9 AM	One Section on Cinema 3 Sections on Tracks. Water supply. Officers Visited & returned to F&CM Bowlby.	
W20c.		2 PM	An officer & pioneers 27mn camp sile with Adj. CRE, Company 7mm. 2 PM. Officers returned Fit C.M. Bowlby.	
	29		Company moved to W20c when they interjoined 115 & 24 Fd Coy. 2 Sections from EQUANCOURT Transport W102.	
	30		Reconnoitering & Combining Tracks. W.S.T. & Pty. worked on 115 & 24 Fd. Coy Ground Extension for Fd. C.M Bowlby.	

Casualties. (Deported) 1 Cpl. 15 Sept. 1 Hospital Gas. (6-9-18) 2 O.R. Hospital sick.
Reinforcements. 2 O.R. 1 Sgt (Bn) to England to Command.
3 O.R. from Hospital. 1Q O.R. from Base. The latter has never no instruction in cement regulation and was much undermanned, trained for that reason. 1 C.S.M. Walker 30.9.18. Announced promotion Diana of O.S.M. HARDING R.E. who will
2 Sappers Eff. Co. rank 14-8-18. on Admission for a Fd. C.M. at R.E. Boy Trouser and lanxman lent returned to present for Country's duty Court Martial and learn fryer was kept abased.

Courses. 1 Sergeant M. R.E.T.C. Route from 6-9-18
4 Sappers to Cookery Course for 13-9-18.
1 Mt. Cpl. to Veterinary course at ABBEVILLE 13-9-18 to 27-9-18.
2 Officers 33 OR.

Leave. Veterinary Casualties NIL Reinforcement NIL Deserters 1 Officer Clang. (10 huh)

G.M.Bowes
1/10/18

WW 35

Army Form C. 2118.

151st Field Company R.E.

OCTOBER 1918.

WAR DIARY
or
INTELLIGENCE SUMMARY.
(Erase heading not required.) PAGE 1.

Place	Date	Hour	Summary of Events and Information	Remarks and references to Appendices
	OCTR 1918			
Sheet 57 C. W.20.c.	1.		Company under orders of C.R.E. Repairing Huts for Divisional Rest Camp at W.13.t. (FINS)	
	3.	14.00	Came under orders of 115 Infantry Brigade with instructions ready to move at 2 hours notice.	
		14.00	Orders received move at 15 hours.	
F.15 a.5.8.		17.30	Company moved to F.15.a.5.8.	
F.17. d. F.21.b.9.5.	4.	05.00	Ordered to move at 07.00. Moved off 08.15 hours to BONY halting on the road at F.17.d. from 09.30 to 16.30 hours. Arrived BONY 18.00 hours. F.21.b.9.5. Brigade ordered Sections out to consolidate line. 2 Officers each with 2 Sections went out with advanced Battalions. Owing to delay relief sections only reached front line positions at dawn having marched about all night and doing nothing. Returned to Camp at 07.00 hours on the 5th.	
	5.		O.C. Company arranged with G.O.C. 115 Infantry Brigade to attach one Officer with his section to each advanced Battalion leaving two Sections with Headquarters. A Battalion Commander reported to Brigade at LE CATELET town. O.C. with one Officer reconnoitering Bridge and alternative sites in the afternoon. Two sections left camp 16.30 hours, with local material, a Bridge suitable for all Horse Transport by 00.05 hours 6th. Other 2 sections joined their Battalions.	
Sheet 62 A. N.W. A.4.d.4.7.	6.	07.00	One Officer and his Section detached from company to work directly under C.R.E. on water duties. This Officer with his Section still detached at head of the month.	
	7.	12.00	Company moved to A.4.d.4.7. where Sections from Battalions rejoined, neither having done any work.	
		07.00	3 Sections working on Roads LE CATELET – PUTNEY, and eastwards under orders C.R.E.	
		17.00	Orders from Brigade. Company required to consolidate. O.C. arranged with G.O.C. 115th Brigade as sections had worked all day, they should report to Battalion Commanders at 05.00 hours.	
Sheet 57 T. 3.24.a. T.16.b.	8.	03.00	3 Sections paraded under Section Officers and proceeded to Battalion Headquarters with tools, to consolidate.	
		14.00	Company Headquarters moved to 3.24.a.	
		16.30	Company Headquarters moved to sunken road at T.16.b. where 3 sections rejoined company. Sections follow the Infantry all day being used as Infantry – no further work having been done at all.	
	9.	13.30	C.R.E. ordered Company to move to ELINCOURT and commence work on roads at once. C.R.E. took O.C. Company on to inspect the roads ELINCOURT-CLARY. On arriving at ELINCOURT Company marched on to brigade ELINCOURT-CLARY. Road and bridged same that night.	
	10.	07.00	One Officer and 3 Sections doubled Road over Crater made last night and made good road craters in CLARY Village.	
	11.		"A" and "B" Sections Transport joined together at ELINCOURT. Company resting. Baths arranged locally.	

CONTINUED

Army Form C. 2118.

WAR DIARY or INTELLIGENCE SUMMARY.

(Erase heading not required.)

151st Field Company R.E.

OCTOBER 1918.   PAGE 2.

Place	Date	Hour	Summary of Events and Information	Remarks and references to Appendices
	OCTR 1918.			
Sheet 57 t P.A.t. 05.90	12.	09.00	Company with all transport moved to Billets in LE FAYT. P.A.t 05.90. Took over eleven bridges over River SELLE from 222 Field Coy R.E.	
	13.		Company had orders of Brigade. Officers reconnoitring line - men employed making foot bridges.	
	14.		Kind of 22 strong posts marked out during forenoon, dug at night by 3 Sections R.E. and 375 Infantry. Owing to shelling and gas work at night not completed.	
	15.	09.00	06 attended conference called by C.R.E.- Reported to 115 Brigade Headquarters for orders. Arranged for 3 Sections R.E. and 40 Infantry to finish posts not completed last night.	
	17.		One Officer and 2 Sections drawing and improving posts previously dug by the Infantry.	
	18.		One Section with 2 pelits of 60 and 40 Infantry digging slits for Brigade and Battle Headquarters. Two Officers with Sections putting foot bridges across River SELLE (16 Bridges erected on front of 140 yards)	
	19.	19.00	One Officer and one Section taking approaches to bridges from main MONTAY- NEUVILLY Road and maintain approaches. Section billeted in Cellars of MONTAY CHATEAU.	
	20.	10.30	C.R.E. ordered 2 Sections to turn out at once to assist 123 Field Coy R.E. bridging River SELLE. Sections moved at once.	
	21.		Pontoon Bridge and improved approaches to same.	
	23.	07.00	Section on bridge maintenance relieved after 2 Sections working on bridge approaches. Headquarters and 2 Sections moved forward to MONTAY, picked up 3rd Section at MONTAY CHATEAU.	
K.12.a.8.8.		11.00	Headquarters and 3 Section moved to K.12.a.8.8.	
	24 + 25.		Waiting all day in Billets for orders. 19.00 hours Brigade wired "Probably not move tonight."	
F.A.A.	26.	14.00	Company moved to F.A. a (P01x D11 M01D) with one Officer and a Section of 124 Field Coy.R.E. attached. G.O.C. 115 Infantry Brigade ordered O.C. Company to River - with C.O. Battalion and work with them consolidating and wiring assisting line.	
	27.		O.C. Company spent all day with C.O. Battalion going around the line and arranging posts that should be wired and strengthened.	
	28.		The attached Section divided into 3, one/two attached to each of Company Sections. 3 Sections R.E. working each one Infantry Coy front improving posts, wiring and cutting lateral communications in helipo.	
	29 + 30.		Attached Section from 124 Field Coy R.E. ordered to rejoin 124 Field Co R.E. Two Sections wiring, one section in Billets bathing.	
	31.	11.30	O.C. Company attended C.O's conference. Received orders to cut gaps in all wire, improve lateral communications and make communications from village of ENCLEFONTAINE forward to front line.	
			REMARKS. A large proportion of the Month the Company was working directly under Brigade orders.	
			CONTINUED	

Army Form C. 2118.

WAR DIARY
or
INTELLIGENCE SUMMARY.
(Erase heading not required.)

151st Field Company, R.E. PAGE 3
OCTOBER 1918

Place	Date	Hour	Summary of Events and Information	Remarks and references to Appendices
			REMARKS (continued)	

experience shows that Sappers so attached are most wastefully employed. Brigades not being able to make, or see, opportunities for R.E. work, attach the Sappers to Battalions who are still too able to do so with the result that the Sappers trail about following the Battalions, carrying their tools frequently missing their rations, and seldom doing one hours useful work in 24. Further, R.E. Transport is not suited for working with the Battalions, — pack animals cannot carry sufficient tools for their actions, and only rarely can they follow the Battalions into the line.

The efficiency of the Company was much impaired by an epidemic of influenza, which reduced the Mounted Section by 30% and the dismounted section by 25%. This necessitated the dismounted being further weakened to find men to look after the horses. Further causes of weakness were

LEAVE. 3 Officers and 61 O.R. during the month, and
One Section (One Officer and 27 other ranks) detached from 6/10/18.

CASUALTIES. 2 Officers, 1 Sergt, 11 Sappers, 1 Mounted Corporal & 7 Drivers to Hospital (sick). 4 Sappers to Hospital wounded (G.S.W.) 1 Driver to Hospital accidentally injured.

COURSES. 1 Corporal to R.E.T.S. Rouen from 7/10/18. 1 Corporal on Lewis Gun Course from 10/10/18.

REINFORCEMENTS. — 1 R.S. Corpl. and 1 Sub Lieut from Base

VETERINARY. CASUALTIES. 2 L Draught, 1 Rider Horse, & 2 Mules evacuated 26/10/18. REINFORCEMENTS — Nil

12/11/18 S.W.C..... MAJOR, R.E.
O.C. 151st FIELD COMPANY R.E.

Army Form C. 2118.

WAR DIARY
or
INTELLIGENCE SUMMARY.
(Erase heading not required.)

151st Field Company R.E.

November 1918 Page 1.

WO 36

Place	Date	Hour	Summary of Events and Information	Remarks and references to Appendices
Sheet 57 c. F.4.a.	NOVR: 1918. 1st 2		Sections at work cutting lateral communications through hedges and wire between the front line posts.	
	2	14.15	O.C. attended conference called by C.R.E. Company put under orders of Brigade.	
		17.30	O.C. reported to G.O.C. Brigade – received instructions to commence in the morning marking out, and in conjunction with C.O's Battalion, digging jumping-off trenches, which were completed by the afternoon of 3rd.	
	4th		Attack on ENGELFONTAINE. One Officer with 2 sections detailed to assist Divisional Signal Coy getting their advanced signal line through the Forest. One section in reserve under O.C. Company at advanced report centre on the outskirts of ENGELFONTAINE. One Company of Pioneers detailed by C.R.E. to work under O.C. 151st Field Coy R.E. whilst employed on roads.	
Sheet 57A A.I.C.8.b.	5th		Company moved to billets in ENGELFONTAINE A.1.C.8.b, and worked during the day at the Crater S.20.c.3.0. and roadway S.20.d.30 to S.27.a.3.7.	
	6th		Company still working on roads.	
C.2.	7th		Company moved to RIBAUMET. C.2. Sappers stopped on road to bridge Crater at LE CROISIL INN. Work not completed at dark – company moved to new billets.	
	8th	8:00	Company ordered to repair and make good, for transport, temporary bridge at AULNOYE STATION. L.29.	
L.29.	9th	14.00	Company moved to Billets near Bridge at L.29.	
			Work continued on Bridge.	

Army Form C. 2118.

WAR DIARY
or
INTELLIGENCE SUMMARY.
(Erase heading not required.)

151st Field Company R.E.

November 1915. Page 2.

Place	Date	Hour	Summary of Events and Information	Remarks and references to Appendices
Sheet 57 A.	NOVR 1915.			
F.12.c.	10th		Company moved to Billets F.12.c. (RUE HAUT)	
	11th		3 Sections scraping Roads WATTIGNIES watersheds. 4th Section under Lieut M.C. Burke rejoined Company from duty on water supplies under C.R.E. Orders received from C.R.E. to reconnoitre route at X.22.d (SOLRINNES)	
	12th		Working on Bridge. One section bathing.	
	13th		2 Sections on Bridge. One section bathing.	
X.22.C.0.7.	14th	14.00	Company moved to SOLRINNES X.22.C.0.7.	
	14th, 15th & 16th		Company employed on Bridges. Trestle wagon fetching decking from AULNOYE Station.	
	17th		Sunday – holiday –	
	18th & 19th		Working on Bridges.	
	19th	20.00	Orders received mov. 22nd inst to BERLAIMONT, billets to be reconnoitred	
	20th	11.00	C.R.E's conference attended by O.C. Coy at H.Q. of 124 Field Coy R.E. All Company working on Bridges.	
	21st	16.00	Bridges completed. 3 – 15 foot bays, 14ft roadway, axle load 20 tons, – built of rough timber	
11.21.C.	22nd	8.30	Company moved to BERLAIMONT 11.21.C. Roads very slippery – horse transport moved at great difficulty.	
	23rd		Company employed drawing pontoon equipment, cleaning and painting wagons for inspection by G.O.C. Division on 26th inst.	
	24th		– ditto –	

Army Form C. 2118.

151st Field Company R.E.
November 1918.   Page 3.

WAR DIARY
or
INTELLIGENCE SUMMARY.
(Erase heading not required.)

Place	Date	Hour	Summary of Events and Information	Remarks and references to Appendices
Sheet 57.A	Nov 1918			
	25th	11:00	Rehearsal of Parade under C.R.E. for inspection by G.O.C.	
	26th		Inspection by G.O.C. Division.	
	27th-30th		Squad & Section drill under Section Officers.	
			CASUALTIES. 1 Officer, 4 N.C.O.s. 7 Sappers & 4 Drivers to Hospital (sick)	
			LEAVE :- 1 Officer, 34 Other Ranks granted Leave to U.K. 1 Sapper Leave to Paris.	
			COURSES 1 Sergt to R.E.T.S. Rouen from 4/11/18	
			REINFORCEMENTS:- 2 Lieuts, 1 Cpl, 1 L.Corpl, 12 Sappers & 4 Drivers. 1 Sergt returned to Base 29/11/18 - surplus to establishment - 1 Officer re-joined Unit from Base 24/11/18.	
			VETERINARY :- CASUALTIES - nil. REINFORCEMENTS - 2 L.D. Horses	

W Wilson Capt
O.C. 151st Field Company R.E.

Army Form C. 2118.

WAR DIARY
or
INTELLIGENCE SUMMARY.
(Erase heading not required.)

151st Field Company R.E.
DECEMBER 1918.

182 37

Place	Date	Hour	Summary of Events and Information	Remarks and references to Appendices
Sheet 57A.	DEC 1918.			
	1.	10.00	Mounted Section left BERLAIMONT to proceed by road to "CORBIE TRAINING AREA". Orders received for dismounted personnel to move on the morning of the 2nd	
	2"	09.00	Dismounted Personnel of Company left BERLAIMONT to proceed by Motor Lorries to ENGLEFONTAINE. Rested at ENGLEFONTAINE the night, and at 08.00 hours on the morning of the 3rd proceeded by march-route to SALESCHES and entrained for VILLERS BRETONNEUX, at which place Company detrained at 15.00 hours on the 4th inst. Proceeded by march-route to Camp	
Sheet 62 D N.b.c. 9.3			at DAOURS - Company billeted in Huts.	
	5		Dismounted - Squad Section Drill under Section Officers.	
		12.00	Mounted Personnel arrived at DAOURS.	
	6th to 3rd		No 2 Section proceeded to BLANGY TRONVILLE and No. 4 Section to GLISEY, and remained there for work on Huts at Camps preparing for arrival of Infantry Battalions, 115th Brigade. Nos 1 and 3 Sections working on Huts at DAOURS Camp till 12th inst. On 13th proceeded to BLANGY TRONVILLE, GLISEY and LA-MOTTE for work on Camps.	
	25th & 26th		Holidays granted to Company on Saturday afternoons and Sundays. Holidays.	

Army Form C. 2118.

WAR DIARY
or
INTELLIGENCE SUMMARY.
(Erase heading not required.)

151st Field Company R.E.

DECEMBER 1918.

Place	Date	Hour	Summary of Events and Information	Remarks and references to Appendices
	DECR 1918.		**REMARKS:-** The efficiency of the Company was much impaired during the month owing to the Company being considerably understrength, chiefly on account of all Miners (23) being transferred to Class "W". The release of Pivotal Men. This, and other causes reduced the Mounted Section by 25% and the dismounted by 30%, which necessitated the dismounted Section being further weakened in order to provide Men for Mounted Section to attend to Animals. **CASUALTIES:-** 1 Sapper died, 2 Sappers & 2 Drivers to Hospital (sick) 1 Sergt., 5 R/Corpls, 10 Sappers 7 Drivers transferred to Class "W" (Miners) 1 2/Cpl. & 1 Sapper demobilized as Pivotal Men. **COURSES** 1 N.C.O. on Chemistry Course from 29th **REINFORCEMENTS:-** 1 Officer re-imforement & 1 Officer rejoined Coy from Base. 6 Sappers, 1 Mounted R/Corpl & 8 Drivers from Base. **LEAVE.** 1 Officer and 11 O.R's granted leave to UK during the Month. **VETERINARY.-** Casualties - NIL - Reinforcements - NIL -	

W. Thynne Capt. R.E.
O.C. 151ST FIELD COMPANY R.E.

Army Form C. 2118.

WAR DIARY
or
INTELLIGENCE SUMMARY
(Erase heading not required.)

151st Field Company R.E.
January 1919

Vol 38

Place	Date	Hour	Summary of Events and Information	Remarks and references to Appendices
SHEET 62D N6C93			Company H.Q. and Mtd Section living in and working on Hutment Camps for Infantry at DAOURS. Section living in GLISY & BLANGY. Sunday all day; Wednesday and Saturday afternoon observed as Holiday. The first half of the month mild and wet the second half - Frosty and dry.	
			Casualties	
			To hospital 1 N.C.O. 2 Driver. 1 N.C.O. Sick when on Leave	
			Courses 1 N.C.O. (Chemistry)	
			Reinforcements 1 Officer 17 O.R.	
			Demobilisation 1 Officer 7 N.C.O. 22 Sappers 7 Drivers	
			Leave 1 - 1 - 2 - 1 - (1 Sapper Sydenham)	
			Veterinary 17 Horses to ENGLAND Y horses. 1 Mule evacuation Sick	

7/2/19

SM Burns

Army Form C. 2118.

WAR DIARY
or
INTELLIGENCE SUMMARY.
(Erase heading not required.)

151st Field Company R.E.
FEBRUARY 1919

Place	Date	Hour	Summary of Events and Information	Remarks and references to Appendices
Sheet 62D N6c9.3	5		Detachments from Stray and Blangy (Baillie-Courts) came lgths at DAOURS	
	6		1 Officer 50 O.R. to POULAINVILLE. Personnel Demobilization round. 14 hours/day. 1 Hot. Meal. Cook house etc. The work was completed in a fortnight. Men then employed on Company Billets. Barracks and Recreation Rooms etc. Owing to very bad weather (snow in the first fortnight of the month, a thaw set in 14th after which the weather was much damp and dull.	
			Casualties. 1 Sapper to Hospital Sick 2 Drivers " " " (Bronchitis)	
			Demobilisation. Offrs NCO Spr Drvr Shoe mkr. 2 19 26 7 16 4 Leave 1 Offr. 5 O.R.	

3/3/19

MAJOR, R.E.
O.C. 151ST FIELD COMPANY R.E.

Army Form C. 2118.

WAR DIARY
~~INTELLIGENCE SUMMARY~~
(Erase heading not required.)

25th 151st Field Company R.E.
MARCH 1919

Place	Date	Hour	Summary of Events and Information	Remarks and references to Appendices
Sheet 62.D No C9.3			Small parties employed repairing damage resulting of Civilian Claims in Village with french. During Heavy and Dewulyshen of men and horses any Littlework could be done.	
			Casualties NIL	
			Dewulyshen	
				Officer NCOs Spr Dvrs Mules
				0 6 32 9 22 12
			Leave	
				1 Officer 18. O.R.
			Transfers	
				1 Officer to 200th Field Company R.E.
				1 Driver to 529th Field Company R.E.

C.J.Morris ....MAJOR, R.E.
O.C 151ST FIELD COMPANY R.E.

3/4/19

WAR DIARY
or
INTELLIGENCE SUMMARY.
(Erase heading not required.)

Army Form C. 2118.

151st Field Company RE

Month April 1915

Place	Date	Hour	Summary of Events and Information	Remarks and references to Appendices
Sheet 62D N6 C9 3			Small parties employed repairing damage civilian property in neighbouring Villages. In settlement of Claims. Tools Stores & Mob. Equipment checked over and all deficiencies issued for. Casualties :- C.S.M. to Hosp. Sick. Drivers 1 Sapper 1 Drum Leave 1 Officer 12 O.R.	

G M Bowes
O.C. 151st FIELD COMPANY R.E.

1/5/15

WAR DIARY
or
INTELLIGENCE SUMMARY

(Erase heading not required.)

Army Form C. 2118.

From 31.5.19. to 6.6.10
From 5.6.19. to 6.6.10

151st Field Company R.E.

May 1919

Place	Date	Hour	Summary of Events and Information	Remarks and references to Appendices
Steel 62D N 6 6 93			Small parties of men employed repairing damage to civilian property in the neighbourhood. Leave reopened at the end of the month for Returnees O.R. only, all report on returning from Leave to C.R.E. 6th Midland Division Rhine Army.	R.5
			Casualties	
			1 Sapper 1 Driver Hospital	
			Denud 1 Officer appointment to 15 JH.Q. 1 W.G.C. 2 Cpl promotion to A.T.S. 1 Rider (Officer Charger) 1 x mule	
			Leave 1 Officer 6 O.R.	

31/5/19

C M Bows .... MAJOR R.E.
O.O. 151ST FIELD COMPANY R.E.

Army Form C. 2118.

151st Field Company R.E.
June 1919

WAR DIARY
INTELLIGENCE SUMMARY.
(Erase heading not required.)

Instructions regarding War Diaries and Intelligence Summaries are contained in F.S. Regs., Part II. and the Staff Manual respectively. Title pages will be prepared in manuscript.

Place	Date	Hour	Summary of Events and Information	Remarks and references to Appendices
Sheet 62.D	5		Small jobs repairing civilian property 5th Village.	
N6c93	6		Handed all surplus stores & equipment to I.C.S. POULAINVILLE. 1 Officer transferred to Imperial War Graves Commission S.Omer. 12 O.R. (Release personnel Dunkerque vi. Corps Dump Camp SAVEUSE.	
	7		29 O.R. (Returned men) Transferred to C.R.E. 6th Midland Division COLOGNE. 1 Officer 1 O.R. (Volunteer, who are absolutely reqd) Transferred to C.E.N's Army FLUX COURT. Company then automatically ceases to exist. 5 Returned O.R. now granted leave will march to CR.E. 6th Midland Div. upon return.	

7-6-19.

J M Bonn
O.C. 151st Field Company R.E.
Major R.E.

www.ingramcontent.com/pod-product-compliance
Lightning Source LLC
Chambersburg PA
CBHW080901230426
43663CB00013B/2595